More Than Mere Money:
The Life of Dorothy Lewis

Nancy Anderson

A division of Indigo Custom Publishing, LLC.

Indigo Custom Publishing, LLC.

Publisher	Henry S. Beers
Associate Publisher	Richard J. Hutto
Executive Vice President	Robert G. Aldrich
Operations Manager	Gary G. Pulliam
Editor-in-Chief	Joni Woolf
Art Director/Designer	Julianne Gleaton
Designer	Daniel Emerson
Director of Marketing and Public Relations	Mary D. Robinson

Printed in the USA.

Library of Congress Control Number: 2006928692

ISBN: (13 digit) 978-0-9776711-1-3
(10 digit) 0-9776711-1-9

Indigo Custom Publishing, LLC. books are available at quantity discounts with bulk purchase for educational, business, or sales promotional use. For information, please write to:
Indigo Custom Publishing, LLC., SunTrust Bank Building, 435 Second Street, Suite 320, Macon, GA 31201, or call 866-311-9578.

Frontispiece photo of Dorothy Ann Vits as a high school senior, courtesy of St. Mary-of-the-Woods College Alumnae Office.

Table of Contents

Preface and Acknowledgements

The inspiration for this project came from Jerry Harrell, Dorothy Lewis's lawyer, who began thinking about it in the mid 1990s. He had met Mrs. Lewis when she first sought legal advice from Cubbedge Snow Jr., shortly after joining the Georgia Bank Board in 1975. After nearly twenty years of regular contact, however, contact which engendered great respect for her business acumen, Harrell still knew little about his reclusive client. Yet the size of the foundation she planned to endow would make her one of Macon's most significant philanthropists. In 2000 he persuaded the other trustees of the Dorothy V. and N. Logan Lewis Foundation to underwrite the research that led to this book. Foundation President Dave Jeffords, who began assisting Mrs. Lewis with her affairs when he came to Georgia Bank as a trust officer in the early 1980s, was also instrumental in getting the work off the ground.

My involvement has been enhanced by having been acquainted with both the Lewises, albeit distantly. In 1963, as my husband's Army tour neared its end and we planned our move back to his hometown, we contracted to rent "the little brown house" not far from the Lewis home which Logan Lewis had purchased while developing Country Club Estates in the 1950s. Eager to explore our future abode during a leave, we drove out unannounced one Saturday morning; there we discovered our landlords in old clothes busy applying a fresh coat of paint to the kitchen. I was immediately drawn to them: Logan because he was so welcoming and friendly, Dorothy because, like me, she was a Yankee transplant, and obviously thrifty. Years later I came into contact with Mrs. Lewis again through my work as director of the Museum of Arts and Sciences, to which she made a number of gifts. Of course, given the folkways of the American South, living in the same community for forty years provided numerous opportunities to know *of* both Mr. and Mrs. Lewis. Nevertheless, acquaintanceship does not equip one to write the story of a person's life, even as it increases the interest in it.

That would not have been possible without the active participation of numerous individuals who have graciously shared their recollections and identified avenues for further research. Interviews with Bib Hay Anderson, who befriended Dorothy Vits at the Finch School, and her sister, Betty Hay McCook Curtis, perhaps her closest friend, were particularly helpful. Logan Lewis's friends Laura Nelle Anderson O'Callaghan, Henry P. "Pink" Persons Jr., John Comer, and Frank Jones provided similar insight about her husband; additionally Mr. Persons and Mrs. O'Callaghan read and commented on early drafts. McIntosh State Bank (formerly Farmers National Bank) President Thurman Willis, Jr., who was devoted to Mrs. Lewis, and retired banker Robert C. "Neal" Ham, who had a similar relationship with her husband, gave key assistance at important junctures. Dorothy's cousin Jane Zeman Protz, was enormously helpful, especially as I prepared to go to Manitowoc for research; she informed me, for example, that the bed and breakfast where I planned to stay had originally been the home of her (and Dorothy's) uncle, Charles Zeman. She also suggested other family members for me to interview, including Vits cousin Amy Brady and Florence Vits's nephew Michael Place; the latter thoughtfully shared an album filled with invaluable family photographs. While in Manitowoc I also met with John Spindler, the attorney who had helped to settle Abby Vits's estate. Cubbedge Snow Jr., Herbert M. "Buddy" Ponder, George Hall, Richard Domingos, Robert. L. McCommon Jr., Don Gordon's widow, Lucy, John F. Rogers Jr., and James W. "Jimmy" McCook III, were sources of information on the Georgia Bank, and Joe E. Timberlake III, whose father was on the original Georgia Bank board, helped me better understand the banking business. J. Alan Neal, President of First National, later SunTrust Bank of Middle Georgia, N.A., provided a community-wide banking perspective. President Cecil Coke Jr. was a source on Mrs. Lewis's affiliation with Riverside Cemetery. Bill McCowen, who managed properties for the Lewises, and who, as Dorothy Lewis's nearest and oldest neighbor became a solicitous friend in her last years, had helpful insights, as did her physician Dr. John O'Shaughnessey. St. Joseph's Catholic Church's former pastor, Monsignor John Cuddy, former Mt. De Sales principals Sister Rosina Bayliss and Sister Fidelis Barragan, and congregants RoseMary McKelvey and Bebe Reichert, increased my understanding of Mrs. Lewis's devotion to her faith and Catholic education. Architect James Berg recalled his work in designing both the Lewises' Old Club Road home and the Georgia Bank and Trust's building at the corner of Third and Mulberry. Anne Bryant's son David provided details of his mother's long relationship with the Lewises, and William C. (Bill) Epps was a similar source on Mrs. Lewis as an accounting client of his former partner, Sidney McNair. Harriet Fincher Comer shared a scrapbook of her experience in the 1952 Macon/Manitowoc exchange. Albert P. Reichert helped me interpret Logan Lewis's World War II experience, and brought me in contact with Oliver Bateman, who had knowledge of Dorothy Lewis's political activities. Arlan Ettinger, who met Mrs. Lewis when he sought to purchase one of the storied Lewis automobiles, shared recollections of a friendship formed late in her life, and Dixie Stewart described her arrangements for the ambitious trips Mrs. Lewis made while wheel-chair bound in the early 1990s. Crockett Rader Sellers graciously lent an album of clippings and photographs put together by her namesake, Crockett Odom. Betty Sweet Simmons and Jean Bush gave advice as to whom to interview, and Ralph Birdsey, whose father had been a close friend of Logan Lewis's in high school, submitted to questioning and read an early draft. My sister, Susan Briska Zeman West, an inveterate reader, and my good friend, Mary Anne Richardson, a reader, writer and teacher of history, also read and critiqued several early drafts.

I began this project before Mrs. Lewis's 2002 death, at a time when her fiduciaries could not give me any assistance. After her death, however, I had access to her home and its contents. As I expected, almost all letters, photographs, and personal items had been disposed of; most intriguing was a scrapbook in which every pasted-in memento had been torn out. Tellingly, however, Mrs. Lewis had left her financial records intact. Stored in a file cabinet in a small room off the kitchen, they yielded considerable information on the Lewis enterprises that laid the groundwork for her later financial success. Her habit of drafting letters on scraps of paper or the backs of envelopes—and piling them into a kitchen cabinet, possibly for future drafting—also provided helpful insights. These materials, identified here as the Lewis Archives, will be donated to the Middle Georgia Archives housed at Washington Memorial Library's Genealogical and Historical Room.

Dorothy Lewis's penchant for privacy, coupled with her careful disposal of almost all memorabilia, made firsthand oral sources such as those above crucial to telling her story. Libraries served to confirm and fill out recollections. Much of the information there might have been inaccessible, however, without the careful stewards who devote their professional lives to helping researchers locate what they need. I am particularly grateful to Muriel McDowell Jackson, Willard Rocker, and Chris Stokes at Washington Memorial Library's splendid Genealogical and Historical Room and Middle Georgia Archives, who were unfailingly courteous despite my numerous queries, and made many helpful suggestions. Thank you too, to the generous Macon people who have donated their papers, books, and photographs to those collections; they will benefit local historians for years to come and it is fitting for the Lewis papers to be placed there. In addition the reference librarians upstairs at Washington Library enabled me to obtain a number of important sources through the fabulous Interlibrary Loan Program. The Manitowoc Public Library was also of considerable assistance. Since much of its catalog is online I was able to identify what I wanted to look at before traveling there, where of necessity my time was limited; Public Service Coordinator Hallie Yundt Silver helped me to make the most of the hours I had in several ways (including waiving normal procedures which restrict the number of times one can get change to feed the photocopy machine!) and after I got home David Ellison located citations I had failed to record while there. The Manitowoc Heritage Center, also in Manitowoc, has a fine collection of useful materials, most of which have been assembled and catalogued by dedicated volunteers, which are opened to the public by still other volunteers. Michelle Holler of the Alumnae Office at St. Mary-of-the-Woods College, and Sister Eileen Ann Kelly of the Sisters of Providence Archives provided photographs and other materials explicating Dorothy Vits's experience at the no-longer-extant St. Mary-of-the-Woods Academy in Terre Haute, Indiana. Arlette Copeland in Special Collections at the Jack Tarver Library at Mercer University helped me find information on Logan Lewis and the other members of his family who were students at that school. The Library of Congress offers a class in how to use its extensive resources, at which participants were advised not to hesitate to request assistance, and I didn't; a "readers' card" there gave me access to numerous maps, manuscripts, magazines, and books on Manitowoc and the aluminum industry which greatly enlarged my understanding of both. The Atlanta Public Library on Forsyth Street downtown has a well-equipped local history room, and both it and the Atlanta History Center's Archives provided useful data on Logan Lewis's ancestry as well as the property inherited from his Lewis, Callaway, and Jones forbears. I also utilized numerous public records in courthouses in Bibb, Dougherty, Fulton, Lee, and Monroe counties in order to trace the Callaway, Jones, and Lewis real estate holdings; Tom Bass graciously provided a letter of recommendation to enable me to use the Bibb Record Room after hours and on Saturdays.

Many other people, not all of whom show up in footnotes, have provided encouragement and tidbits of information—it seems I have not gone anywhere in the last five years without talking to someone who knew something about my subject. Carey Pickard Jr., Giles O'Neal, Bill Simmons Jr., Sara Landry, Mary Burt, Joan Baggs McKenzie, Dr. Brown Dennis, Frankie Lynch, Eleanor Lane, Richard Keil, Holst Beall Jr., Jack Thomas, and George Haskell were among them.

Thanks too, to the past presidents at the Museum of Arts and Sciences whose retirement gift of computer and software gave me the equipment on which to produce the manuscript. Since at the time I believed being retired meant never having to write another thank you note, their generosity was not properly acknowledged.

Most of all, I am grateful to my long-suffering spouse, Lanier Anderson. His legal background left him vulnerable to numerous dinner-table interrogations that he endured with patience. Doubtless pleased that I chose research and writing over shopping, he has given unstinting support, encouragement, and advice throughout, only occasionally letting his eyes glaze over as I discoursed on the latest discoveries.

Nancy Anderson
Macon, Georgia
2006

Introduction

Savings represent much more than mere money value. They are the proof that the saver is worth something to himself. Any fool can waste. Any fool can muddle. But it takes something more of a man to save, and the more he saves, the more of a man he makes of himself. Waste and extravagance unsettle a man's mind for every crisis. Thrift, which means some form of self-restraint, steadies it.

—Author Unknown

This paragraph must have resonated with Dorothy Lewis because she went to the trouble of copying it by hand onto a sheet from a yellow legal pad. After her death it was found in a pile of notes and drafts—many on old fliers or envelopes—in a kitchen cabinet, undated, but written in the strong script of her middle years.

By any measure Dorothy Vits Lewis was an extraordinary woman. She was stunning. Intelligent. Well born. Devout. And enormously wealthy.

Of more than mere money value, however, the seventy million dollars with which Dorothy Lewis endowed a foundation in honor of her husband is "proof that the saver [was] worth something to [her]self;" that she was no fool... and certainly, that she made something of herself.

What is intriguing about Dorothy Lewis's story is not that she came to be wealthy—she was born into a hard-working family whose efforts created substantial assets that her marriage augmented—but how a woman with the education and experience imposed by her gender and class was able to exponentially increase those assets.

She grew up in an era in which girls became ladies who, regardless of age, deferred to fathers and husbands. She was taught by nuns until being sent to a "finishing school" which required students to visit art museums during the day and attend theater and opera at night; classes covered domestic and fine arts, certainly not matters, like business, which men were expected to handle. She did not have a career, and what volunteer work she did consisted of behind-the-scenes service to her church, staging chic social events, or promoting her conservative political perspective. While she had opportunities for travel, her trips were mostly recreational outings to the places her husband hunted, played golf, or raced cars.

She did have considerable advantages. She grew up in a community settled by immigrants whose vigorous work ethic generated a surprising number of profitable business ventures; one of her brother's kindergarten classmates left a foundation worth $40 million. The company founded by her grandfather and led first by her uncle and then by her father, became the largest of its kind in the world, a circumstance that naturally opened doors. She married a handsome, well-connected man whose financial instincts and success in banking left her a significant platform upon which to build. Nevertheless, these advantages do not entirely account for the size of the estate that became the Dorothy V. and N. Logan Lewis Foundation.

After the premature loss of her husband, Dorothy Lewis absorbed herself in the management of their diverse enterprises, becoming an astute businesswoman at a time when most of those with whom she did business would not have thought of putting the two words—"business" and "woman"—together. While she didn't invent a widget or hold a high-powered job, build a company or develop a new line of services, she did pay careful attention to her assets, making sure they were always at work. Productively at work.

Breaking barriers was not on her agenda; she dealt with the world as it was. A keen observer with a quick mind, she informed herself by reading business journals and annual reports, deftly applying what she learned. Not at all shy about seeking professional advice, she often grilled her advisors. Then, information in hand, she kept her own counsel as she set her course. Independent, "a gutsy lady" who "could accomplish and do," as an old chum described her, she enjoyed being the hands-on manager of her holdings, and she did not hesitate to use her position to protect and enhance them.

Though she lived in Macon for sixty-five years very, few Maconites knew her. Even those closest to her realized that there was much about her life she preferred not to share; in all likelihood their respect for that privacy is why they remained close. She would not have been pleased to find herself the subject of this narrative.

Those to whom she entrusted her affairs, however, believe that the future generations which will benefit from the philanthropy made possible by her financial success should meet the remarkable woman behind the Lewis Foundation.

This, then, is Dorothy Lewis.

Chapter 1

-•◦•◦•-

The Stunning Young Woman
from Wisconsin

Family Background

Dorothy Lewis was born in Manitowoc, Wisconsin, although exactly when even her trust officer admitted he could not say with certainty.[1] Once, in her later years, she responded to a cousin's inquiry regarding her age with a smile and a laugh, confiding that she'd lied about it for so long that she was no longer sure herself.[2]

Indeed, school records cite conflicting months, though they are consistent in giving the year as 1909 and the date as the eleventh.[3] A newspaper notice of her arrival adds to the ambiguity: the August 19, 1909, edition of the *Manitowoc Pilot,* a weekly published on Thursdays, reported that "A daughter was born Friday to Dr. and Mrs. Vits," which would seem to indicate that the date was the thirteenth. Nevertheless a certificate on file in the Manitowoc County Courthouse certifies that the birth occurred Wednesday, August 11, 1909.[4]

Both of her parents came from large families with an entrepreneurial bent. The year before her birth two maternal uncles had organized their own business, a grain elevator. Shortly thereafter her paternal grandfather and uncles merged their growing aluminum manufacturing business with two similar firms, launching an enterprise that remained Manitowoc's largest employer until 2001. That same year too, her father, who had been a stockholder in the family business since 1902, gave up his dental practice to join his relatives and their one hundred thirty employees at what locals still remember as "The Goods," but which became known outside Manitowoc as the Mirro Company.

As Dorothy Lewis grew up the Aluminum Goods Manufacturing Company grew as well, becoming increasingly large and successful, providing not only

1 Dave Jeffords, Oral Interview, May 11, 2000.
2 Jane Protz, Oral Interview #1, September 28, 2000. Sister Rosina Bayliss, R.S.M. who took Dorothy communion every Monday for many years, said that Mrs. Lewis had told her the same story. Oral Interview, June 10, 2000. Perhaps this was a graceful way of avoiding having to reveal the number; according to Jane Protz Dorothy's mother never acknowledged her age either.
3 The 1914-15 kindergarten register from the Park (formerly Luling) School in Manitowoc records her birthday as September 11, 1909, while 1921-22 and 1922-23 McKinley School class registers for the seventh and eighth grade note it as August 11, 1909. (Manuscript records, Manitowoc County Heritage Center Library.)
4 State of Wisconsin Birth Record (#767), issued by Preston F. Jones, Register of Deeds, Manitowoc County, August 17, 2001.

financial security but expanding influence and opportunities for those who founded and led it. In fact, the growth of that company and the prominent role it played in the city as she matured surely had an enormous—perhaps the primary—influence on her perception and understanding of the world around her.

Manitowoc County, Wisconsin, was settled in the mid-nineteenth century after a Chicago land speculator acquired large holdings there, printed maps in German, and began promoting sales in Germany. Early ads touted a climate and topography similar to those of the fatherland, although both proved harsher in actuality. Sales went well. Besides the turmoil created by struggles between church and state, Germany was an autocratic, militaristic society with no opportunities for advancement. The American broadsides promised low taxes, cheap land, unheard of political freedoms, and limitless possibilities for those willing to work - and to endure hardships. More than a million Germans immigrated to the United States between 1846 and 1856.[5] Wisconsin, thanks both to the large number of German-speaking immigrants already there (which made newcomers feel less like strangers) and to the easy access provided by the Great Lakes, was a primary destination. Among those making the three-week journey was Dorothy Lewis's paternal grandfather, Henry Vits.

Young Vits was just thirteen when he arrived in America in 1855. His father, William Henry Vits, had made an exploratory trip from Germany to check out the region the previous year. What he found must have pleased him for he bought land, and despite the fact that his wife had died while he was in America, he returned with his four children to establish a grist mill in the Meeme Township in the south end of Manitowoc County. Henry Vits, the only son, had had some schooling in Germany, but farm work kept him from continuing his studies in America. In 1860 he began a three-year apprenticeship with a tanner in the city of Manitowoc, and then spent a year each in both Chicago and Milwaukee to perfect his knowledge of the trade. Upon his return to Manitowoc he served as foreman for his former employer for two years before going into partnership with another tanner, eventually buying a firm of his own in the mid 1870s. During that decade Manitowoc led the state in the production of leather,[6] and despite tribulations that included the unprecedented experience of having his tannery struck by lightning three times in one night,[7] the young immigrant's business thrived.

An early biographical sketch painted a laudatory picture of Henry Vits:

5 Edward Ehlert, *German Influence in Manitowoc County*, Manitowoc County Historical Society Occupational Monograph Number 20, 1973. How fast the county grew is evident from the following: the 1850 census lists 3720 residents, of which 2093 were foreign born (1378 German); by 1860 the population had shot up to 22,412. By 1900 the County population totaled 42,261, of whom 11,786 lived in the City of Manitowoc.
6 Ellen D. Langill, *Manitowoc County, A Beacon on the Lakeshore*, Milwaukee Publishing Co., Milwaukee, WI, 1999, p. 49.
7 "Monday night lightening struck Henry Vits' tannery three times, thus proving untrue the old adage that lightening never strikes twice in the same place. No damage done." From the *Manitowoc Pilot*, Thursday, September 13, 1888, as quoted in biographical listings at www.2manitowoc.com.

He is a thoroughly practical tanner, familiar with every detail of the business, and manufactures a high grade of leathers that finds a ready market. As a businessman he is known for his promptness, reliability, integrity and enterprise. As a citizen he has an interest in anything that tends to benefit the city and community. . . . He is a man of social disposition, generous-hearted and cordial, and greatly enjoys the companionship of his friends.[8]

He served as postmaster during the Cleveland administration, and in addition to running his successful tannery he helped to organize the Manitowoc Mutual Fire Insurance Company and the Manitowoc Gas Light Company. His public and civic activities covered nearly forty years and included intermittent service on the city council, county board, school board, and state assembly, as well as efforts on behalf of numerous charitable endeavors such as the county insane asylum. According to an effusive obituary[9] in the *Manitowoc Herald-News* the "trust and confidence" the community had for him were demonstrated when a large delegation of citizens urged him to accept the mayoralty; he declined the honor. Sharing his countrymen's proverbial love of music, he belonged to several singing societies; he was also an Elk, an Odd Fellow, a Democrat, and a Lutheran, being a member of the First Reformed Church in Manitowoc.

Henry Vits had married Mary Hockemeyer in 1866, daughter of another German immigrant, and they had nine children, of whom Dorothy's father, Albert John ("A.J."), born in 1870, was the third. (See Family Tree on pp. 216-217.) They lived at 918 South 14th Street,[10] around the corner from the tannery on the south side of the Manitowoc River, and they prospered as the small city grew in size and economic strength.

By the end of the 1880s, however, it was becoming apparent that Manitowoc County's ample supply of tamarack trees, source of the tannin that had spurred the development of local tanneries, was not inexhaustible. Though his firm was then producing about 3,000 hides a year, a prudent man like Henry Vits began to consider other ventures. Perhaps in response to that situation, and despite the fact that all of the Vits sons had been involved in the business at one time or another, during this period A. J. decided to go to Milwaukee to study dentistry at what later became Marquette University, hanging out his shingle when he returned in 1900; younger brother George apprenticed himself to a local tailor.

As it happened, events elsewhere opened new opportunities for Henry

8 *Biographical Dictionary and Portrait Gallery,* p. 607.
9 December 8, 1921, p. 1.
10 Wright's 1894 *City Directory.* This is the earliest city directory to confirm the address, but once the Vitses settled in Manitowoc they never moved.

Vits and his family. Digressing to explore the story, intriguing in and of itself, provides insight into the circumstances in which Dorothy Lewis grew up.

In 1886, a twenty-two year old Oberlin graduate named Charles Martin Hall had discovered an electrolytic process by which to extract aluminum from alumina. Napoleon III had been enthusiastic about this highly regarded "white gold," believing it would make ideal breastplates for his army save for its $545 per pound price, so Hall knew his discovery had potential. Aluminum was abundant in nature, extremely lightweight and malleable, and yet possessed of strength approaching that of cast iron; in addition, it was virtually rust free and non-tarnishing. In Europe utensils made from it were more highly valued than those of gold and silver. The difficulty of extracting it, however, had kept its price too high for extensive use.

Hall moved quickly to capitalize on his method, collaborating with a group of young Pittsburgh businessmen to organize what became the Aluminum Company of America (later Alcoa), to produce the metal. But as remarkable as aluminum was, and in spite of a precipitous drop in its price (from $8 a pound in 1888 to $.78 by 1893[11]), there were not many places to sell it: "Practically no one wanted" it, Hall wrote to his partners.[12] The company's efforts to attract customers with the lower prices it achieved through economies of scale would have failed, save for its companion strategy of cultivating markets.[13] Developing new end uses for aluminum, the visionary young businessmen energetically promoted them (even seeking customer acceptance by organizing door-to-door sales and teaching buyers how to clean and polish the metal), and then supported the establishment of firms to manufacture those objects, firms that would purchase the necessary raw materials from the Aluminum Company of America. The nascent industry spawned increasing interest, and as the potential of the new metal caught on an industry magazine, *The Aluminum World,* began publication in 1894.[14]

One of the promotional efforts Hall's firm put together was the largest commercial exhibit in the Columbian Exposition at the 1893 Chicago World's Fair. That display, and German novelties made of aluminum that were exhibited with it, so intrigued Joseph Koenig of Two Rivers, Wisconsin, that he founded the Aluminum Manufacturing Company in a warehouse there in 1895.[15] Dorothy's grandfather, Henry Vits, was similarly interested; he studied the potential for such a business for several years before, at the age of fifty-six, dismantling his tannery,

11 George David Smith, *From Monopoly to Competition: The Transformations of Alcoa,* 1888-1986, Cambridge/New York, Cambridge University Press, 1988, p. 34. Alcoa commissioned outsider Smith to write this history but gave him "complete freedom of interpretation" (p.xxx) so that the book is both more comprehensive and more balanced than that of Charles Carr, cited below.
12 Ibid., p. 33.
13 Ibid., p. 82.
14 Charles C. Carr, *Alcoa: An American Enterprise,* New York, Rinehart & Co., 1952, p. 110. Carr, a former journalist, did public relations for the company for fifteen years before writing this account after he retired.
15 He rented the warehouse from J. Edward Hamilton, the furniture entrepreneur who later chaired the board of the combined Aluminum Goods Manufacturing Company. Dan Juchniewich, "The American Hamilton Industries of Two Rivers, Wisconsin, 1880-1980," Manitowoc County Historical Society, Occupational Monograph # 42, 1980 series, p. 11. Koenig is pronounced "Kane-ig."

retooling the building that had housed it, and opening the Manitowoc Aluminum Novelty Company. That was in 1898, and his eldest son, William Henry Vits, and new son-in-law William F. Pflueger, were the firm's other officers.[16] Like Koenig's, the Vits firm produced combs, hairpins, thimbles, and matchboxes, etc. Years later one employee recalled beginning work at the Manitowoc Aluminum Novelty Company at age fourteen for four cents an hour; he made novelties with ingenious machines for Henry Vits, he said, a man so frugal that he knocked apart the wooden boxes in which supplies were delivered to save the lumber—and even the nails—for future use.[17] The Two Rivers and Manitowoc operations continued in business for another ten years before the advantages of combining their efforts became apparent.

Meanwhile, the promise of the new products, as well as the general business climate of the era, encouraged something of a free-for-all in the young industry. To curb misplaced enthusiasm and establish some standards, a trade association was formed in 1901;[18] among its officers was W. F. Pflueger, Vice President, who, having been involved in interstate commerce as a drug salesman for many years before joining the Vits firm, no doubt brought valuable experience and an outgoing personality to the position. An important side effect of the association was the opportunity it gave the manufacturers to become acquainted as they worked to solve common problems. After William Vits's untimely death[19] his younger brother George joined the business and accompanied Pflueger to the 1902 meeting in Pittsburgh.

It is George Vits that company histories credit with having had the vision to merge the Vits and neighboring Koenig firms with the New Jersey Aluminum Company under a new name, the Aluminum Goods Manufacturing Company (the consolidation which, as noted above, took place just before Dorothy Lewis was born.) As its historian George David Smith points out, however, Alcoa, which monopolized aluminum production until 1909 by virtue of patent and tariff protection, was able to exercise "powerful leverage" with its external customers, among whom were the three aluminum companies.[20] Smith writes that Alcoa "chartered the Aluminum Goods Manufacturing Company" so as to "properly promote the rapid growth of [a] business for which the future held great promise" given the improved credit base and capital position of the

16 Leonora Kadow, "The History of Aluminum," Manitowoc County Historical Society, Occupational Monograph #18, 1972 series, p. 2.
17 William Kohl, Manitowoc County Historical Society Newsletter, Volume 11, Number 5, p. 69.
18 Carr, ibid., p. 116.
19 William Vits' health apparently failed him within months of the new company's formation; according to a notice in *The Aluminum World* (Vol. VIII, No. 1, October, 1901, p. 14) he had "removed" to Denver and appeared to be on the way to recovery when "complications set it and death resulted." He was 32; his wife Louise and three sons continued to live at 915 S. Fifteenth Street in a house whose back yard connected to that of his parents, which faced Fourteenth Street. All three of William's sons, and a grandson, eventually became principal executives with Mirro. Shortly after the above notice the *World* reported that "Many aluminum men will regret to hear that W.F. Pflueger has withdrawn from the Manitowoc Aluminum Novelty Company of Manitowoc, Wisconsin. Mr. Pflueger will take a rest before definitely deciding upon his future plans. The new officers are Henry Vits, President, William Hockemeyer, Vice President, and George Vits, Secretary." (August, 1902, Vol. VIII, No. 11, p. 219) Mr. Hockemeyer was in all likelihood related to Henry Vits' wife Mary, whose maiden name was Hockemeyer.
20 *From Monopoly to Competition*, p. 102.

combined firm. Alcoa also wanted to mitigate the pre-merger competition amongst the companies which had "threatened to diminish the . . . market for sheet and ingot aluminum." For its efforts in organizing the venture, Alcoa took a twenty-five percent interest in the new company and appointed its top two officers to the new board of directors. A.G.M.C. was at first based in New Jersey under the leadership of New Jersey's Gustave Kruschnitt, but at the 1911 annual meeting thirty-four year old George Vits, then Vice President and General Manager, was named President in his stead.[21]

Joseph Koenig (of Two Rivers) had been the original Vice President of the consolidated firm, and continued in that role and as one of the five-member board of directors until his death in 1929, when he was replaced by his son. The A.G.M.C. board was chaired by another Two Rivers entrepreneur, J. E. Hamilton, founder and President of the Hamilton Manufacturing Co., until his death in 1940. Significantly, in addition to George Vits and his father Henry, the other directors were Arthur Vining Davis and Roy A. Hunt of Pittsburgh, at that time President and Vice President, later Chairman of the Board and President, respectively, of the Aluminum Company of America; they remained with A.G.M.C. until at least 1941. Davis, in particular, was an industrial giant in early twentieth century America, having begun helping Charles Hall get his company going as early as 1888; through Davis and Hunt the Vitses had ties to the Pittsburgh Mellons who were the bankers, then stockholders, and then directors of Alcoa.[22] Henry Vits stepped down from the board, to be replaced by Dorothy's father, A. J. Vits, in 1914.

The Manitowoc firm had begun to produce cookware as early as 1907, and while the product was well-received, being lightweight[23] and easy to handle as well as heating quickly and evenly, the limited quantities in which it was manufactured had kept its price out of the reach of most people. George Vits decided to expand the Wisconsin plants, using mass production to lower the price. The wisdom of that decision became apparent when the Quaker Oats Company commissioned a double boiler that racked up sales of over a million. The high quality, heavy gauge, but affordable cookware for which the company became famous was soon rolling off assembly lines in large quantities. Called "Viko," a name coined from combining the first two letters of the two founders' names (Vits and Koenig), it was sold almost exclusively under private brands through distributors and mail order houses.

21 Kadow, ibid., p. 2, and *The Mirro Mixing Bowl*, Vol. X, Number 3, March 1948, p. 3. According to Donald H. Wallace, an assistant professor of economics at Harvard, shortly after the formation of A.G.M.C. "internal dissension arose between the Wisconsin and New Jersey members" of the partnership, which led to the western interests purchasing the eastern out. Alcoa then entered into an agreement with G. A. Kruttschnitt and J.C. Coleman whereby the latter pledged not to enter the aluminum business in the United States east of Denver for twenty years. Donald H. Wallace, *Market Control in the Aluminum Industry*, Cambridge, Harvard University Press, 1937, p. 397.
22 Carr, ibid., pp. 33-47.
23 This was no small advantage! Women were cooking primarily with cast iron, which was very heavy.

In 1915 the firm acquired yet another manufacturer in Two Rivers, the Standard Aluminum Company, and diversified further by contracting with Dodge, Studebaker, and Buick for the production of automobile hubcaps.

The company had not yet offered its own line of cookware, but, in 1917, A.G.M.C. developed the "Mirro" brand for the retail market, promoted it through full page ads in such wide-circulation magazines as the *Saturday Evening Post,* and *Ladies' Home Journal,* and at the same time greatly enlarged its sales operation. Dorothy's father A. J. handled the marketing end of the business, and was named Vice President in 1921.

World War I also contributed to A.G.M.C.'s success: with no shortage of raw materials and enormous demand for canteens, mess kits, etc., only production capacity limited sales. That problem was promptly addressed, first by the acquisition of another plant in St. Louis, and then by building five large additions to the facilities in Manitowoc and Two Rivers. An R. G. Dun & Co. report dated March 1, 1918,[24] reflects the firm's rapid growth, noting that its net worth increased from $1,072,098 in 1913 to $3,267,093 in 1917; total assets were $5,298,705.

By all accounts A.G.M.C. was well managed. The same R. G. Dun report cited above noted that "The interested parties are well regarded in personal respects and . . . men of good business ability." George Vits made the welfare of his employees a priority, through personal contact in the early days, and via enlightened policies as the company grew. By 1917, to both promote and reward loyalty, he pioneered an employee insurance plan, purchasing a group life policy worth $1500 for males and $1000 for all employees under 21. In 1923 Vits began presenting gold watches to every employee who had served "the Goods" for twenty-five years. A company newsletter engendered a cohesive atmosphere; there were company teams in almost every sport, a company band (of which Vits was an honorary member), and an annual company picnic and parade day that was an eagerly awaited and joyfully celebrated summer event.

In the twenties the firm continued its growth, though divesting itself of the St. Louis and Newark facilities in order to concentrate on the plants in Wisconsin. Aggressive advertising and campaigns designed to capitalize on the retail stores being opened by mail order houses kept production high. Sales offices had opened in Detroit, Chicago, and New York by the end of the decade, and a diversified line of approximately 2,500 articles was being distributed throughout the United States, Canada, and Latin America, as well as in other countries. A 1931 R. G. Dun report[25] (citing net worth that had risen to $15,754,447) notes that A.G.M.C. "has had outstanding success and steadily

24 Typescript; in the Manitowoc County Heritage Center Library.
25 Typescript; ibid.

and consistently developed and expanded its properties through re-investment of its earnings. A new seven story office and warehouse building and a new five story plating building . . . were completed during 1929 at a cost exceeding $800,000 and . . . something like $675,000 [was] expended for new machinery, equipment, etc." Yet "the company is in a strong cash position and at the close of business December 31, 1930, had no borrowings from banks . . . no fixed debt and . . . a ratio of current assets to current liabilities [of] better than five to one." Despite a forty-two percent decrease in profits "naturally . . . effected [sic] by general business conditions" during the last year, the report concludes, management had reduced expenses in operations and administration to such an extent that "prospects continue propitious." Clearly, and fortuitously, the firm was in a strong position to face the coming economic downturn.

As the largest producer of cookware in the nation, A.G.M.C. was by far the largest employer in the Manitowoc County, providing work for 3400 people before the Depression hit. Lincoln High School yearbooks in the Manitowoc Public Library show that a remarkable 18-37 percent of each graduating class between 1920 and 1927 took jobs at "the Goods" after graduation. By this time, too, nearly all of Dorothy's paternal relatives were working there—her father and uncle George, her cousins Earl, William, and Albert, her uncle Hugo, her aunt's husband Joe Topic, her brother, Albert J. Vits, Jr. and his brother-in-law, Jimmie Place—even a distant German cousin, a nephew of her grandfather's named Walter Laufs, were all employed at "the Goods."

The premium the company placed on a loyal workforce, the strong financial position it enjoyed going into the Depression, and its significant place in the community's economic well-being, all contributed to its determination to keep as many people as possible on the payroll during the darkest days of 1931-32. Despite a 65 percent decrease in sales, A.G.M.C. laid off only one quarter of its employees, a feat that is still gratefully remembered in Manitowoc.

When George Vits died prematurely in 1933, Dorothy's father A.J. took over as president,[26] instituting a strict program to cut expenses as well as the development of numerous "tie-in" promotions with companies such as Folger Coffee, Pillsbury, Colgate, Carnation Milk, etc. When sales began to climb employees were brought back so that the number of workers hit 2700 before the end of the year.[27] Increased sales and frugal management allowed the company to continue paying dividends throughout the '30s, and by 1936 it was able to announce a retroactive 5 percent pay increase.[28]

During the years in which "the Goods" grew in success it was not the

26 He remained president of the company until his death in 1955. Two of William's sons, Earl O. and Albert L., served as vice president; Albert also served as President from 1960-67.
27 Kadow, ibid., p. 4, and *The Mirro Mixing Bowl,* Vol. X, Number 5, May, 1948, p. 3.
28 *New York Times,* November 17, 1936, 10:5.

only venture in which George Vits exerted leadership. He was also president of the Handwear Manufacturing Co., a director and officer of several banks and insurance companies, and helped to organize and then presided over the Manitowoc Hotel Corporation, the Lakeside Country Club, and the Rotary Club; he chaired the Advisory Committee that expanded the local hospital, as well as the executive committee of the Boy Scout Council that developed extensive new camping facilities, among many other local good works. His and his company's reputation led to a seat on the board of the National Manufacturer's Association,[29] and he was active in politics. Because he was aligned with the conservative wing of the Republican Party at the time when liberal Robert LaFollette was the state's Senator, the national party under Herbert Hoover selected him as Wisconsin's National Committeeman, from which position he dispensed the state's federal patronage.[30] Though he resided in a small Midwestern city, his death (from arteriosclerosis) rated nine column inches in the *New York Times*.

Such visibility and connections had their downsides. The very success of the Aluminum Company of America made it a target of several governmental investigations, and by virtue of its close business relationship, the Aluminum Goods Manufacturing Company came under scrutiny as well. In 1922 the Federal Trade Commission investigated a complaint of unfair competition in the cooking utensil business in which it was alleged that Alcoa controlled A.G.M.C; after extensive hearings the case was closed when it was determined that the charges were not sustained by the evidence. In 1937 the Department of Justice filed a sweeping anti-trust case that included allegations of monopolization of cooking utensils centered around Alcoa's ownership of a minority interest in A.G.M.C., which was also named as a defendant. The Court found that vigorous competition had always existed between A.G.M.C. and the Aluminum Cooking Utensil Company, Alcoa's WearEver subsidiary, and that A.G.M.C.'s policies were directed by the Vits, Koenig, and Hamilton families, longtime majority owners of the business.[31] Although both firms were eventually exonerated, the proceedings were doubtless tiresome sidebars to an otherwise exhilarating history of increasing business success. In addition, they no doubt contributed to Dorothy Vits Lewis's negative attitude towards the federal government.

Dorothy Lewis's maternal grandfather, Frank Zeman, was born in Bohemia in 1842, the same year that Henry Vits was born in Prussia, and migrated from there to Wisconsin in 1850, shortly before the Vits family. While less is known about the circumstances of the Zemans' arrival, the reasons for Bohemian migration were not unlike those of their German neighbors.

29 *The Manitowoc Herald-Times*, November 16, 1933, p. 1.
30 *New York Times*, December 7, 1927,1:6, and August 2, 1928 3:2.
31 Carr, ibid., p. 204, 223.

The capital of Bohemia, Prague, had been a center of political and cultural influence in twelfth century Europe, but the kingdom fell victim to Teutonic imperialism and had completely lost its independence by 1620. Leaders were massacred, land confiscated, and the native nobility dispossessed, in addition to the religious and cultural oppression of the common people. In the nineteenth century, however, a renaissance of native language and literature, combined with the revolutionary currents swirling across the continent after 1848, especially the end of serfdom in Austria, raised popular aspirations enormously. Peasants could now own land, though it was likely to be in the mountains where soil was thin and rocky, since the fertile flatlands remained in the hands of Austrian nobles. Given the onerousness of compulsory military service, autocratic officials, and heavy taxation, coupled with persistent droughts, peasants whose holdings were too small to comfortably support a large family opted to convert their land to funds for travel to a new country rather than to eke out a living farming their native soil. Those who left published promising reports of their success in Bohemian newspapers, and the agents who profited by the migration ran advertisements touting their services in German and Austrian papers. While their numbers were not as extensive as those of the Germans, more than 40,000 Bohemians came to America between 1850 and 1870.[32]

Most came to the Midwest where homesteads were available for clearing and planting, hard work that was rewarded in the second generation. Literate, industrious, and progressive, Bohemians did well in the new land. After the Erie Canal opened in the 1820s, Wisconsin was easily accessible by water from Buffalo. The state also maintained a salaried "immigration commissioner" in New York to divert newcomers which helped it draw a substantial percentage of them: the 1850 census showed that one out of three Wisconsin residents were foreign born.

Despite the enmity between their countries back home, the Bohemians had more in common with the Germans than any other ethnic group. Customs and mode of life were similar, and language was a particular tie since most Bohemians had attended German language schools. While they mingled freely with Germans, the Bohemians remained fairly clannish, flocking to communities in which they could do business and socialize with others from their former country outside the American mainstream. Having lived in villages in the old country, the "intensely social" music and dance-loving Bohemians found Midwestern farms lonely and isolated. They formed a tightly knit community

32 Kenneth D. Miller, *The Czecho-Slovaks in America,* New York, George H. Doran Company, 1922, p. 43. The cultural group to which the Zemans trace their roots came from the provinces of Bohemia, Moravia, and Silesia in eastern Europe, and at the time of their nineteenth century migration they were generally called Bohemians; after World War I, when the country obtained full independence from Germany under the name Czechoslovakia, the nomenclature changed to "Czechs." Slovaks, while sharing many cultural characteristics with the Czechs and speaking a closely related language, are a separate group. The background on migration included here is based on Miller's discussion of the same, pp. 1-60.

in Manitowoc County, which by 1870 ranked among the top dozen Bohemian settlements in the country.[33]

Frank Zemen's obituary in the *Manitowoc Herald News*[34] indicates that he followed a typical path, locating first on a farm in Manitowoc County before moving into the city around 1880. He, too, became a prominent citizen in his new country, serving as a trustee of the Czech fraternal lodge SCPS #132, which helped organize the popular Ceske Slovanska Lipa Opera House, among other civic efforts. He was a Democrat "in days when the party controlled the County;"[35] he was elected to several terms on City Council, as Sheriff in 1889, and later to several terms as County Treasurer, "testifying to his capable administration . . . He was known as a man who enjoyed the esteem of all who knew him as a man of character and integrity." He married fellow Bohemian Anna Wanek in the 1860s, and they had seven children. (See Family Tree on pp. 218-219.) Dorothy Lewis' mother, born in 1873 and named in honor of her mother, was the third.

Zeman owned and operated the Star Hotel at the corner of North Main and Buffalo, in which he and his family lived until well after the turn of the century. The Star is described as a "saloon and boarding residence" in the 1911-12 *City Directory*,[36] but the description fails to convey the turn-of-the-century context of the genre. According to Czech historian Thomas Capek, saloon keeping was the first business opportunity seized upon by newly arrived Bohemians: it required little preliminary training, start up capital was provided by the brewer, and there was no language barrier since most of the customers were one's own countrymen. In the latter half of the nineteenth century saloons and their keepers enjoyed great influence as centers of community life; nearly every lodge and club organized got their start in a neighborhood saloon. After World War I, however, Capek reports that the saloon-keeper's power declined as so-called "National Halls" (community centers containing movie theaters, restaurants, meeting rooms and ball rooms), sokols, public reading rooms, and libraries competed for patrons' time—and schools and temperance societies taught the young to abhor liquor traffic. As a result, the author concludes, the saloon-keeper's "former prestige is now but a tradition . . . a tradition . . . utterly incomprehensible to the latter-day immigrant."[37]

After working with his father at the hotel for some years, the older son, Frank, Jr., took it over and ran it until shortly after 1912, when he apparently

33 Thomas Capek, *The Cechs (Bohemians) in America: A Study of Their National, Cultural, Political, Social, Economic and Religious Life*, Boston/New York, Houghton Mifflin Co., 1920, pp. 25-38. One of the ads cited reads: "Come! In Wisconsin all men are free and equal before the law. . . . Religious freedom is absolute and there is not the slightest connection between church and state. . . . In Wisconsin no religious qualification is necessary for office or to constitute a voter; all that is required is for the man to be 21 years old and to have lived in the state one year."
34 June 21, 1926, p. 2.
35 Ibid.
36 1911-12 *City Directory*, published by Zorn's Directory of the City and County of Manitowoc, WI; Milwaukee, Joseph P. Steiner Co.
37 Capek, ibid., pp. 77-78.

moved to Chicago. The younger brothers, Charles and Edward, however, to whom Anna Zeman Vits remained particularly close throughout her life,[38] became successful businessmen in Manitowoc. Charles, President of his Senior Class, graduated from Northside High in 1900, then worked for Armour and Company in Chicago before returning to clerk with the Northern Grain Company in Manitowoc. In 1908 he and Robert Ritchie became partners in the Northern Elevator Company, which he served as president until it was sold in 1950. Their business prospered. In a short piece on Charles Zeman included in his *History of Manitowoc County,* local historian Louis Falge writes that "In both social and business circles he well merits the regard in which he is held, and the financial success to which he has attained is well deserved."[39] He married Bess, the daughter of Dr. and Mrs. R. K. Paine in 1913, and they had one daughter, Valerie.

Edward Zeman graduated from Northside in 1903 and immediately went to work for Northern Grain, where he remained until 1908 when he joined his brother in organizing the Northern Elevator Company, of which he was Vice President until the firm was sold. Among other ventures, Edward Zeman was an original stockholder of Eastman Manufacturing Company and a director at the time it was merged with Imperial Brass Co. of Chicago. He was also a stockholder and director of Eastman Atlantic Manufacturing Co. of Wilmington, Delaware, a director of Capitol Building Corp. of Manitowoc, and an officer and director of the Lakeside Packing Company for more than twenty years. He married Minnie Klackner in 1912 and they had three daughters, Jane, Pauline, and Marion. Like their father, both Zeman brothers were Elks.

According to family tradition[40] Anna Zeman, with her sisters Mary[41] and Emma, helped out at the hotel before her marriage, but the 1897 City Directory lists her as a clerk at Mendik and Mulholland. She and A. J. Vits were married in 1902, after which they moved from their parents' homes to one of their own at 912 St. Clair Street on the north side of the Manitowoc River.

Manitowoc

Manitowoc takes its name from indigenous peoples whose words *munedoo,* meaning "great spirit," and *owk,* meaning "home" were combined to create "Home of the Great Spirit." The city appears to have lived up to its nomenclature, for on many counts it is a remarkable place.

It is located on Lake Michigan about 175 miles north of Chicago, at the mouth of the Manitowoc River. The first settlers of European descent landed

---

38 According to Edward's daughter Jane Protz, this closeness may have resulted from losing his mother in 1899; only fifteen when she died, Edward spent a great deal of time with his sister Anna and A.J. Vits after their marriage in 1902. Interview #1.
39 Dr. Louis Falge, *History of Manitowoc County,* volume II, p. 140, c. 1911-12. Reprinted 1979 by Manitowoc Genealogical Society.
40 Protz interview, ibid.
41 Mary married and moved east; Emma married A. J. Auton. Another brother, Joseph, died as a youth.

there in 1836, two years after the Menomonee Indians signed the area over to the American government. The village was chartered in 1852, and a city charter granted in 1870 when the inhabitants numbered just over 5,000.

The unpublished autobiography of social critic Ernest A. Hooten[42] provides an engaging description of the city just before Dorothy Vits's birth. Hooten was a parson's son who went on to chair Harvard's Anthropology Department; his intelligence and scholarly background are evident in an account that is enlightening, if dated in its use of ethnic stereotypes. He had just entered adolescence in the fall of 1898 when the Methodist church moved his family to Manitowoc, "the most congenial place my father ever preached, a city which harbors the pleasantest memories of my youth."[43] His memoir puts a human face on historical data.

Originally traversed only by planks mounted on pilings, or later by ferry, the Manitowoc River divides the city into northern and southern sections, and according to Hooten "the educational, social, and religious separateness of the two . . . was virtually total. On the north side lived most of the families of English and Scandinavian extraction; on the south side were many Poles, along with most of the factories, shipyards, grain elevators, railway freight yards and the depot. However, the Germans, who constituted the majority of the population, or very close to it, lived on both sides of the river, and so did the Czechs, generally known as Bohemians." There were a few Irish sprinkled in but no other distinguishable nationalities.

Hooten seemed most impressed by the Germans who "were, for the most part, descendents of the crowd which came to Wisconsin after 1848, headed by the patriot Carl Shurz. They were Lutherans and very substantial and moderately prosperous people. Some of them were wealthy, especially the brewers and other manufacturers and those connected with the lake shipping industry." Poles and Czechs, he said, enjoyed less social standing and tended to keep more to themselves; most of the wealthiest families were of British descent.

By outnumbering other groups the Germans exerted noticeable influence on the city. "There were beergardens, Turnvereins,[44] Mannershoren,[45] skat clubs (in which some sort of intricate card game was played) and many other German organizations. Most of the elder generation spoke German [despite having been] born in Wisconsin, and not a few . . . had fought on the side of the North in the Civil War. They believed in education . . . had considerable civic pride, and were passionately fond of music. . . . I have seldom had the privilege

42 Earnest Albert Hooten, *The Autobiography of Earnest Albert Hooten, 1887-1954,* typescript, n.d., Library of Congress.
43 Ibid., pp. 94-96.
44 These were athletic clubs, probably something like YMCAs. Interestingly, the Bohemians developed a similar organization called "sokol."
45 These were singing societies; Henry Vits belonged to several. The members of one, the Concordia, welcomed him and his wife back from a European trip by conducting an impromptu serenade in the street in front of their home at 918 S.14th Street (*Manitowoc Pilot,* Thursday, August 13, 1908.)

of associating with a finer class of people."[46] While Hooten doesn't mention it, another indication of the predominance of German immigrants and their descendants in the city was the presence of two German language newspapers, *Nordwestern* and *Die Wahrheit (The Truth);* they continued publication until World War I when the United States went to war against the fatherland.

Hooten's "perennial companion" was Walter Spindler, the youngest son of a local capitalist who lived diagonally across from the parsonage.[47] Walter's widowed father was a "portly, taciturn Teuton" whose coachman drove the boys all over the countryside behind a handsome pair of matching bays. The Spindlers' "magnificent stone house" was styled like a French chateau with a turret-topped tower at one corner and an interior that Hooten describes as typical of a wealthy German American of the period.[48] A golden-oak paneled ground floor tower room was lined with glass-fronted bookcases surrounding a table covered with magazines and newspapers. The front room contained a piano and overstuffed furniture; the living room was full of leather chairs, spittoons, and ashtrays, its walls adorned with steel engravings, oil paintings, and the stuffed heads of animals that Mr. Spindler had shot. A phonograph with wax cylinders sat in one corner. Upstairs the bedroom closets bulged with guns and fishing gear, and the third floor housed a billiard and pool table with multiple racks of cues. "The kitchen and pantries were vast and spotless," Hooten adds, smelling "of rich German food, particularly sauerkraut."[49]

Farther down the street "across from the Spindler barn was a tumbledown, unpainted house" where another playmate, Aloysius Hogan, lived. "His father was a saturnine, black-bearded Irishman who worked in a coal yard and drank. The house looked as if he had wiped the coal dust off his hands and face all over its outside." Though Hooten and Spindler befriended him, young Aloysius "was regarded askance by our parents not so much because he lived in a poor house as because his family were Roman Catholic, though they eventually had to admit that he was a nice boy, despite his antecedents."[50]

German Lutherans, says Hooten, while standoffish towards other Protestants until they got to know them well, then became friendly and hospitable. The Scandinavians, "blond, blue-eyed and placid," had their own Lutheran Church; "the Poles and Czechs did not count with us, especially the former." (Hooten describes his own family as of "lower middle class English stock.") Nearly all Protestant families were Republican, the party having been founded at Ripon, Wisconsin, in 1855, but foreigners and Catholics were likely

---

46 Hooten, ibid., pp. 94-6.
47 Young Spindler, interestingly, grew up to head the Aluminum Specialty Company, a major competitor to the Vits family firm; his nephew John, was an attorney who counted Dorothy Lewis' brother Abby as a client near the end of his life.
48 Ibid., p. 101.
49 Ibid., p. 100.
50 Ibid., p. 102.

to be Democrats.[51]

The work ethic was an important factor in civic and family life: "All small town parents in those days believed in teaching children to work rather than to play. No matter how wealthy your father might be, you were expected to turn to and help shovel snow in winter, to chop wood and keep the wood boxes full, to cut the grass in summer, rake leaves in fall. Girls learned to sweep and dust, to wash dishes and make beds, even if their mothers kept a 'hired girl'. . . .There was not much interest in exercise and physical development through games." Bringing up wood and coal to start the fire, and planting gardens were, after all, necessities in that era.[52]

That work ethic set the tone for public as well as private life. Having defeated Manitowoc Rapids in a bid to become the county seat, the settlers who founded Manitowoc donated a site for the courthouse in the 1850s, and sought the aid of their Republican Congressman in getting the federal government to help dredge the harbor, already one of the best natural ones on Lake Michigan, in the 1860s. In 1873 the city bonded itself to secure a railroad and built a grain elevator.[53] With such an infrastructure Manitowoc was well on its way to industrial success by the time Hooten moved there, despite lacking the capital available in older Eastern cities, and the bustle is evident in his narrative. The river, navigable for several miles from its mouth, hosted both shipbuilding and commerce. "Enormous, open sterned car ferries plied across the lake between Manitowoc and Ludington,"[54] Michigan, Hooten writes (a route that facilitated delivery of A.G.M.C.'s hubcaps to Detroit automakers twenty years hence), and freighters went back and forth to Chicago and Mackinaw. The grain elevators and dry dock wharves were busy, and pea-canning factories drew many workers, including Hooten, who earned fifteen cents an hour there during the summer.[55]

Most of the author's recollections, however, are less analytical. Five blocks east of his house lay Lake Michigan, its waves pounding narrow clay, gravel, and pebble beaches that lay thirty to fifty feet below steep, crumbling bluffs. While the boys were more likely to swim in the river than the lake, which was cold and rough, they rode surf on planks there in summer and enjoyed rudimentary coasting and skiing in the winter. A boardwalk leading out to the lighthouse made for a pleasant Sunday stroll and the foghorn on the breakwater two hundred yards from shore was a reassuring presence in not-infrequent thick weather. Vacant buildings and clay pits in an abandoned brickyard "made a terrain suitable for all sorts of war games, for which, owing to the Spindler propensity for firearms," the boys were usually well equipped.

51 Ibid., pp. 94-96.
52 Ibid., p. 61.
53 Wright's Manitowoc *City and County Directory,* Milwaukee, 1938, p. 14.
54 Hooten, ibid., pp. 94-96.
55 Ibid., p. 172.

Then there was Fourth of July: "a wild and adventurous day at the turn of the century."[56] Boys saved their money for weeks to lay in a store of explosives, most of which were shot off before breakfast. In the afternoon the town band (no shortage of good musicians given the numerous German and central European émigrés) led a parade to the cemetery that featured Company H of the National Guard "uniformed and armed to the teeth," Spanish American war heroes, and "bearded, cane-wielding veterans of the Civil War accompanied by a fife and drum corps." A rabble of carriages bearing the Mayor and Aldermen, accompanied by the orator of the day and hundreds of school children waving flags, came next. The parade and speeches were followed by an extravagant fireworks display. While the festive Fourth may have been Manitowoc's biggest event, summer concerts in the park every Saturday evening found people from all over town seated on iron benches around the bandstand eating popcorn and swatting mosquitoes in the hot weather while they listened to the music.

Each fall the Manitowoc County Fair transformed the fairgrounds northwest of the city with fresh paint, flags, and pennants so that barkers could promote the usual round of hurdy-gurdies, sideshows, and ring-the-cane stands, while tight wire artists, acrobats, and clowns entertained cracker-jack munching audiences between harness races every afternoon for a week.[57] On other occasions Buffalo Bill's Wild West Show visited the fairgrounds, as did the Congress of Rough Riders. Winter brought sleigh rides under a cold moon to a roadhouse out in the country.[58] John Phillips Sousa's band included the Opera House on its tours more than once.

Interestingly, considering the place in which Dorothy would spend her married life, "the Civil War was still a vivid memory," Hooten writes. "In doctor's and dentist's officers one was very likely to see lithographs adorning the wall showing Pickett's Charge at Gettysburg, or some similar battle scene. The men from the South were always dressed in spotless gray uniforms . . . faced by equally immaculate boys in blue, all firing point-blank at each other . . . . A few dead and wounded were scattered about in dramatic poses, together with shattered cannons." Fictional literature was likewise preoccupied to a great extent, with stories about the Civil War.

Hooten graduated from the 180-student Northside High School in the same class as Dorothy Lewis' uncle, Edward Zeman, 1903. It was a school, he writes, that "existed principally for its football team in the fall," usually illegally recruiting alumni for tough games. In fact the team became so notorious for

56 Ibid., p. 109.
57 Ibid., p. 180.
58 Ibid., p. 120-25.

playing "ringers" and ineligibles that it was blacklisted by other schools until a new principal cleaned up the system.[59] But the "ability to sing or play an instrument was a social asset that bulked larger than athletic proficiency"[60] and it was the amount of time spent on music (Hooten recounts being pulled from class for whole days to practice performances in the auditorium) that got the Welsh principal Harry Evans fired. At the end of Hooten's sophomore year the school board held a public hearing to discuss the issue, only to be dismayed when the students rallied to the principal's support; nevertheless the man was dismissed and "replaced by Paul Keller who really got the school in shape, though he was not popular."[61]

This charming glimpse into turn-of-the-century Manitowoc life ends, unfortunately, with Hooten's departure for Lawrence College in the fall of 1903.

The city continued to grow in the twentieth century, its population increasing from approximately 12,000 when Dorothy Vits was born to approximately 25,000 when she was married in 1937. At just under 35,000 today, it is still a small city. What is impressive, particularly given its size, is the number of nationally known industries that have been developed there. Besides Mirro, which was the largest, it is home to the Manitowoc Company, a leading designer and manufacturer of high capacity cranes and excavators, as well as refrigeration equipment, and the Burger Boat Company, known worldwide for its custom luxury motor yachts. The Rahr Brewery that so impressed Hooten had a difficult time during Prohibition but came back and has now been bought out by Budweiser. Numerous other manufacturers enjoy success, especially when considered with the "twin city" of Two Rivers, home base of the Hamilton Manufacturing Company.

Place is important. In telling the story of Alcoa's growth Charles Carr points out that Pittsburgh did not give birth to aluminum because it was rich in bauxite or hydroelectric power; it has neither. What it had was a business climate in which creative genius could get a hearing and the financial backing necessary to transform an idea into an industry. Manitowoc did not have access to the capital or experience available in Pittsburgh, but its citizens, overwhelmingly immigrant Americans, had the drive, imagination, and capacity for hard work that enabled them to build a thriving and prosperous community.

Dorothy's Life Before Her Marriage

Dorothy Lewis was the second child of Anne and A. J. Vits. Her older

59 Ibid., p. 127.
60 Ibid., p. 120.
61 Ibid., p. 185.

brother Albert J. Vits, Jr., known to his family as "Abby," was born in 1905, three years after his parents' marriage. They were still living on St. Clair on the north side of the river then, and Dr. Vits was still practicing dentistry from a second floor office on North 8th Street.[62]

Dorothy came along four years later. In an early portrait of mother and children she is seen as a pretty baby with dark eyes and very little hair, peering up curiously at the photographer while snuggling closer to her mother's breast; her handsome, curly-haired older brother stands behind, looking over his mother's shoulder. Anne appears serene.

Although 96 percent of Bohemians had been Catholic in the old country, many became Protestants after coming to America, perhaps, Capek says, a reflection of the association between Catholicism and the Austrian empire, as well as Bohemian traditions going back to the fifteenth century dissenter, Jan Hus. Wisconsin, however, with its heavy concentration of Bohemians, had a very high concentration of Catholic congregations, and the Zeman family followed that faith. While A.J. Vits was presumably raised as a Lutheran, his wife was an unusually devout Catholic and he converted to her faith, possibly before their marriage since it was in a Roman Catholic ceremony, and thereafter regularly attended church with her.[63] Cousin Jane Protz remembers a needle pointed "kneeler" that "Aunt Anne had in her bedroom, where she prayed." Religious affinity may have been part of the reason that the family appears to have been closer to their Zeman than their Vits kin.

According to a local genealogist[64] all of the Catholic churches in Manitowoc were organized from St. Boniface, founded in 1853 on the south side of the river. Nineteenth century Roman Catholic parishes that served largely immigrant populations were typically "organized by nationality rather than territory," which allowed "each group to worship and pray in its own language, following the tradition and customs of the Old World."[65] Manitowoc seems to have followed that pattern although there were no specifically Bohemian congregations. St. Boniface was German-oriented, Saint Mary's (founded in 1870) was characterized as Polish, and Sacred Heart (1902) as Irish. The Zemans had originally worshiped at St. Boniface, but when Sacred Heart opened on State Street between Seventh and Eighth on the north side of the river, just a few blocks east and north of the Star Hotel, they went there. Anne and A.J. Vits

62 *Schmidt's Directory of the City and County of Manitowoc*, 1909-10 (compiled by Frank Zorn), Manitowoc, Schmidt and Zorn. A German-language ad for his practice was discovered in a book about German immigration in the Library of Congress: Karyl Enstad Rommelfanger, *Einwanderer, A True Story About German Immigration to America*, School Yard Press, 1997.
63 Protz, Interview #3, March 20, 2004. Mrs. Protz said she had not known that "Uncle Al" hadn't "always been Catholic" until being apprised of the fact by an older relative long after her childhood.
64 Richard N. Cote, *The Genealogists' Guide to Manitowoc County, Wisconsin*, Manitowoc, 1977, p. 34.
65 Jay P. Dolan, *In Search of An American Catholicism: A History of Religion and Culture in Tension*, 2002, Oxford University Press, New York, p. 60.

set up housekeeping on St. Clair Place, also just a few blocks north of Sacred Heart, and that is where Baptismal and First Communion records for both of their children are located. Sacred Heart also operated an elementary school that both Abby and Dorothy most likely attended. In 1932 when yet another Catholic church, Holy Innocents, opened on Waldo Boulevard, just north of where the Vitses were then living on Michigan Avenue, they began worshipping there. Funeral services for both of Dorothy's parents and for Abby and his wife were held there, and it was in Holy Innocents' parish house that Dorothy Vits married Logan Lewis in 1937.

Both Abby and Dorothy attended kindergarten in the same public school, named Luling when Abby was enrolled 1910-11, and Park when Dorothy went in 1914-15.[66] The teacher's roll book lists the parent's name as "Dr." A. J. Vits on Abby's record, and "Mr." on Dorothy's, perhaps reflecting the fact that A. J. stopped practicing dentistry around 1910. The addresses given are also different, indicating that the family had moved from St. Clair to 407 Park Street by the time Dorothy was enrolled. The latter home was slightly larger and just a block from the lake; the 1905 Sanborn Map[67] shows it as having an outbuilding in the back yard, which might have been either a garage or a rental unit. The most remarkable part of Dorothy's class register, however, is that she does not appear to have been present from the end of October until the beginning of March. In later years the family "wintered" in California but whether that, or illness, explains her absence is unknown.

Despite a very complete, well-organized and catalogued collection of school registers, however, the Manitowoc Heritage Center Library has no elementary school record for either child. Presumably that is because they went to Sacred Heart, a parochial school run by Franciscan Sisters; Abby's obituary confirms that he was educated there and Jane Protz, who also attended Sacred Heart, is certain that Dorothy, too, studied there. Zorn's City Directory for 1915-16 lists a school of which Sister M. Carmelita was principal, but it has long since closed, and the Diocese of Green Bay was not able to verify its rolls.

Heritage Center school records for Dorothy reappear in 1922 when she entered the seventh grade at McKinley School on Huron Street. By that time her family had moved to the large home at 1304 Michigan Avenue, just a few blocks from the school, which it would occupy for the next seventy years. Her attendance is again considerably less than that of her classmates, 156 days of a 190-day year, though her grades (three A's and three B's) were better than most of those who had been in class all year. Her best marks were in reading, spelling, and language; her worst subject seems to have been arithmetic, but her lowest

---

66 Indexed and catalogued School Registers, Manuscript Records, Manitowoc County Heritage Center Library.
67 Ibid.

mark would have pleased many of the other students. She was promoted to the eighth grade and her attendance improved that year: 174 of 185 days. Her grades, unfortunately, were not as good, with her only "A" being in spelling.

During those years Dorothy's uncle, George Vits, was on the school commission, and Manitowoc opened a magnificent new high school, an architecturally impressive building with a Gothic tower rising high above a sixteen-acre lakeside campus. One of its remarkable features was a splendid, $100,000 "natatorium" contributed by members of the Vits family in memory of patriarch Henry Vits, who had seen and been impressed with such a facility on one of his trips back to Germany. Dorothy Vits and her brother Abby, however, were sent away to high school. Abby went to Georgetown Prep in Garret Park, Maryland, and Roxbury Academy in Cheshire, Connecticut, before matriculating at Notre Dame University. Excerpted yearbook pages displayed in a family scrapbook[68] reveal his interest in athletics: "He has contributed his services to the junior athletic field with a great deal of success . . . [having been] concerned with all junior athletic teams for the past four years in some capacity or other . . . as player, captain, manager and coach." His younger cousin Jane recalls Abby as a dashing figure during his college years, wearing a raccoon coat and driving a yellow roadster; photographs in the same album show him with both.

After finishing the seventh and eighth grade at McKinley, Dorothy was sent to St. Mary-of-the-Woods Academy, a Catholic girls school five miles northwest of Terre Haute, Indiana, founded by a French order[69] of the Sisters of Providence in 1841. Soon after her graduation in 1927 the academy was relocated to Indianapolis, but a four-year college of the same name remains on the site as the oldest Catholic liberal arts college for women in the nation.

The school was reputedly a beautiful, sylvan place with broad lawns and giant trees on a seventy acre tract adjoining 1230 acres of farm lands and orchards which the Sisters managed so as to provide foodstuffs for the school; the nuns even had a coal mine to produce fuel for the boiler. A 1915 Bulletin effusively describes "a stately sweep of classic buildings extending over a thousand feet in a curving line, with a lovely conventual church set in the midst like an exquisitely carved gem of purest ray, surrounded on all sides by a charmingly varied natural environment."[70] It was a school, reads a flyer of the same era, "where young women are guided understandingly and successfully to beautiful and efficient Christian womanhood." To which sentiment a quote from Indiana author Booth Tarkington (whose mother attended the Academy) adds this testimony: "The manner of St. Mary-of-the-Woods is what remains most deeply

---

68 Scrapbook compiled by Abby's wife Florence Place Vits, in the possession of her nephew Michael Place, Manitowoc.
69 According to Notre Dame church historian Jay Dolan, "upwardly mobile Catholics" considered France the center of culture and its Catholic aristocracy the model for middle class refinement and gentility, hence convent schools administered by religious orders of women from France had become popular in the late nineteenth century. ibid., p. 89.
70 Vol. V, Number LV. Photocopies of this and other documents cited were provided by Michelle Holler of the Alumnae Relations and Annual Giving Office at St. Mary-of-the-Woods College, December 2000.

impressed upon me. It always springs to my mind whenever I delve for the true meaning of lady."

In the Catalogue for the "eighty-seventh year, 1927-28" the first sentence under "General Regulations" advises that "In order to secure a select student body it is required that strangers placing pupils at St. Mary-of-the-Woods send *social and business references from respectable and reliable sources.*" [Italics in the original.] The regulations go on to outline a requirement that students have chaperones on "visits to the city," for whose services a fee will be charged. There were also prohibitions on phone calls and weekend visitation (such interruptions being detrimental to a student's progress), limitations on foodstuffs mailed to students (fruit only, no candy), and rules for the uniforms (a simple dress of any color could be worn for "entertainments" but it "should have sleeves and should not have a low neck.") Clearly, the fashionable style of dress for which Dorothy later became known remained under wraps at St. Mary-of-the-Woods. Students were also advised to bring their own "table service, consisting of knife, fork, fruit knife, soup spoon, tea and fruit spoons, and six table napkins."

Music classes included instruction in piano, harp, violin, pipe organ, and voice, as well as harmony; art, domestic science, and riding were also taught, in addition to English, Latin, modern language, mathematics, history, and science, which courses must account for the sixteen units of work outlined by the Indiana State Department of Education. Archives held by the Sisters of Providence indicate that fees were paid on Dorothy's behalf for catechism, church history, Bible study, arithmetic, physics, literature, history, current events, botany, French and Latin. Fees were also paid for Sodality (a devotional association), art, piano lessons, vocal lessons, swimming, and horseback riding. A Macon friend remembers that Dorothy had been an accomplished horsewoman "back in the days before we knew her,"[71] and she may have acquired or honed her skills in Terre Haute.

In recalling the benefits of her own Catholic education, writer Mary McCarthy has endorsed the practical value of absorbing "a good deal of world history and the history of ideas before you are twelve," which, like a language learned early, makes them "indelible." More important, however, than "knowing more, at an earlier age, so that it becomes a part of oneself, [a Catholic education] is also a matter of feeling," especially for "something prior to and beyond utility ('Consider the lilies of the field, they toil not, neither do they spin.')" For McCarthy the most valued consequence of Catholic school "was the sense of mystery and wonder, ashes put on one's forehead on Ash Wednesday, the blessing of the throat with candles on St. Blaise's Day, the purple palls put on the statues after Passion Sunday . . . the ringing of the bell at the Sanctus . . . . In these exalted moments of altruism the soul was fired with reverence."[72]

71 Betty Hay McCook Curtis, Oral Interview #1, June 15, 2000.

So it may have been for Dorothy Vits at St. Mary-of-the-Woods. In keeping with the tradition of baroque piety that characterized the era in which it was built, the conventual Church of the Immaculate Conception where the girls were encouraged to attend daily Mass with the Sisters had an inspiring Italian Renaissance exterior and an elaborate, old-world interior. Among other sacred places and shrines on the grounds was the Our Lady of Lourdes Grotto, a replica of the famous French shrine commemorating the appearance of Mary, Mother of God, to a young girl in France, which featured an 1879 European statue. In May 1925, the middle of Dorothy's time as a student, the National Shrine of Our Lady of Providence was canonically erected at the school. Centered around a copy of Scipione Pulzone's painting *Mater Divinae Providentiae,* long venerated in Europe, the shrine's purpose was to encourage families to make Mary the queen of their homes. A confraternity[73] was established and affiliated with the archconfraternity[74] based in Rome. The April-May 1926 issue of "The Bugle Call," the newsletter for Sisters of Providence students, urged young people to give their mothers a copy of the Madonna that appeared on its frontispiece instead of a Mother's Day card.[75]

Religious devotion was a long-standing tradition in all of the schools where the Sisters of Providence taught, and Dorothy's experience at St. Mary-in-the-Woods must have reinforced her lifelong commitment to devotional activities. The school's foundress, Mother Theodore Guerin (who was beatified in 1998), had started a chapter of the Children of Mary at the Academy "to encourage love of God and of neighbor in imitation of the Blessed Virgin Mary by the practice of virtues, prayer, attendance at daily Mass and the reception of Holy Communion;" it later became affiliated with the Sodality of the Blessed Virgin Mary in Rome. Dorothy Vits was among the members attending monthly meetings. Minutes of the Catholic Students Mission Crusade list her as being elected the director of spiritual activities for one of the groups in 1925-1926.[76]

72 *Memories of a Catholic Girlhood*, Harcourt, Brace & Co., 1957, London/New York, pp. 24-27.
73 An association of laity dedicated to promoting public devotion.
74 A confraternity with affiliates.
75 Information drawn from the Sisters of Providence website, http://www.spsmw.org/heritage/congregationhistory/tidbits
76 Email correspondence from Sister Eileen Ann Kelly, Sisters of Providence Archives, December 13, 2001. Several sources suggested that Dorothy Lewis at one time considered becoming a nun herself; if that is so it may well have been while she was at St. Mary-of-the-Woods. The following excerpt from Jay Dolan's description of Devotional Catholicism will give non-Catholic readers a better appreciation of Dorothy Lewis' faith: "In the 1920-50 era devotional Catholicism reached its high-water mark. The two main features of this style of piety were the widespread practice of a 'Mass and sacraments' Catholicism and devotion to Mary. . . . For Catholics the Mass was immutable. As far as most people knew, the Mass had never changed and never would. They sat in church as quiet spectators and said their own private prayers. A holy ritual, and at times a spectacle, the Mass reinforced the trademarks of devotional Catholicism that had emerged in the nineteenth century. The centrality of the priest in the ritual of the Mass underscored his authority in the community. Without him there was no Mass, and without the Mass Catholicism was bankrupt. Since the Mass also emphasized the sinfulness of the human person, only those free of sin could receive Communion. Because of this, Confession, the sacrament of penance, became another major ritual for Catholics. Confession and Communion-these were the major Catholic miracles. At Mass Jesus became present in the midst of the congregation, uniting himself with the devout in Communion. In Confession God forgave the sins of the penitent. In both rituals the priest was the key mediator who escorted the divine into the human community. Authority, sin, ritual, and the miraculous were the key ingredients of the Catholic ethos. . . . Devotion to Mary was especially popular in this period and was generally identified with women. The recitation of the rosary, the spring ritual of May crownings of Marian statues, and the celebration of Marian feast days occupied a prominent place in the lives of Catholics. . . . The increased emphasis on miracle and the growth of shrines that encouraged this focus on the miraculous stood in stark contrast to the modern emphasis on the scientific method and positivism." ibid., pp. 169-71. In the introduction to his book, which examines the relationship between Catholicism and American culture, Dolan uses W.E.B. Du Bois' concept of "twoness-an American, a Negro, two souls, two thoughts, two unreconciled strivings" to illuminate his own experience as both a Catholic and an American-a twoness grounded in religion rather than race.

Another clue to her religious development at that formative age is a souvenir brochure containing a salutation and seal from Pope Pius XI that commemorated the Holy Year 1925; found in her desk after her death, it suggests that she was one of thousands who made the great pilgrimage to Rome during that Anno Santo.[77]

There were twenty-one girls in the Class of 1927, from which Dorothy Vits was elected Vice President. Her yearbook photo (frontispiece) reveals a strikingly beautiful young woman with dark hair and eyes, and a remarkably direct, almost challenging gaze. In the group class photo she stands in the front row, as likely befit her office, and while the picture is not as flattering, she seems a swan amongst ducklings.

Following high school in Indiana Dorothy went to the equally exclusive, if quite secular, Finch School in New York City. Later known as Finch Junior College and then Finch College, the school was widely considered one of the country's most prestigious 'finishing schools.' "This fashionable institution of learning was . . . designed to 'finish' the enrolled student. She was trained to be the darling of society, with polished manners, discreet decorum, prepared to be the lady of the house when Mr. Right appeared. There she would reign supreme on her pedestal."[78] Though the term 'finishing' was never part of the institutional name, the sobriquet was so common that that was the name given it by the Manitowoc paper in Dorothy's engagement announcement.[79] By whatever nomenclature "it was *the* school for young ladies in that day."[80]

Located on the upper east side between Park and Madison, the school had had an interesting origin. It was founded by an early Barnard graduate who felt the classical education she had received there was irrelevant to the life women lead. Jessica Cosgrave once declared that her four years in college

77 Brochure is now in collection of Lewis Foundation Archives. Jane Protz believed it very likely that Dorothy and her mother had made that trip: "Business was booming and Aunt Anne was very religious." (Interview #3.) After Anne Vits' death Dorothy gave Jane a cape and rosary beads which had belonged to her mother, saying, "I think these have been blessed by the Pope." That this 1925 trip to Rome was not her first to Europe is evidenced by an amusing vignette handed down in Macon's Allen Dennis family. According to that story Mr. Dennis' brother-in-law Brown Wemberly ("a bon vivant cotton merchant" according to his nephew) met Dorothy Vits and her brother on a cross-Atlantic voyage not long after World War I, the occasion made memorable by Abby Vits' assistance to an overweight passenger who encountered some difficulty with a tub. The story, originally shared with me by Allen Dennis' son Brown in a phone interview on October 17, 2002, was corroborated by a 1983 letter from the older Dennis to Dorothy Lewis found in her bedroom desk after her death. (Now in the Lewis Archives.) Enclosing the photocopied bio of one Elliott White Springs from an unidentified compendium, he wrote: "I think this is the Col. Springs your brother rescued from under the bath tub." Mr. Dennis and Dorothy Lewis were both serving on the board of the Riverside Cemetery at the time the letter was written.
78 Laura Augusta Reddington, *My Memoirs of Finch*, Martin Printing Col., New York, 1964, p. 13. Ms. Reddington ran the switchboard at Finch for thirty-five years beginning in 1928, and had an apartment at the school. Years after they had left Finch Betty Hay McCook Curtis sent Dorothy a small card titled "Finch School Maxims" which she had found in the bottom of a drawer, with a handwritten note asking, "How long has it been since you have seen these?" They also reflect the atmosphere at the school: "1. Remember that believing in people usually brings out the best that is in them. 2. Remember there is always another side: suspend judgement [sic]. 3. Remember there is always a way out. Do not waste time in self-pity but find it. 4. Remember in all your decisions to be influenced by proportion. 5. Remember that your actions always affect others and that other people's feelings are just like your own; be considerate. 6. Remember that other people are just as intuitive as you are and judge you from trifles just as you do them. 7. Remember that in the long run everyone will find you out and will judge you by your true self and not by your pretensions; be sincere. 8. Remember that snobbishness of any kind is a sign of limitation. 9. Remember that all happiness comes from efficient action; recreation must be to re-create work. 10. Remember that optimism is a duty. Cheerfulness and depression are both contagious and you have no right to inflict despondent moods on others. 11. Remember that you must be worthy and capable of love to be able to give or to keep it. 12. Remember that you have a soul just as truly as you have a body and a social self. Do not starve it." Lewis Archives.
79 *Manitowoc Herald Times*, Saturday, June 12, 1937, p.8.
80 Vivian Hay Anderson, Oral Interview, May 18, 2000.

"were years of . . . apathy as far as any mental contact with the great facts of life was concerned."[81] A woman of determined mind who described herself as an "orthodox" Socialist and feminist, and also the person credited with coining the term "current events," Mrs. Cosgrave started Finch as a "protest" against colleges with such conventional programs as Barnard's. The thirteen-student school she opened in an apartment on Madison Avenue in 1900 was designed to teach her pupils "some of the things of the life they are living," and to provide them with a strong cultural background.[82] Academics, per se, were not emphasized.

With a board of trustees made up of both educators and members of some of the city's most socially prominent families, the school had grown to approximately 150 students (some boarding, but mostly day students) by the time Dorothy enrolled in the fall of 1927. Mrs. Cosgrave was referred to as the "Headmistress" and she set a schedule in which students spent half their time on class work and half on painting, music and the theater. Fencing, dancing, interior decoration, and home making were among the subjects taught, although the latter was not practiced: chambermaids arrived early to close the windows, serve breakfast, clean the rooms, and prepare and serve dinner, a formal affair with candlelight and linen tablecloths.[83] Students did sew themselves suits of clothing, learning the intricacies of French seams in the process.[84] The young ladies were required to use chaperones anytime they left the school, even to shop,[85] and with their chaperones they went to the opera every week where Finch maintained a box next to that of the Met's General Manager. The *New York Times* reported on such social activities as teas and luncheons for the students; a contemporary of Dorothy's also remembers seances.[86] The school was housed in five brownstones on East Seventy-seventh Street across from the Carlisle Hotel, and though it closed in 1976, there was still, in the summer of 2000, at least one elderly bellman at the Carlisle who well-remembered the hullabaloo that surrounded the arrival of prominent young women like Anne Ford at the start of a new term.[87]

It was at Finch that Dorothy met a pretty, voluble girl from Macon, Georgia, a connection that altered the course of her life. Vivian ("Bib") Hay, afterwards Mrs. Halstead Tindal Anderson, was the daughter of a wealthy insurance entrepreneur to whom the old saw "never met a stranger" would be particularly applicable. During an interview in her ninety-first year Mrs. Anderson recalled that the two "hit it off very well." Her description of the origins of their relationship reveals a hint of the remoteness for which Dorothy

81 *New York Times*, November 1, 1949, 27:1, Obituary of Jessica Garretson Finch Cosgrave.
82 Ibid., October 21, 1944, 19:7, reporting a speech made by Mrs. Cosgrave.
83 Reddington, ibid., p. 22-3.
84 Anderson interview, ibid.
85 Reddington, ibid., p. 21.
86 Curtis interview, ibid.
87 Oral Interview, May 27, 2000. Unfortunately, the author did not record the name of the bellman to whom she spoke on this day.

later became known, as well the expectations of young women in that era: Dorothy "was popular at school, but she was never with anybody. I don't' know why, but she took a liking to me . . . she invited me to Wisconsin—and my father let me go."[88] How different Dorothy Vits's life would have been had Mr. Hay said "no." Dorothy's own father, A.J. Vits, in Chicago on business, met his daughter's guest at the station where she had to change trains, accompanying her to Manitowoc, and then on to the Vits's summer home at Elkhart Lake.

It was the beginning of a friendship that endured long after they left school, indeed to the ends of their lives, expanding to include Bib's younger sister Betty, who followed them to Finch. The young women visited back and forth frequently in the late twenties and early thirties, usually for several weeks at a time. Mrs. Anderson remembered the Georgia visits as including more social opportunities than those in Wisconsin, and believes Dorothy enjoyed them for that reason. The Hay family home[89] was the largest in the city with an expansive ball room, and Mr. Hay had provided a variety of musical instruments for entertaining the numerous young people who gathered there in evenings for music and dance, "even on school nights," Mrs. Anderson remembers, although of course the girls were not in school during these visits. Macon "people were warm to her," she said, smiling.

Dorothy Vits "was the most gorgeous thing I ever saw," another contemporary recounts; "She was more than just pretty. She had a great style about her and beautiful skin and black hair. She was stunning, and she knew how to dress."[90] Unsurprisingly, she did not lack for beaux when she was in town. A number of Macon admirers sought her company, but Basil Hall was her most frequent date, and even followed her home to Wisconsin on occasion. Crockett Odom was another escort, and he, too, drove up to Manitowoc and Elkhart Lake with Bib and her new husband, "Andy" Anderson, one summer after they married in 1934. Manitowoc "boyfriends" included Bobby Testwuide who adopted that title in introducing himself to guests at Dorothy's wedding, while testifying as to what a "wonderful girl" she was.[91]

Dorothy's formal education did not end with her studies at Finch. After obtaining an associate degree in New York City she spent a year abroad, matriculating at the Villa des Sorbiers in Versailles, France; unfortunately nothing else is known about her studies there. When she returned to the United States she pursued an aspiration to become involved in theater. Her engagement announcement noted that she had "spent much of her time in the East following

88 Anderson interview, ibid.
89 Donated to the Georgia Trust for Historic Preservation in 1978 by the Hay family, the 24,000 SF house was built in 1855-60 and designated a National Historic Landmark by the U. S. Department of the Interior. It is now open to the public six days a week.
90 Laura Nelle Anderson O'Callaghan, Oral Interview, September 15, 2000.
91 Ibid.

her interest in dramatics,"[92] but where or with whom she studied is unknown. She boarded in the dorms at Finch, according to Mrs. Anderson's younger sister Betty Hay McCook Curtis, then a student there, who graduated in 1933. Mrs. Curtis remembers Dorothy's mother taking them to tea at the Savoy when she came to New York to visit. "Everybody was . . . enamored with Dorothy because she was glamorous looking and was doing theater."[93] Her friend does not believe that she ever got farther than an apprenticeship, however, because "we would have gone to see her if she had" performed. Still, it was a strong interest; books on drama and theater arts, anthologies of plays from the early thirties, and New York theatre programs from the late twenties were still on her bookshelves after her 2002 death,[94] and her bedroom desk contained a "Guide Programme" for the 1929 Season at the Theatre Albert 1er; featuring a company, the English Players, which produced "a repertory of English-speaking plays" for Paris audiences; it was likely a souvenir from the year she spent at Versailles after leaving Finch.

By this time Dorothy's brother, Abby, had been married awhile, having eloped with a beautiful blonde before finishing college. A few years his senior, Florence Place was a bandleader, and an orphan from South Bend who was responsible for looking after three younger brothers. While the union was doubtless not what the Vitses would have chosen for their son, they accepted Flo, as she was known, and two of her brothers, Ira and Jimmy, moved to Manitowoc with her; a friend remembers them being introduced at the Vits-Lewis wedding as "adopted brothers."[95] Ira went to work for "the Goods," taking a sales position out of town but returning home for Christmas and holidays. It was during one of those returns that he met local belle, Gerta Hempel, whom he later married, going on to work in and eventually manage her family's chemical business, the Heresite Company. Jimmy, still in his teens when Florence and Abby married, continued to live with A.J. and Anne after Abby and Flo moved to California in the early thirties, making himself useful while attending Lincoln High School, and later after he too, had gone to work at "the Goods." Following his marriage he and his wife Toni and son Michael continued to spend a great deal of time with the older Vitses. (The oldest Place brother moved to Chicago after Flo and Abby's marriage.[96])

Abby and Flo had one child, a daughter they named Gretchen Ann, who died in infancy, on July 29, 1932, and was buried in the Zeman family plot in Evergreen Cemetery, Manitowoc. Abby had joined A.G.M.C. in the jobbing

92 Ibid.
93 Curtis interview, ibid.
94 For example, *The Best Plays of 1934-5* and *Yearbook of the Drama in America*, Burns Mantle, ed., Dodd, Mead and Company, New York, 1935; *Sarah Bernhardt, The Art of the Theatre; The Plays of Henrik Ibsen*, Otis Skinner's 1923 *Footlights and Spotlight: Recollections of My Life On Stage*; 1928's *An Introduction to Drama*; and 1931's *Ellen Terry and Bernard Shaw: A Correspondence*. Intriguingly, a 1934 edition of Noel Coward's *Play Parade* containing Dorothy Ann Vits' bookplate, and inscribed from Basil Wise Hall, has half the frontispiece torn out.
95 O'Callaghan interview, ibid.
96 Michael Place Oral Interview, October 20, 2000.

sales department in 1928, was transferred to Syndicated Sales in 1931, and joined Central Sales in 1933; soon after their baby's death he transferred his work to Los Angeles and was named Pacific Coast Sales Manager in 1952. He and Flo appear to have enjoyed a merry life in California, developing friendships with numerous celebrities, including syndicated columnist and author Patricia Barham, who visited them in Manitowoc,[97] and renowned singer Bing Crosby. Abby retired in 1976 but he and Flo continued to live in Beverly Hills, spending part of each year in the Vitses' Michigan Avenue home in Manitowoc or at the summer place at Elkhart Lake, until moving to the former for good in 1982; he died in 1985. Flo moved out of the family home after that but remained in Manitowoc until her death in 1992. Living at a distance and in different manners, Dorothy and her brother were never close.

Even before Abby moved west for "the Goods," the Vitses had been in the habit of wintering in southern California, and during the early thirties Dorothy spent considerable time in Coconut Grove. Mrs. Curtis recalls visiting her friend there before either of them married, a trip that included a side excursion to the Hearst Castle, San Simeon. A page torn from a magazine entitled *California Outdoors and In* (April, 1932, p. 8) that was found in her bedroom in 2002 depicts "Miss Dorothy Vits" posing for "the celebrated young Viennese portrait painter, Professor Fritz Werner" at "the Ambassador Hotel—a place . . . that people of beauty and character . . . frequent as a second home." In the accompanying photograph Dorothy is seen sitting pristinely on a raised platform, looking like a character from the Renaissance in a scoop-necked velvet gown and pendant cross, with a large ring on her right hand; the painter and his nearly finished portrait are in the foreground.[98]

If winters were spent in California, summers found the Vitses at the charming Victorian resort of Elkhart Lake in the northwest corner of Sheboygan County, just south of Manitowoc County. Hotels in the tiny town offered gambling which A. J. enjoyed, but there were numerous other recreational opportunities, including auto races that were run on village streets until Road America opened a twisting four mile course south of town in 1955.[99] The Vitses built a lakeside house that was readily accessible—just an hour from Manitowoc—and they were in frequent residence there.

As was typical for young women of her station in those years, employment

97 Newspaper clipping from Manitowoc paper found in scrapbook compiled by Florence Place in possession of Michael Place, Manitowoc.
98 Found in Mrs. Lewis' desk after her death; now in the Lewis Archives.
99 Jane Protz, March 20, 2004. Dorothy was married to Logan Lewis by the time the Road America track was constructed in 1955, and they bought a modest 10 shares of stock in the company formed to build it and manage the four or five races staged every summer; Dorothy held the stock until her death. "Respected the world over as one of the great road racing courses, Road America's 500 acres of woodland and grass provide a unique pastoral setting for the twisting 4-mile circuit on which some of the best national and international drivers compete for the checkered flag. (From the 25th anniversary brochure, Road America File, Lewis Archives.) Dorothy's old "boyfriend," Robert Testwuide, who became Chairman of the Board of Schreier Malting Company, was Vice Chair of the Road America board for many years.

was not part of Dorothy's post-formal-education life. Twenty-seven when she married, "at home" fills the blank on her marriage license next to "occupation."

When her friend Bib Hay married Halstead Anderson in a sumptuous 1934 ceremony, Dorothy Vits was one of her six attendants. The next year Bib's younger sister, Betty, married Jimmy McCook and Mrs. Anderson said that Dorothy came to Macon for that wedding also. Jimmy McCook's best man was the handsome scion of an old Georgia family, a debonair bachelor named Logan Lewis, termed by one of his friends "our prince."[100] A year and a half after that wedding he and Dorothy were married, and when she returned to Macon following their 1937 honeymoon, it was as a permanent resident.

Dorothy as an infant cuddles next to Anne Vits; brother Abby stands behind them. Photo courtesy of Michael Place.

Henry Vits, Dorothy's paternal grandfather, was the founder of the Manitowoc Aluminum Novelty Company, one of the forerunners of the Mirro Company, the world's largest manufacturer of aluminum cookware. He is shown with his wife, Mary, in this undated photo. Courtesy of Michael Place.

100 O'Callaghan interview, ibid.

Dorothy Vits stands in the front row, fourth from right, in this picture of the 1927 graduating class of St. Mary-of-the-Woods Academy, Terre Haute, IN. Photo courtesy of St. Mary-of-the-Woods Alumnae Office.

The Vits' Michigan Avenue home. Photo courtesy of Michael Place.

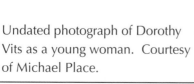

Undated photograph of Dorothy Vits as a young woman. Courtesy of Michael Place.

Dorothy Vits poses for Viennese portrait painter, Professor Fritz Werner, at the Ambassador Hotel in California. Photo from *California Outdoors and In*, April 1932, p. 8.

Bib Hay Anderson, Crockett Odom, and a pant-suited Dorothy Vits relax in the sunshine at the Vits summer home at Elkhart Lake in 1934. From the Crockett Odom Scrapbook, courtesy of Crockett Rader Sellers.

Chapter 2

————◆•◆•◆————

The Debonair "Prince"
from Georgia

Family Background

The man whose Macon friend described him as "our Prince"[1] was born February 8, 1908, if not to royalty, certainly to an old Georgia family, every branch of which had enjoyed wealth and prominence since the early nineteenth century; indeed one of his great-great-grandfathers had been referred to as "the Prince of Meriwether."[2] It was land, commerce, and banking, however, rather than manufacturing, that enriched the Georgians.

Their roots in the state dated to its earliest post-colonial history. As Dorothy Vits's perceptions of the world were shaped by the growth and success of the Aluminum Goods Manufacturing Company, Nathaniel Logan Lewis's were formed by his family's position and accumulated fortune. Perhaps more so; given the small size of his immediate family—his mother and himself—the extended branches of the family tree exerted a more-than-ordinary influence over the house in which he grew up, filled as it was with the material remnants of their time on earth. Ancestors, as represented by their former possessions, were a living presence in every corner of 717 Vineville Avenue. Having been in ill health for several years, his mother filled a composition book with a penciled inventory of the objects with which they lived shortly before her death: portraits, furniture, china, linens, silver, even clothing. Beginning with simple family charts that showed her son's descent from the Jones, Strozier, Callaway, Logan, Hardeman, Lewis, Butts, and Jelks clans (in that order), each piece was described and its ownership history recounted.[3] One oil portrait of his great-grandfather George Logan had been a gift from his great uncle Alec; another had come from a second cousin, once removed in North Carolina. A brass candlestick had been used by his great-great-grandmother Elizabeth Strozier Jones when

1 Laura Nelle O'Callaghan, Oral Interview #1, September 15, 2000.
2 J.L.S., "Old Citizens," *The Meriwether Vindicator*, February 24, 1905, quoted in *Pioneers of Meriwether County, Georgia as reported in the Meriwether Vindicator,* compiled by Clare Isanhour, Smyrna, GA, 1991, Coweta County Genealogical Society, Newnan.
3 She also noted to whom the things should be distributed if he decided not to keep them, but added "Only remember, don't be too hasty-things become dear from association." Composition Book Inventory found in the Lewis kitchen after Dorothy Lewis' 2002 death, now in Lewis Archives.

she got up in the night with her children; the needlepoint on the ottoman had been done by his great-grandmother Ann Jones Callaway; a cane with a gold knob had belonged to his grandfather Robert Gallatin Lewis and had been used by his father; a small music box had been purchased on a trip to New York by that same grandfather Lewis for his wife, Mary Jelks Lewis. Evidence of the interests and travels of the extended clan still filled the book shelves of the Lewis living room on Old Club Road after Dorothy Lewis's death: Annie Callaway's guide book to *Cairo of Today* dated 1904, Alex Logan's *New Conceptions in Science,* 1908, Tero Callaway's *The Habits of Good Society: A Handbook for Ladies and Gentlemen,* published in 1871, Robert Gallatin Lewis' 1883 edition of the *Complete Works of Dickens,* the 1903 copy of Emerson's essays that had belonged to his widow Mary Jelks Lewis Mallary, and the numerous leather-bound collections (Shakespeare, Stevenson, Tennyson, etc.) with E. N. Lewis, Logan's father, inscribed on the frontispiece. Clearly, to know his family is to better know Logan Lewis.

Logan Lewis' paternal great-great-great-great-grandfather, Jacob Lewis (1750-1812) had been an ensign with the Virginia troops during the Revolutionary War, taking part in the expedition to Fort Pitts under General McIntosh.[4] Like thousands of others whose service entitled them to bounty grants once the battles were over, Jacob Lewis migrated to Georgia to claim land in Burke County[5], perhaps drawn by Georgia's willingness to couple headright grants with veterans' bounties.[6] He eventually settled in Burke County in the eastern part of the state, remaining there until his death in 1812. His son Jacob Lewis Jr. (1779-1820) lived in adjacent Screven County and drew land in Wilkinson County in the 1807 Lottery.[7] Jacob Jr.'s son, however, John Benjamin Lewis (1805-1884), relocated to Dooly (later Crisp) County in southwest Georgia, where he became a large landowner, paying taxes of $12.55 on 1950 acres, twenty-three slaves and two buggies in 1851.[8] Another source, perhaps reflecting Lewis' increasing prosperity over the decade before secession (the 1860 Slave Schedule shows him owning fifty-five slaves)[9] sets his holdings at 3300 acres, and notes that during the "stressful times" of the Civil War John Benjamin Lewis "distributed wagonloads of provisions among the needy of his community."[10]

4 *Historical and Genealogical Collections of Dooly County, Georgia,* volume III, compiled and edited by Nora Powell and Watts Powell, p. 219.
5 Rev. Silas Emmett Lucas, Jr., *Index to the Headright and Bounty Grants of Georgia, 1750-1909,* published by Georgia Genealogical Reprints, 1970, p. 385.
6 Kenneth Coleman, ed., *A History of Georgia,* 2nd Edition, University of Georgia Press, Athens, 1991, p. 106.
7 Rev. Silas Emmett Lucas, Jr., *The Second or 1807 Land Lottery of Georgia,* Vidalia, Ga., Georgia Genealogical Reprints, 1968, p. 118. A Jacob Lewis Sr. and Jr. from Wilkes County also drew land in the second lottery but since they were residents of Wilkes, they are presumably another father-son combination of the same name since individuals could only draw from their home county and according to the Dooly County history cited above, John Benjamin Lewis' father resided in Screven County.
8 *Historical and Genealogical Collections of Dooly County, Georgia,* ibid., vol. I., p.91.
9 Dooly County Census Records on microfilm in the Washington Memorial Library Genealogical and Historical Room.
10 W. P. Fleming, *Crisp County, Georgia Historical Sketches,* reproduced from the 1932 edition with a new index by Carleton J. Thaxton, The Reprint Co., Spartanburg, S. C., 1980, p. 128.

It was John Benjamin's son, John Falton Lewis (Logan Lewis' great-grandfather, 1830-1879) who moved the family from farming into business and banking. According to the Crisp County historian W. P. Fleming, Colonel Lewis got his start in merchandizing at Cork's Ferry, just south of where Cedar Creek empties into the Flint River.[11] The fact that his property on Stagecoach Road was located along "the chief artery of land commerce in that particular section"[12] may have contributed to his new venture; family history also credits his wealthy father-in-law, who had built some of the first boats on the Ocmulgee, Flint, and Chattahoochee rivers, with encouraging him to transport cotton to New York for sale after the Civil War.[13] Many merchants in the rural sections of Georgia were also farmers or planters,[14] and given the dearth of financial institutions, they found it was frequently a short step from commerce to credit, with one merchant known to have dispensed loans from a trunk under his bed.[15] In 1853 J.F. Lewis had married Lavinia Butts, daughter of another of Dooley's largest planters,[16] and they settled near their parents in Gum Creek (now Coney) where they raised a large family. (See Family Tree on pp. 220-21.) An effusive sketch in *Memoirs of Georgia* describes John Falton Lewis as "one of those self-made men who forged to the front by reason of superior financial acumen. His was a mind that was quick to perceive and ready to act upon the opportunities of life. And long before he had reached the zenith he had impressed his individuality upon the business world of all south Georgia."[17] The memoirist then goes on to quote a posthumously published eulogy from the *Montezuma Weekly:* "Noble spectacle it was to behold him, while in life, surrounded by his young sons like a chieftain upon the field among his lieutenants, teaching them to plan and succeed, carefully carrying out in every detail the operations of the largest business of the country."

In 1869 J.F. Lewis established another mercantile and banking business just up the Flint in neighboring Macon County, this time in partnership with William Minor,[18] after whom he later named one of his eight children. He put his eldest son, Elijah, then just seventeen, in charge of it.[19] Eventually his sons

11 Ibid., p. 44.
12 Ibid., p. 48.
13 Ione Lewis McKenzie, "The Lewis Family," in Louise Frederick Hays, *History of Macon County, Georgia,* Spartanburg, South Carolina, The Reprint Co., 1979, p. 575.
14 Coleman, ibid., p. 154.
15 In her study of the background of Macon County business, Chamber of Commerce executive Nanita Gottman wrote that inn-keeper/farmer "Nathan Bryan . . . became a rich man. He kept his savings under his bed in a rawhide trunk and it was said to be mostly in gold. His wealth became known and his neighbors called upon him for loans. . . .[A] neighbor simply sent a boy on horseback with a message stating the amount he wished to borrow, Bryan dropped the note in the trunk, sent the money, and let the scrap of paper remain there until the money was returned." Quoted in "History of Macon County Banks Begins in 1830's," *Macon Telegraph,* October 27, 1965, Two Star Edition, p. 14A.
16 Elijah Butts, who had been born in Connecticut in 1808, was listed in the 1860 census as having real property valued at $34,000 and personal property valued at $22,520; the 1860 slave schedule credits him with thirty-six slaves and eleven slave houses.
17 *Southern Historical Association, Historical and Biographical Memoirs of Georgia,* vol. II, 1895, Reprinted by Southern Historical Press, Easley, S. C., 1976, pp. 707-08.
18 I did not uncover the source of Lewis' relationship to Minor but the 1860 Dooly County federal census lists him as an eighteen-year-old "merchant" residing in the J. F. Lewis household; by the time of the 1870 census Minor was counted in Montezuma, Macon County, where as a "retail merchant" with $5000 in real and personal property, he was a member of the Daniel Kelsoe household. (Davine V. Campbell, *1870 Federal Census for Macon County,* Warner Robins, Central Georgia Genealogical Society, 1989, p. 31.)
19 Hays, ibid., p. 195.

headed banks all across south Georgia:[20] Elijah Banks Lewis,[21] who later served as mayor and represented the Third District in Congress for a dozen years[22], ran the Lewis Banking Company and organized the First National Bank[23] in Montezuma, the two of which were reorganized as the Citizens National Bank under the leadership of the youngest brother, William Minor Lewis, following Elijah's 1921 suicide;[24] John F. Lewis Jr. (who married Mary Lee Lamar of Macon) headed the Citizens Bank in Valdosta; Sheribiah Butts Lewis presided over a bank in Albany until his 1890 death at age thirty;[25] and William Minor Lewis organized and was president of the Fourth National Bank in Macon as well as a bank in Atlanta and the one in Montezuma mentioned above. The "Colonel"[26] and his third son, Robert Gallatin Lewis (Logan's grandfather, 1858-1892), selected Hawkinsville to establish the Lewis-Leonard Banking Company in partnership with in-law Dr. Bothwell Leonard of Vienna, who had married John Falton's oldest daughter, Eva, in 1876.[27] An 1877 clipping from the Pulaski County newspaper notes that John F. Lewis of Gum Creek, D. B. Leonard of Vienna, and Robert G. Lewis, among others, had left for New York, presumably on business.[28]

Robert Gallatin Lewis was not long out of Mercer, where he was said to have taken a particular interest in mathematics, when he and his family resettled themselves in Hawkinsville in 1879; unfortunately the Colonel died before the year was out.[29] Nevertheless young Lewis seems to have managed their financial venture well. His bank "was one of Hawkinsville's best financial assets for a number of years," and "of great value in the making for better business in the

20 *Memoirs of Georgia,* ibid.
21 Some sources (Fleming, ibid., p. 43; Pulaski County History, p. 375) give the middle name as Butts; others (Powell, ibid., p. 220; Hays, ibid., p. 389) say it is Banks. The sketch in the Macon County history, however, was written by E. B. Lewis' daughter Ione Lewis McKenzie, which gives it more credibility than the others. The confusion may stem from the fact that he was named for his maternal grandfather, Elijah Butts, and most primary sources refer to him as "E. B." or "Elijah B." causing some chroniclers to understandably assume that the "B." must stand for "Butts."
22 Where he served on the Banking and Currency Committee, eventually becoming Democratic Minority Leader of that committee.
23 *Memoirs of Georgia,* ibid., p. 197.
24 *The Macon Telegraph,* February 24, 1921, p. 9A.
25 Corroborating evidence has not been found for this *Memoirs of Georgia* assertion; the *History and Reminiscences of Dougherty County* compiled by the Thronateeksa Chapter of the D.A.R. (Albany, 1924, p. 313), claims that the first bank organized there was the First National Bank of Albany in 1888, just two years before Sheribiah Butts Lewis' death in 1890-indeed nine years after John F. Lewis, who is credited with having established that bank, is said to have died of pneumonia in Hawkinsville. The *History* also credits Capt. John A. Davis with that bank's organization. It seems clear, however, that Sheribiah Butts Lewis is the Sherrie B. Lewis, husband of Nettie Coley, who is buried in Oakview Cemetery in Albany (*Dougherty County Cemeteries,* Book I, published by Southwest Georgia Genealogical Society, Inc., Albany, 1984) because the birth and death dates match his; evidence that he was in Albany is also found in another part of the Dougherty County history: a newspaper story on March 15, 1885 listed Mr. S. B. Lewis as a member of the Committee on Conveyances set up to support a meeting of the Georgia Press Association in Bainbridge (ibid., pp. 68-69.)
26 This may have been the southern honorific when used in the *Memoirs of Georgia* sketch cited above; while John Falton Lewis did serve in the War, according to Lillian Henderson, comp., *Roster of the Confederate Soldiers of Georgia 1861-1865* (Georgia Division of the United Daughters of the Confederacy, 1994 reprint of 1959 publication), his highest rank was Captain of the 32nd Inf., Co I, which surrendered at Greensboro April 26, 1865.
27 Despite being spread around Georgia the Lewis family apparently maintained close ties; fifteen years after his death descendants of a number of Robert Gallatin Lewis' siblings turned up at the wedding of his son Nat to Johnnie Logan in 1906: *The Macon Telegraph* reported that children of Elijah (Mrs. W.H. McKenzie of Montezuma), John (Misses Caro and Laura Lewis of Valdosta), Eva (Misses Bertha, Sallie, and Helen Leonard of Vienna), and Mattie (Mrs. Will Dodson of Americus) were among the out of town guests at the ceremony. (*The Macon Telegraph,* "Society", December 13, 1906, p. 3.)
28 Tad Evans, comp., *Pulaski County, Georgia, Newspaper Clippings,* Vol. II, 1876-1881, self-published, Savannah, 2001, p. 110.
29 Curiously, a J. F. Lewis (49) is listed as a resident of Dooly County in the 1880 census, with an S. B. Lewis (20) as son, the ages of both consistent with the ages shown in the 1870 census data for John F. Lewis, 39, husband of Lavinia, and father of "Sabriah," age 10. Lavinia Lewis, however, was counted as a resident of Pulaski County in 1880, showing up as the head of a household that included Robert G., age 22, John, age 16, Mattie, age 13, Pearl, age 10, and Minor, age 5. Yet the sketch of Robert Gallatin Lewis in the Pulaski County history as well as the one of "Colonel John F. Lewis" in *Memoirs of Georgia* give the father's death date as December of 1879.

town."[30] A local history claims that he was "held in high esteem for his financial ability, brilliant mind, and moral integrity. As a leader in business, social and religious life, R. G. Lewis was the first citizen of his community."[31]   He helped to found the Public Library and Literary Society in 1882 and was eventually one of its directors.[32] An 1887 Pulaski County newspaper cited an instance of particular beneficence: in connection with the death of a wounded, widowed Civil War veteran named Julius Bagby, the paper reported that Lewis had enabled Bagby to keep up payments on a $5000 life insurance policy that would otherwise have lapsed, thus preserving an estate for his orphaned children.[33]

In 1883 Lewis married Cox College graduate Mary Jelks (Logan's grandmother, 1865-1925), a member of the prominent Jelks-Polhill clan which had settled Hawkinsville early in the nineteenth century.[34] Mary's paternal grandfather, James Oliver Jelks, Sr., was a merchant planter of Welsh descent who served in the legislature during the 1830s; her maternal grandfather, James Polhill, was a judge of the southern circuit for many years. J. O. Jelks Jr., Mary's father, built the city's first store, mercantile business having previously been conducted from dwellings, and enjoyed considerable success in growing his firm; the Pulaski County history describes him as "truly a literary person" despite his lack of formal education, given that he "read and traveled rather extensively."[35] Her mother, Elizabeth Phillips (or Phelps in some sources) had taken honors in music at LaGrange College in 1862;[36] she and J. O. Jelks Jr. were married in 1863 and Mary was born in 1865. Mary Jelks Lewis must have inherited her mother's abilities because she too was known as a talented musician. She and Robert Lewis were active members of the Baptist Church. They had three children, of whom Logan Lewis' father, Elijah Nathaniel Lewis, born in 1885, was the first, and at ten pounds, probably the largest.[37] Their third child was just a year old when tragedy struck the young family in 1892: Robert Gallatin Lewis died of pneumonia at age thirty-four.

The twenty-eight year old widow had a number of family connections with the larger city of Macon, some forty miles north of Hawkinsville on the Ocmulgee; her husband's sister, Pearl, had moved there after her marriage and her uncle E. N. Jelks, having married a Macon girl, ran a fertilizer firm in the city. How she met Macon businessman Edgar Y. Mallary is unclear, although another uncle, John Jelks, was living just around the corner from where E.Y. Mallary was

30 Hawkinsville Chapter of the Daughters of the American Revolution, *The History of Pulaski County, Georgia* 1808-1935, Bicentennial Edition, OmniPress, Inc., Macon, Georgia, 1975, p. 112.
31 Ibid., p. 375.
32 Ibid., p. 381.
33 Evans, ibid., Vol. III, 1882-87, p. 409.
34 *Memoirs of Georgia*, Vol. I, p. 383.
35 Ibid., P. 359.
36 *Memoirs of Georgia*, Vol. II, p. 704.
37 Evans, ibid., p. 344.

living with his brother in 1893.[38] In any event, Mary Jelks Lewis and E. Y. Mallary were married the year following Robert Lewis's death.

Mallary, a widower with two sons and a daughter, had been born in Cuthbert[39] where his Baptist preacher father, Rollin D. Mallary, had been President of Southwestern College.[40] Having come of age and married Blanche Nelson in North Carolina while the elder Mallary served in a similar capacity at Shelby College there, E. Y. Mallary had attended Mercer University[41] and moved to Macon permanently in the 1880s. He worked as a traveling salesman before organizing a wholesale machine manufacturer/distributor that he ran with his younger brother, Frank Lorraine Mallary. The year after marrying Mary Jelks Lewis he commissioned architect Peter Dennis to build a substantial home for his enlarged family in the rapidly suburbanizing village of Vineville,[42] just north of the city limits and across the street from his brother. All six of the children by their prior marriages, as well as another daughter born in 1895,[43] were reared in that house. Meanwhile, as reported by the Pulaski County newspaper in 1894, Mallary had filed to take his wife's place as the guardian of the persons and property of R. G. Lewis, in 1894.[44] That same year he relinquished primary responsibility for the machinery business to his brother Frank and became president of the newly organized Dime Savings Bank. Shortly thereafter his business interests expanded further to include the Macon Seed and Mercantile Co; the Merchants and Mechanics Building and Loan Association; and Cobb, Mallary and Stetson, an insurance firm. In 1898, he organized the Commercial and Savings Bank with capital of $50,000 and a surplus of $12,500;[45] he was president, his wife's brother E. Nat Jelks was vice president, and his sister's husband, J. J. Cobb, was cashier; Commercial National Bank followed. Soon after the turn of the century he expanded his business interests yet again, becoming one of the founders of the kaolin industry, and helping to organize the Eagle River Mining Company, which operated gold mines in Alaska. He was president of the Georgia Kaolin Company until his death in 1926, apparently well deserving of the encomiums in his obituary, which described him as one of the "foremost" men in the industry.[46]

38 The 1893 City Directory shows Edgar Mallary boarding with his brother Francis at the southeast corner of Vineville and Cleveland avenues, a near neighbor of John Jelks, who lived on Cleveland.
39 Obituary, *Macon Telegraph*, February 8, 1926, p. 1A.
40 Clara Nell Hargrove, Julius Gholson, and Ida Walker Young, *A History of Macon, Georgia*, Macon: Macon Women's Club, 1949, p. 687.
41 Both his maternal and paternal grandfathers were Baptist ministers who were involved with Mercer in its early years, the latter having raised the $120,000 that put the school on a firm financial basis in the 1830s and 40s, and the former having served as President of the university from 1844-55. (A.B. Caldwell, "Edgar Young Mallary," in *Men of Mark in Georgia*, 1733-1911, ed. by William J. Northen, Atlanta, A. B. Caldwell, publisher, 1912. vol. VI, p. 248.)
42 Macon Architectural and Building Survey, 1970, Carl and Russell Feiss, Unpublished Working Papers, Volumes I-XX, in the Historical and Genealogical Room, Washington Memorial Library, p. 4291. Materials for these papers were gathered by volunteers and while useful, contain errors; the homes built by Carlton and Ann Callaway, and their daughter Tero, for example, now numbered 2427 and 2437, respectively, are confused.
43 Intriguingly, they apparently honored their two first spouses (Robert Lewis and Blanche Nelson) by naming this daughter Blanche Roberta Mallary. (*Men of Mark in Georgia*, ibid., p. 252.)
44 Evans, comp., *Pulaski County*, ibid., Vol. IV, p. 274.
45 According to the 1899 *City Directory* it was the smallest of Macon's eight banks.
46 This description of Mallary's business career is drawn from year-by-year comparisons of information listed in Macon city directories from 1887 through Mallary's death in 1926 (various publishers), as well as the *Telegraph* obituary and the *Men of Mark in Georgia* sketch cited above.

Logan's father, Elijah Nathaniel Lewis (1885-1918), the oldest of the seven step-siblings, grew up to become "one of the best known young men of Macon."[47] He began working at his stepfather's bank while still in his teens, first as a clerk, then bookkeeper, rising eventually to assistant cashier and cashier.[48] But according to his obituary, "when that institution was purchased by the American National Bank" around 1915, "he devoted his time to his personal interests, he and his wife having extensive realty holdings."[49] In December of 1906 he had married Miss Johnnie Logan, the only daughter of another prominent and wealthy Vinevillian.

If Johnnie Logan wasn't the girl next door she was the girl several houses down the street. Her paternal grandfather (Logan Lewis's great-grandfather) was George M. Logan (1812-71). The circumstances of George Logan's arrival in Macon, or even Georgia, remain unknown to this writer, although a death notice for his brother, General John M. Logan, states that he came to America from County Donegal, Ireland, in the early 1820s, settling in Guilford County, North Carolina, where he was Clerk of Court for sixteen years;[50] one might assume that the brothers emigrated at the same time, though no evidence supports the assumption. A George Logan, albeit with no or varying initials, is mentioned in Macon newspaper clippings beginning in the 1830s,[51] as an officer in the City Guard and stockholder in the Central Railroad, among other things. He is not found in the Georgia index to either the 1840 or 1850 census, but a printout of the Bibb County section of the 1850 tally lists him as an Irish-born merchant with a twenty-three year old wife, Pauline, and $10,000 worth of property, some of which was in slaves since the 1850 Slave Schedule shows him owning seven Negroes.[52] An 1852 deed for the property at the corner of Second and Cherry where the firm of Logan and Atkinson was located indicates that his business was a dry goods store.[53] In 1854 the *Macon Messenger* carried a notice that he and James Meara had leased the Lanier House Hotel,[54] and that "no exertions will be spared to sustain the established reputation" of the facility.[55] The 1860 census

47 Obituary, *Macon Telegraph*, November 30, 1918, p. 1A.
48 This description drawn from Macon city directories 1904-1915.
49 Obituary, ibid.
50 Willard Rocker, *Marriages and Obituaries from the Macon Messenger 1823-1870*, Easley, S.C., Southern Historical Press, 1988, pp. 149-50.
51 Tad Evans, *Macon, Georgia, Newspaper Clippings*, Vol. II, 1831-1836, published by the writer with assistance of the R. J. Taylor Foundation, Savannah, Georgia, 1999, pp. 156, 185, 246, 325.
52 With Logan apparently somehow omitted from the index his listing in the microfilmed pages of the 1850 census could not be confirmed; this information came from the book *1850 Bibb County, Georgia Census* published by Genealogical Enterprises, Morrow, Ga., 1968. The age given (forty-five) is very likely an error as the 1860 and 1870 censuses record him as forty-eight and fifty-eight respectively. He is included in the 1850 Slave Schedules (Jack C. Cox, comp., *The 1850 Census of Georgia Slave Owners*, Baltimore, Genealogical Publishing Co., 1988, p. 188) but was not located in the microfilmed version of 1860's in the Washington Library Genealogical and Historical Room. He died July 8, 1871.
53 Bibb County Record Room, Book L, p. 295, dated February 6, 1852.
54 The hotel may have been owned by a group of Macon men, including Robert Sampson Lanier, whose father, Sterling, had opened it in 1850. (Richard Iobst, *Civil War Macon, the History of a Confederate City*, Macon, Mercer University Press, 1999, p. 88, quoting a letter from R.S. Lanier to Clifford Anderson.) According to William Thomas Jenkins, *Antebellum Macon and Bibb County, Georgia*, UGA PhD Dissertation, Athens, Georgia, 1966, p. 265, the incorporators were Sidney C. Lanier, Edwin Groover, Thomas Wood, Charles Cooper, and Edwin B. Weed.
55 Tad Evans, comp., *Macon, Georgia Newspaper Clippings*, Vol. VI, 1852-1854, p. 324.

shows him as the proprietor there, with $2500 in real and $7500 in personal property, as well as three children, including a six-year-old named John.[56] Eventually the Logans had seven children,[57] of whom John Thomas (1853-1885), who became Johnnie Logan's father (Logan Lewis' maternal grandfather) was the second.

George Logan's wife, Pauline, was a member of the prominent Hardeman family. One of her brothers, John Thomas Hardeman Jr.,[58] was a state legislator who served as speaker during both Confederate and Reconstruction sessions, a congressman both before and after the Civil War, and an orator[59] who twice ran for Governor; he became so famous as the Confederate officer whose troops flew the first Stars and Bars over Georgia that the local UDC chapter is named for him. Another brother, Robert Ulla Hardeman, enjoyed a statewide following as Georgia state treasurer for a number of years at the end of the nineteenth century. One of Pauline's uncles, Robert Vines Hardeman, was a state senator and judge in Jones County; another, Benjamin Franklin Hardeman, was a state senator from Oglethorpe County and Solicitor General of the northern circuit. The Hardemans, like the Jelkses of Welsh descent, had settled in Virginia before Pauline's grandfather (Logan's great-great-great-grandfather) John Hardeman moved to Georgia's Jackson (later Oglethorpe) County after the Revolution. John's son, Thomas Hardeman Sr., (Logan's great-great-grandfather) was born there in 1797, had a lucky draw in the 1821 lottery,[60] and married Sarah Blewett Sparks of Eatonton in 1821; he served as sheriff and clerk of court in Putnam County before moving to Macon in 1832 where he established a cotton warehouse that became one of the largest in the state.[61] Early newspaper clippings provide glimpses of Hardeman's extensive business and community activities; deeds on file in the Bibb County Courthouse indicate that he encountered difficulties during the financial panic of the early 1840s, but the firm of Hardeman and Sparks was on a sound footing by the time of his 1861 death, just days before the firing on Fort Sumter.

---

56 As noted above, the author could not find George Logan's name in the 1860 Slave Schedule.

57 Reconstructing from various sources they were (in addition to John Thomas): Fanny (1851-1874), George H. (1855-1880) who married Helen Gustin, Robert H. (1858-9), Louise (1860-65), Alex S. (1863-1922), and Pauline (1866-1935) who married Richard Findlay. □ window at the Lanier House in 1865; this was very likely George and Pauline Logan's child, whose cause of death is described as an "accident" in the *Record of Interments, Rose Hill Cemetery, Bibb County, Georgia 1840-1871*, comp. by Lawrence Edward Hallman and Linda Moore Hallman, Thomaston, Georgia, 1996, p. 152.

58 Presumably Pauline Hardeman Logan named her son (Logan's grandfather) John Thomas in honor of both her father and brother.

59 Macon histories cite numerous ceremonial occasions on which Thos. Hardeman, Jr. took the platform, and the effusive sketch in *Memoirs of Georgia* claims that "as an orator Col. Hardeman had no superior in the state; the agricultural population flocked to him; the merchant and mechanic were charmed, while on literary occasions his audience was held spell-bound, and on the stump he was almost matchless." A sample quoted there illustrates his flair. Speaking to the first legislative session after the fall of the Confederacy he reportedly said: "Georgia, though prostrate, will rise again; though desolated, her fields will gladden once more with waving harvest the hearts of her husbandmen; though stricken with poverty, her hills will enrich with their hidden treasure and her commerce whiten with her sails her ocean waters, and though her schools are deserted and her colleges suspended, learning will decorate her brow with the wreaths of science and religion rekindle her fires upon the desecrated altars of her faith. Though joined to the rock of an irresistible destiny, she will sever the cords that bind her, and with stately step and graceful mien resume her onward and upward march to glory and to greatness." *Memoirs of Georgia*, Vol. I, p. 343.

60 Lucas, *The 1821 (Fourth) Land Lottery*, ibid., p. 120.

61 *Memoirs of Georgia*, ibid., p. 340.

Macon was a frontier town in those days, eager to accept newcomers who exhibited talent and industry, so family connections do not account for George Logan's success in his new country; indeed he and Pauline did not marry until 1850 and references in Macon histories to his civic involvement begin much earlier.[62] He was active in the Democratic Party in the 1840s, served on various public committees, and was elected Mayor three times, in 1848, 1849, and 1850. While mayor he managed to bring the city's debt under control, and also led a group of citizens in posting a $4000 advance to bring the Georgia Agricultural Fair to Macon in 1851, an event that drew 7000 people from six states—at a time when the city's entire population was just 7052, including 2961 slaves.[63] Later in the 1850s, perhaps as a result of the influence of his wife's relatives and his "close friendship" with Macon's wealthiest resident and most ardent secessionist, planter John B. Lamar,[64] he became involved in "southern rights" efforts, working to help southern emigrants to settle in Kansas.[65] After Lincoln's election he added his name to a list of citizens "in favor of the South . . . and of immediate secession by Georgia from an abolitionist Union,"[66] who were calling for a meeting to nominate candidates to a state convention. The next spring, showing his support for the southern cause in another way, he invited "members of the Bibb County Cavalry to join him [at the Lanier House] in a glass of wine" following a parade and military maneuvers.[67] Logan's hotel was apparently doing well: in early 1860 it underwent extensive expansion, adding forty-eight rooms and stretching over an adjacent alley to present a 135-foot front along Mulberry Street, a facade decorated with iron cornices and a balcony that ran its entire length, as well as a cupola. The building was "well ventilated and furnished in the finest and most fashionable style."[68] Even a destructive 1863 fire in the attic, which left the hotel "a monument of desolation," did not breach its operations for long.[69] Unfortunately, as the "principal"[70] hostelry in the city it was the obvious choice for General James Wilson's headquarters when the Yankees occupied Macon after the war; Logan rented the former John B. Lamar home for his family, only to see it subsequently commandeered by another Yankee officer.[71] While he is not listed in the 1866 City Directory, the 1867 directory records him as the proprietor of the Lanier House. Perhaps reflecting the economic

62Hargrove, et al., ibid., pp. 115, 116, 135, 139, 143, 144, 146, 150, 153, 175, 204, 226, 305, and John C. Butler, *Historical Record of Macon and Central Georgia*, Macon, 1879, reprinted 1958 by Macon Town Committee of the Colonial Dames of America, J. W. Burke Co., pp. 189 and 198.

63 A detailed discussion of Macon's efforts to bring the fair can be found in Jenkins, ibid., pp. 208-214. Hargrove, et al, ibid., p. 153, claims attendance of 20,000.

64 Iobst, ibid., p. 9 (as to the wealth of J. B. Lamar), and p. 415 (Logan's relationship to Lamar.)

65 Hargrove, et al, ibid., p. 175.

66 Ibid., p. 204.

67 Iobst, ibid., p. 29.

68 *Macon Daily Telegraph*, June 4, 1860, as quoted in Iobst, ibid., p. 10.

69 The fact that the fire was in the attic contributed to the destruction because, at seventy feet above the street, it was out of reach of the fire engines below. Iobst, ibid., pp. 256-7.

70 Ibid., p. 1.

71 Ibid., p. 415-6. Lamar had died in action during the war.

dislocations during Reconstruction, a May 1868 Sheriff's Sale reported in the *Telegraph and Messenger* included furnishings sold to satisfy fi fas in favor of the estate of his late partner, James Meara.[72] By the 1870 census, Logan is termed a "commission merchant"[73] and the City Directory for that year notes that he is a "notary public and ex officio magistrate" who resides in Vineville, close to many of his wife's Hardeman relatives.[74] It may have been the position of "Notary Public," or perhaps his earlier service as mayor, that earned him the honorific "Judge" in a commentary in the *Daily Telegraph and Messenger* mourning his death: "a most worthy, upright and influential . . . old and popular citizen, one universally beloved and respected by all classes. . . . His remains were escorted to the tomb by a large cortege of citizens and were buried with Masonic honors."[75]

While the Lewis/Butts (paternal/paternal), Jelks/Polhill (paternal/maternal) and Logan/Hardeman (maternal/paternal) branches of Logan Lewis's family tree were all populated with prominent people, the maternal/maternal line was the wealthiest. Johnnie Logan's grandfather, Carlton B. Callaway (Logan Lewis' great-grandfather, 1818-1900; see Logan Family tree on pp. 222-223), was descended from a large family which, originally from Maryland, had migrated to Delaware and then North Carolina before settling in Wilkes County[76] soon after the Creeks ceded the Savannah River back country as payment for their trading debts in the 1780s. Carlton's great-grandfather Job Callaway (Logan's great-great-great-great-grandfather, 1741-1804) received several headright and bounty grants of land[77] in Wilkes and purchased even more property so that he had acquired approximately 2000 acres along Long and Clark's Creeks by the time he died in 1804;[78] 1794 tax records show him owning 16 slaves, among the largest number listed.[79] Job's son, Jacob (Logan's great-great-great-grandfather, 1760-1833), and his siblings inherited and added to those holdings.[80] Jacob's brothers (Joshua and Joseph) and his son, Parker (Logan's great-great-grandfather, 1790-1868), among others in the family, had lucky draws in the Georgia land

72 Evans, *Macon Newspaper Clippings*, ibid., Vol. IX, 1866-1869, p. 161.
73 Jenkins, ibid., provides a helpful description of what such a professional did for his clients or customers: pay taxes, sell property, collect rents, or any other such services.
74 The author did not find any deeds referring the to transfer of the Lanier House either to or from George Logan.
75 July 11, 1871, p. 3.
76 See complete family tree at www.Ancestry.com; it is based on Robert Mercer Callaway, *The Lineage of Peter Callaway and Related Families*. Carlton Callaway's great grandfather was a brother of John Callaway, from whom the well-known Fuller Earle Callaway family of LaGrange, Georgia, is descended.
77 Rev. Silas Emmett Lucas, Jr., *Index to the Headright and Bounty Grants of Georgia*, 1750-1909, ibid., pp. 92 and 385.
78 Job Callaway's acquisitions can be traced in deed abstracts collected in Michael Martin Farmer, *Wilkes County, Ga. Deed Books A-VV, 1784-1806*, published with the assistance of the R. J. Taylor Foundation, Farmer Genealogy, Dallas, Tx., 1996. Frank Hudson Parker in *A 1790 Census for Wilkes County, Georgia Prepared from Tax Returns with Abstracts*, The Reprint Company, Spartanburg, S. C., 1988, shows Job Callaway holding 1201 acres and ten slaves in 1791; his sons Joseph, Jacob, and Job, Jr., appear to have accumulated less than half that and only a few slaves.
79 Ruth Blair, *Some Early Tax Digests of Georgia*, Atlanta, Georgia Department of Archives and History, 1926, p. 299.
80 Abstract of Wills dated April 5, 1803, in Farmer, ibid., p. 745 and p. 818.

lotteries,[81] land which they probably sold so as to use the proceeds to buy additional property in Wilkes County.

Carleton Callaway's bride came from an even more prosperous family. Her father, "Cotton John" Jones (another of Logan's great-great-grandfathers, 1802-1874) was among the largest planters in the state, an enormously successful agriculturalist of whom it was said "everything he touched turned to money."[82] He earned his nickname in the cotton markets at Griffin where he was known to bring as many as 1000 bales to sell during "the high tide of his activities."[83] Originally from Lincoln County, he migrated to Wilkes, where he married Elizabeth Strozier (1808-1892), the daughter of Reuben and Pheraby Callaway Strozier,[84] in 1824. Late in the same decade they moved to Meriwether County where their nine children included Logan's great-grandmother, Ann Jones Callaway (1832-1920).[85] Considered a practical man of sound judgment, and an energetic manager of plantations that totaled nearly 12,000 acres in Meriwether as well as in Baker and Dougherty counties, Jones served on the Inferior Court of Meriwether County and was a director of the State Bank of Georgia. Master of three hundred thirty-seven slaves, he gave each of his nine living children "a small fortune" before the Civil War,[86] and was rumored to have half a million dollars even after it, though the freeing of his slaves and depreciation in land values, as well as the failure of the Bank of the State of Georgia contributed to what were doubtless heavy losses. After forty successful years in Meriwether

81 The large Callaway family was remarkably lucky in acquiring land via the Georgia lotteries established to open new territories to settlement. Job Callaway's brothers Joshua and Isaac, and nephews David and Jonathan, drew prizes in the first lottery (Virginia S. and Ralph V. Wood, *1805 Georgia Land Lottery*, Cambridge, Greenwood Press, 1964, p. 53-4.) Job's sons Joseph and Joshua drew land in Baldwin County and Joseph, along with Joshua's son Edward also drew land in Wilkinson County in the second lottery (Rev. Silas Emmett Lucas, Jr., *The Second or 1807 Land Lottery of Georgia*, Vidalia, Georgia Genealogical Reprints, 1968, pp. 43-4.) The Callaway family was even more successful in the admittedly larger 1820 draw: Parker Callaway (Logan's great-great-grandfather, who had been too young for the earlier distributions) drew land in Gwinnett County while Jacob Callaway had a successful draw in Walton, Eli Callaway in Early and Irwin, Barham and David Callaway in Irwin, Noah Callaway in Early and Habersham, Enoch, Joseph H., and Seaborn Callaway in Early, Joseph M. and Joel Callaway in Habersham, and Luke and Amasa Callaway in Appling (Rev. Silas E. Lucas, Jr., *The Third and Fourth or 1820 and 1821 Land Lotteries of Georgia*, Easley, S.C., Georgia Genealogical Reprints and Southern Historical Press, 1973, pp. 80-81.) In 1821 this success was repeated, with Jesse, Lemuel, Jacob, and Joshua Callaway drawing land in Houston County; Joshua and Susannah Callaway (a widow) successful in Dooly; Jesse, Jesse M., Joseph and Isaac Callaway's orphans drew in Henry (Lucas, ibid., pp. 58-9.) Drury (Carlton's uncle) and Chenoth Callaway are listed in the 1827 Lottery and Enoch, George H., Jesse, Luke (two draws), Chenoth, Barham, Drury, Abram (two draws), Woodson, and Lewis B., all drew prizes in the 1832 Lottery distributing land north and west of the Chattahoochee. (Rev. S. E. Lucas, Jr., *The 1832 Gold Lottery of Georgia*, Easley, S.C., Southern Historical Press, 1976, pp. 122-23.)
82 *Pioneers of Meriwether County, Georgia, as reported in the Meriwether Vindicator*, compiled by Clare Isanhour, Smyrna, GA, 1991, Coweta County Genealogical Society, Newnan, Ga. Not paginated; in alphabetical order.
83 "Enoch Callaway Jones," in Lucian Lamar Knight, *Georgia and Georgians*, Vol. VI, p. 2793-4.
84 Pheraby Callaway (1787-1865) was the daughter of John and Bethany Arnold Callaway; her father and Parker Callaway's grandfather Job were brothers, sons of Edward Callaway (1711-1769.) That made Elizabeth Strozier and Parker Callaway second cousins, and their children, Ann Jones and Carlton B. Callaway, third cousins. Altogether three of Parker Callaway and Elizabeth Strozier Jones' children (including Ann and C. B.) came to marry: Lucy Ann Callaway (1828-c.1912) married Ann's older brother Willis A. Jones (1831-1873), and they moved to Lee County about the same time Ann and C. B. did; Indiana Callaway (1838-1869) was Enoch Callaway Jones' (1838-1916) first wife.
85 I began my search for information on Ann Jones' family background at Ancestry.com, using postings by several genealogists, most notably Ross E. Jones, Elayne Pair, John Pickens, and David G. Richardson all of which were based on the Davidson book cited below and census data, as well as *Wilkes County Vital Records* and Hattie Wilson, *Callaway Tree*, Atlanta, GA, 1922, provided to David Richardson by Henry B. Miller.
86 Isanhour, ibid. It is likely that this amounted to $10,000 to each of the nine who lived to adulthood; in an 1873 will, Jones wrote that his executors were to settle that amount on Orrie, the youngest, "to make her equal with the balance of my children who have already received that amount," unless he had been able to have accomplished the same during life. (William H. Davidson, *Brooks of Honey and Butter: The Plantations and People of Meriwether County*, Georgia, Alexander City, AL, Outlook Publishing Co., 1971, Vol. I, p. 259.) Orrie was probably late in receiving her share because she was so much younger than the others, having been born in 1848; she was actually Jones' granddaughter, but raised as a daughter after her mother died during her infancy and her father, Reuben F. Jones (1825-1892), took a second wife and moved to Alabama.

County, by then sixty-seven years of age, Jones responded to the changed circumstances of the country and more specifically, the burning of his cotton gin in November of 1869,[87] by selling his Meriwether plantations and moving to Atlanta. There, with characteristic foresight, he invested his newly liquid assets in property at the center of the city, only steps away from what was then the railroad terminal and is now Underground Atlanta. When he was killed in a tragic horse and buggy accident in 1874, he left assets in Calhoun, Meriwether, Troup, and Fulton Counties with a total value in excess of $115,000.[88] Ann Jones Callaway had acquired a half interest in a 2500-acre plantation in Dougherty County as part of the gift each of his children received during Jones's life; part of her distributive share[89] in her father's estate was a half interest in a piece of commercial property in downtown Atlanta that Logan Lewis used as collateral to finance business ventures from the 1930s through the 1960s.[90]

In the 1850 census thirty-two year old Carlton Callaway was still listed as a member of his father Parker's household (albeit as having married within the year) and Parker, a farmer, is shown owning property valued at $25,500, again among the most substantial in Wilkes County. In 1854, however, C.B., as he was more usually known, perhaps using some of the funds his father-in-law had settled on his wife, purchased a 1012-acre tract of land in Lee County,[91] then just opening up in southwest Georgia, and moved his young family there; his cousin, Drury, had had a lucky draw in Lee, his brother Miles owned land there, and his and Ann's married siblings, Willis and Lucy Callaway Jones, bought an adjoining farm. Part of Carlton's property was the site where stagecoach teams were changed on the run from Starkville to Lumpkin;[92] perhaps realizing the significance of such a stop he purchased another 202-acre lot of land in 1856 on which the Georgia and Florida Railroad had already obtained a ten-acre right of way for what would be a depot on the line from Albany to Americus.[93] He

87 Jones wrote a letter about the burning which appeared in *The LaGrange Reporter* on Friday, November 5: "It was undoubtedly the work of an incendiary-no one had been working near it for some days and when we reached the lint room door signs of a torch having been thrust through a hole . . .were plainly visible. . . . The house contained almost the entire present crop, amounting to about 25 bales. No insurance. Let us hope that the day is not far distant when law and order will be restored to this unfortunate country, and those who commit such acts brought to justice." To which the editors added their own sentiments: "Hanging is too quick and easy a death for incendiaries. They ought to be burned by some slow and torturing process." The next month Jones advertised his plantation for sale: "$50,000 worth of Real Estate and Perishable Property!!!" Quoted in Davidson, ibid.
88 Fulton County Probate Records, Estate Number 3132. Jones' file includes "Appraisements" of the property in each of the four counties, the 1874 Annual Return and Distribution, the Final Return and Receipt filed in 1904, and the Widow's Election, as well as the original of his will.
89 The other part of her share was forgiveness of the $5500 debt her husband, C. B., owed her father; two sons-in-law and four of his sons owed John Jones money at the time of his death. Each of the nine children inherited property, stock, or cash worth $10,500, ibid.
90 Ann owned the Atlanta and Dougherty County properties with her nephew, John Pope Jones, son of her deceased brother Willis and C.B.'s sister Lucy Ann, who had grown up in Lee County. They sold the Dougherty County property in 1906 for $12,500, but held on to the Whitehall Street lot, on which they built a three-story brick store, leased to the Keely Company, in 1902. (Dougherty Court Record Room Book 15, pp. 31-2; Fulton County Record Room Book W, p. 666 and Book 164, pp. 365-8.) Pope Jones married Mary Wilcoxon of Coweta County and settled there on a 2000-acre plantation that stretched from Wahoo Creek to the Chattahoochee River, breaking records for crop production in a repetition of the agricultural success enjoyed by his grandfather and uncles. (*A History of Coweta County*, GA, compiled and written by the Newnan/Coweta Historical Society, 1988, Male Academy Museum, Newnan, Ga., p. 140.) He died in 1929, nine years after his aunt Ann, leaving four children to inherit his share of the property.
91 Lee County Clerk of Court Record Room, Deed Book A, folios 695-6. Callaway bought what was "known as the Plantation on which Charles Randall now resides," which was spread over five Land Lots; he paid $13,000. A Land Lot typically comprised 202.5 acres.
92 Lee County Historical Society, *The History of Lee County*, Leesburg, Georgia, 1983, p. 36.
93 Lee County Deed Book A, folios 570 (the right of way) and 700 (Callaway's $1775 purchase.)

bought another four land lots in 1858.[94] It was from these holdings that, after the War, he donated property for a Baptist Church[95] as well as, "in consideration of $5 and the benefit and value to him of the location of the County site," land for a Courthouse.[96] The county seat was then moved from Starkville, three miles away, and Callaway's holdings ended up comprising nearly half of the acreage of what became Leesburg. In the 1860 census he is listed as a Lee County "planter" with assets of $30,000 in real property as well as $40,000 in personal property, and the Slave Schedule for that year shows that he owned thirty-eight slaves; he and his wife, Ann, had four children living with them, including a daughter, Tero (1857-1934, pronounced "Tee-row"), age three, who became Johnnie Logan's mother and Logan Lewis' maternal grandmother. C. B.' s father, Parker Callaway, by then sixty-nine years old, was still living in Wilkes County where he is shown holding real property valued at $16,600 and personal property worth $154,000.

After the Civil War, C. B. Callaway relocated his family to Bibb County, purchasing thirty-some acres and a residence in the Vineville district from Eliza Lamar for $4500.[97] According to his obituary he had been "impressed by the beauty of Macon and the attractiveness of its beautiful suburb, which [was] then a large vineyard, surrounded by many orchards. The luxuriance of the growth that abounded everywhere showed the rich resources of the country and Mr. Callaway decided that [that] was the very place for him to locate."[98] The Lee County History, however, reveals what may have been the real reason for the relocation: numerous "fevers" attributed to the county's excessive swamps and poor water supplies, to which the black population seemed immune, contributed to an early version of white flight before the development of artesian wells in the 1880s ended the problem.[99] Additionally, absentee ownership became more feasible with the end of slavery, and two of Ann Jones Callaway's sisters, Margiana and Orrie, had married Macon men and moved to the city.[100] In any event, the 1870 census locates Callaway in his new home, with assets of $7000 in real property, $1,000 in personal property. Bibb County tax records for 1884 list him as owning thirty-two acres valued at $4800, town property worth $1200 and household furnishings and animals valued at $500.[101] The drop in net worth between the 1860 and 1870 censuses is only partly the result of postwar losses (slaves having been counted as personal property): much of his holdings were in other parts of the state. He retained "immense properties"[102] in Lee

94 Deed Book A, folio 702. He paid $9200 for this 740 acres.
95 *History of Lee County,* ibid.
96 Lee County Deed Book B, folio 175; this deed is dated February 7, 1873.
97 Bibb County Record Room, Book AK, page 240, deed record dated January 29, 1869.
98 Obituary, *Macon Telegraph,* August 11, 1911, p. 2.
99 *Lee County Historical Society,* ibid., pp. 23-9.
100 Margiana married W. Raeburn (sometimes spelled Rayburn or Rabun) Phillips, a Jones County planter who moved to Macon and became a Bibb County Commissioner; Orrie married cotton factor William Flanders. They both lived in the downtown section of Macon rather than Vineville.
101 Microfilmed copies on deposit in Washington Memorial Library Historical and Genealogical Room.
102 *Lee County Historical Society,* ibid., p. 305.

County which his only son, John Parker, managed after graduating from Mercer University.[103]

A sketch of John P. Callaway (Logan's great-uncle) in the Lee County history[104] describes him as "probably the wealthiest and one of the most active men who ever lived in Leesburg. In addition to his large mercantile firm, his father owned the Callaway Hotel, a saw mill, cotton gin, livery stable, and a private banking business; he also operated about one hundred plows on his 4000-acre farm." J. P. was active in politics, serving several terms as mayor of Leesburg, as a state representative and senator, and at his death he was president of the Bank of Leesburg.[105] Intra-family deeds on record in Bibb and Lee counties show that Carlton Callaway owned, in addition to his residence in Vineville, the 2100-acre "Leesburgh [sic] Place" in Lee County, a one-third interest in a 2700-acre "Ducker Place" in Dougherty County, land in Leesburg and Macon, and an 850-acre plantation in Monroe County known as "Oak Lawn," on which J. P. lived at least part of the time. (The 1881 and 1894 deeds were recorded in 1906 in Bibb County, at the same time that John Parker Callaway was given power of attorney to handle the properties for his mother and three sisters; they were recorded in the years of execution in Lee County, however, indicating that most of the business they were designed to cover took place there.[106]) Unfortunately, the son became something of an invalid in later-mid life and died intestate in 1911. He had married Mamie Sawyer of Lee County in 1895, but the couple apparently had no children, and J.P.'s mother and sisters bought out his widow's interest for $32,500 and twelve acres in Leesburg.[107]

If substantial portions of the Callaway wealth were in Lee, Dougherty, and Monroe counties, the "home place" in Bibb was propitiously located in what soon became a more thickly settled suburban area. Carlton Callaway began the subdivision of this property about 1888[108] when he built the Victorian house still standing on the corner of Corbin and Vineville avenues, moving there with his wife, aged mother-in-law Elizabeth Strozier Jones, and two younger daughters; the eldest, Lula, remained in the original home, the long drive to it eventually becoming Callaway Street, or lived in the "old Callaway house" in Lorane, near the Monroe County properties. By then a streetcar connected Vineville to downtown Macon and families like the E. Y. Mallarys were flocking to the village;

103 Lee County Book B, folio 269 records a power of attorney in John's favor authorizing him "to make title as fully as if I were personally present." The Callaways began selling lots "in town" as early as 1871.
104 Ibid., p. 305; p. 36.
105 Obituary, ibid.
106 Bibb County Clerk of Court, Book 106, pp. 572-5, executed 1881 and 1894, recorded 1906. Lee County Book B, pp. 574-5 for the 1881 deed, Book D, pp. 283-87, for the 1894 deeds; Book E, pp. 157-8, one of several powers of attorney granted to John P. Callaway.
107 Bibb County Book 171, pp. 732-34, executed September 9, 1911, recorded October 25, 1911. In Lee County these instruments are recorded in Book H, pp. 170-71 and p. 180. Mamie Callaway developed her acreage into Walnut Heights, a subdivision of 57 lots the plat for which is recorded in Book H, p. 624.
108 Perhaps it is chauvinistic to attribute this move to Carlton Callaway since he had deeded his properties to his wife and children in 1881 and the lien filed October 18,1888 against the "new two-story house on the Vineville Road" by contractors S. M. Subers and Joseph Clisby for unpaid "tin work" lists Mrs. C. B. Callaway as the debtor. (Recorded in Book VV, Folio 40, Bibb Superior Court.) Indications are, however, that despite the names on the deeds, C. B. was managing the family's affairs.

as the area became more urbanized commercial development was appropriate and the front footage on the northwestern side of busy Vineville Avenue was given over to a small group of brick stores erected in the late nineties.[109] The family continued to benefit from subdividing, selling and renting this property after C.B.'s 1900 death, building and renting homes in the first block of Callaway as early as 1904; indeed Logan Lewis completed the portion of Callaway Drive between Clayton Street and Carlton Way in 1938, after his marriage to Dorothy Vits.[110]

The section of Bibb County in which the Logans, Callaways, Mallarys, and Jelkses lived took its name, Vineville, from the extensive vineyards of an early resident. Comprised of something over 500 acres, it is about a mile and a half northwest of the valley in which the city of Macon was established, and rests on a low plateau bisected by the "old federal road" from Macon to Forsyth, in Monroe County.[111] The approximately thirty estates there when George Logan and Carlton Callaway moved their families to the village were anchored by large homes facing that road, though set well off it. The population in 1870 was 1644, of whom 498 were white.[112]

The intimacy of this quasi-rural part of the county may explain the marriage of John Logan and Tero Callaway; they were seventeen and twelve years of age, respectively, when their families relocated to Vineville. Tero, however, like her Jones aunts, was sent to Salem Academy in North Carolina and attended Wesleyan College for a time after that; John Logan did not attend college but held several clerk positions downtown. Whatever led to the nuptials, they took place in 1882,[113] heralded in a page one news story in the *Macon Telegraph* under the headline "Tender Ties."[114] In the hyperbolic prose of the times, it told of "a joyous couple, the one esteemed for true gallantry of spirit, and the other loved for many graces of mind and beauty," now "happily united in wedded love." With siblings Alex and Pauline Logan and Annie and John Callaway as attendants, Dr. E. W. Warren of the First Baptist Church officiated at the ceremony in the Callaway residence.[115] The bride was "exquisitely attired in garnet colored surah satin and mole skin trimmed with point lace and iridescent

109 The street directory in the 1897 City Directory lists C.B. Callaway at 529 Vineville, Buford Davis as his next neighbor (# 603) to the west, and E. Y. Mallary on the other side of Davis at number 619. In 1900 J. B. Corbin, grocer, appears at #601, indicating that the store had opened in the interim. According to the *Lee County History* the Callaways were developing stores in Leesburg about the same time. ibid., p. 37.
110 Bibb County Plat Book 9, pp. 134-141.
111 National Register of Historic Places Nomination Form for Vineville Neighborhood, Manuscript in vertical file at Washington Memorial Library Historical and Genealogical Room.
112 Francis A. Walker, Superintendent, *Compendium of the Ninth Census* (June 1, 1870), Washington, Government Printing Office, 1872, p. 138.
113 A marriage license for Mr. John T. Logan and Miss Tero Callaway dated January 9, 1882 is on file in the Bibb County Probate Court.
114 *The Macon Telegraph*, January 11, 1882, p. 1.
115 At this time the Callaways occupied the home known more recently as the A. A. Drake house at 2455 Clayton Street, which illustrates of how far "back from the road" the Vineville estates were originally set. As the Callaways began to subdivide their original acreage in the 1890s, they built a large frame house now at the corner of Corbin and Vineville, in which C.B., his wife Ann Jones Callaway and daughters Annie and Tero lived until Tero built a home of her own next door to it, on the corner of Callaway and Vineville; daughter Lula, who died in 1916, remained in the family's former home on Clayton.

fringe, while diamond pendants glistened from her ears." The list of wedding gifts and their presenters included in the story illustrated the couple's connections to numerous Hardeman relatives, as well as other Vineville neighbors such as the Lamars, Holts, Clisbys, and Schofields.

The newlyweds apparently made their home with John Logan's widowed mother, Pauline, at the southwest corner of what is now Holt Avenue, from whence the young husband commuted to his job at J.H. Hertz, a clothier on Cherry Street. J. T. Logan is listed in city directories from 1872 through the year of his death as a clerk, and then bookkeeper for various Macon businesses, primarily clothing stores. In those years directories do not include the names of wives, though they do give residences, and the directories for 1884 and 1885 show him living at Pauline Logan's home at 56 Forsyth Road in Vineville. Bibb tax records list $250 in household furnishings by his name, but no property;[116] his mother owned two acres valued at $2500,[117] and $100 in household goods. John's younger brother and sister, Alex and Pauline, were no doubt also part of the household, as were two servants;[118] his oldest sister Fanny had apparently died soon after her father, and another brother, George, had married Helen Gustin in 1877 and moved in with her family nearby. The streetcar line, which might have become a means of getting John Logan to Macon to work and indeed, helped spur the transformation of Vineville from farm community to suburb, was not completed until 1888.

But the "tender ties" had been severed by then. At an age uncannily close to that of Robert Gallatin Lewis, John Thomas Logan died November 28, 1885,[119] and was buried in the Hardeman lot in Rose Hill, next to the infant daughter he and Tero had lost in November of 1883.[120] Johnnie, his namesake and only surviving child, was just two weeks old.

City directories indicate that after John Logan's death, his mother and the younger children moved to Washington Avenue, where they boarded, although they continued to pay taxes on the Vineville property. His widow and her baby daughter apparently returned to the Callaway home to live with her parents and unmarried younger sister, Annie. In 1893 (the same year in which Mary Jelks Lewis and E. Y. Mallary wed) Tero married W. B. Amos, a widower with several children who was in the insurance business in Forsyth; that marriage too, was short-lived as Amos died of consumption in June of 1895,[121] after which the then

116 Bibb tax records for 1884 and 1885 on microfilm at the Genealogical and Historical Room in the Washington Memorial Library show John as the agent for Pauline in those years, and the City Directory for 1884 shows him living in her residence.
117 Apparently the Logans moved to Vineville before purchasing property there; a deed in the Bibb Record Room dated May 10, 1872 shows Pauline Logan, Trustee, purchasing two acres of land in the approximate place of 56 Forsyth Road, from Charles A. Nutting for $3500. Book Z, folio 359.
118 They were living there, ages sixteen and thirteen, when the 1880 census was enumerated; after John's 1885 death Alex Logan is listed as head of house on the 1886 tax records.
119 Death Notice, *Macon Telegraph,* November 29, 1885, p. 5.
120 After her death in 1934, Tero Callaway Logan Amos was buried with them in the Hardeman plot, the only Callaway child not buried in the plot with C. B. and Ann. Record of Burials (1841-1959) Rose Hill Cemetery All Sections, City of Macon, 1959.
121 Obituary, *Macon Telegraph,* June 1, 1895.

twice-widowed, thirty-eight year old Tero and young Johnnie returned again to her father's home. A charter member of the Vineville Baptist Church, she lived with her family until around 1905, when she commissioned Sandersville architect Charles Edward Choate to design a substantial chocolate brick classic revival house next door to the large frame dwelling in which her by-then-widowed mother and maiden sister continued to reside. Her daughter, Johnnie, was then twenty, and, having been to Europe in 1904,[122] was likely a student at Wesleyan.

Johnnie Logan and Nat Lewis had much in common. They were both descended from prominent, landed, financially successful and politically well-connected families. They had both been fatherless from an early age, and both of their mothers had remarried widowers with several children, although Johnnie Logan did not grow up in a successfully blended stepfamily; she was only ten when her stepfather died and she and her mother returned to Macon to live with her maternal grandparents. (By that time Pauline Logan, her paternal grandmother, had also died; paternal grandfather George had died long before her birth.[123]) Johnnie and Nat were born in the same year and in all probability they attended the Vineville School, just a few blocks down the street, together after 1895. They grew up in houses even closer to each other than those of John Logan and Tero Callaway; the Callaway/Amos and Mallary homes, then numbered 529/531 and 607, respectively, are both still standing on Vineville Avenue, not much more than a football field apart. Like Johnnie's uncle John, Nat Lewis went to Mercer University. Johnnie, as noted above, attended Wesleyan.

The Logan-Lewis marriage on December 12, 1906, as well as the several parties that preceded it, was given extensive coverage in the *Telegraph*, as might befit the nuptials of "a popular young couple."[124] Members of the extended Lewis family came from all over the state both as guests and as attendants; J.P. Callaway and Alex Logan, uncles of the bride, came from Leesburg and Washington D.C., respectively. Like her mother, Johnnie Logan was married from home, with an elaborate reception following the ceremony. Her attendants included Margaret Corbin, Martha Lewis, Annie Laurie Mallary, Virginia Willingham, and Katie May Arnold of Athens. Nat Lewis's attendants were Nelson Mallary, Eugene Mallary, Julian Lewis, Eden Taylor Jr., and Guyton Park; the flower girls were his sister, niece, and cousins Jelksie Lewis, Lamar Lewis of Valdosta, Rosalie Mallary, and Annie Payne Jelks. The bride's "tall, graceful figure was enveloped in the folds of her long, filmy tulle veil, which was caught

122 *The Baedeker's Guide* she took with her was on the shelves in the Lewis home after Dorothy Lewis' 2002 death. She may have gone with her grandmother and great aunt as city directories show them out of their house that year, and a guidebook with Annie Callaway's name and "1904" inscribed in it was found in the Lewis library.
123 Pauline V. Logan died May 24, 1893 according to the *Macon Telegraph* Obituary Index 1890-94 in the Washington Library Genealogical Room; George Logan died July 8, 1871 according to the date on his tombstone in Rose Hill Cemetery plot adjoining that of his brother-in-law Thomas Hardeman, Jr.
124 November 20, 1906, p. 5; November 25, 1906, p. 3; December 2, 1906, p. 3; December 9, 1906, p. 4, 5 and 8; December 13, 1906, p. 3.

with a handsome diamond crescent, and the lace bertha on her bodice was caught in front with a diamond sunburst, both gifts of the groom."[125] Mr. and Mrs. Lewis caught a 7:20 p.m. train for New York after the 5:00 p.m. ceremony, and also visited Washington, D.C. before returning to Macon to make their home with the bride's mother, next door to that of her widowed grandmother, Ann Callaway, and her unmarried Aunt Annie.

Macon

Macon, Georgia, is not much older than Manitowoc, Wisconsin, having been chartered just thirty years earlier. But its location in the center of the South, a region populated primarily by settlers of British origin who migrated from other parts of the United States, along with the large numbers of African slaves imported to work the land, gave it a very different atmosphere at the time Dorothy Lewis moved there. Macon's fortunes had been tied to a cotton economy that produced prosperity, war, and then a genteel poverty for the city's first hundred-odd years. The myth and romance of the Old South cast shadows that lingered long after the influx of thousands of newcomers during and following the Second World War.

The city was laid out on the western bank of the Ocmulgee River in the central part of the state in 1823. The timing was not incidental. Eli Whitney's invention of the cotton gin less than thirty years before had ensured the economic viability of short staple cotton, the kind best grown in Georgia's inland and upland regions. Andrew Jackson's military victories had convinced the Creeks to sign an 1821 treaty releasing all the land between the Ocmulgee and Flint rivers. Florida, a lawless refuge for pirates, smugglers, runaway slaves, and hostile Indians, had been secured from Spain in 1819, bringing a measure of stability to the area south of the city. And the Georgia legislature, anxious to capitalize on these factors, continued its practice of distributing its newly acquired lands free, via a lottery in which each male citizen of a certain age had at least one chance, or "draw;" additional chances were given to Revolutionary veterans, widows, and heads of families. Between 1800 and 1840 sixty-nine new counties were created and Georgia's population quadrupled, increasing from 162,000 to 691,000.[126] As indicated above, Logan Lewis' forbears were the beneficiaries of this rapid growth. Bibb County, of which Macon was the county seat, was at the heart of it.

Located at the point where the Atlantic Coastal Plain rises to meet the Piedmont Plateau, a juncture known as the "Fall Line" at which rivers become

125 *The Macon Telegraph*, December 13, 1906, p. 3.
126 Kenneth Coleman, *Georgia History in Outline*, Athens, University of Georgia Press, 1978, pp. 30-33.

unnavigable, Macon quickly became the commercial hub of the surrounding agricultural area. Before its tenth birthday, the city was sending upwards of 70,000 bags of cotton down the Ocmulgee to Brunswick, three banks had been organized with capital of more than $1 million, merchandise in stores was estimated at like value, and farmers were coming from more than sixty miles around to do business.[127] Trade became and remained the predominant source of income, even after manufacturing (of bricks, cotton, and ironworks) gained a foothold in the 1850s.

Like Manitowoc, Macon was short of capital to develop its resources, but unlike Manitowoc, it did not fill that gap with skilled labor. A late nineteenth century Board of Trade publication bemoaned the shortage of "mechanics" in the South: "Anyone acquainted with Southern ideas knows there has always existed a false pride and an air of freedom in this section which has been adverse to the apprentice system while learning trades. It has appeared too slavish to the majority of Southern parents to bind their children to men of skill and to corporations having the means of developing talent . . ."[128] Macon, it was said, was "more interested in the graces and pleasures of reciprocal hospitality than in commercial enterprises."[129]

Which is not to say that the city lacked entrepreneurial spirit. As spreading cultivation lessened rainwater runoff, the Ocmulgee narrowed and navigation proved impossible without constant dredging. Realizing that rail offered the best protection for their mercantile interests, Macon businessmen convinced the City to invest in a line to Savannah. Later they convened a statewide meeting that led to the legislature's decision to build track from the Chattahoochee to Chattanooga, extending the reach of the previously constructed Monroe railroad and placing Macon at the center of intrastate rail traffic. By 1860 the city was the fifth largest in the state.

The Civil War interrupted this progress. While military action was limited to an unsuccessful if dramatic assault from the east by an inept Yankee general, Macon expressed its devotion to the cause other than by doing battle: it was a depository for Confederate gold; its arsenal, laboratory, and armory produced tons of needed ordnance; Camp Oglethorpe at Central City Park held prisoners of war who were officers (enlisted men were sent to Andersonville); and many of its buildings became hospitals for nursing the wounded soldiers arriving by rail from battlefields to the north. The bad news from Appomattox arrived in time to change the expected invasion by the general who had torched Columbus's wartime industries just hours before, into an occupation; while that may have not been less painful it was certainly less destructive, despite its dislocation of

127 Butler, ibid., p. 115.
128 Quoted in Nancy Anderson, *Macon, A Pictorial History,* Virginia Beach, The Donning Company, 1979, p. 64.
129 George Herbert Clarke, writing in *The Independent* (a New York magazine) on November 8, 1906 as quoted in ibid., p. 169.

the George Logan family. Still, the city was devastated: the value of personal property (much of which had been in slaves) dropped 74 percent between 1860 and 1870, and there were 487 new widows and 913 new orphans[130] amongst a population numbering little more than 5000 whites. The Ladies Memorial Society, which evolved into the United Daughters of the Confederacy, quickly set about honoring the war dead. In a large section of Rose Hill Cemetery neat white headstones marked the graves of more than six hundred soldiers who had given their lives; until well into the twentieth century Macon school children marched there, en masse, with flowers and flags on Confederate Memorial Day. If, as Hooten claims, the Civil War was a "vivid memory" in Manitowoc, it was a living presence in Macon.

Former slaves, having won their freedom, soon found themselves newly tied to the land via sharecropping and tenancy; that, coupled with agriculture's continued dependence on cotton, served as a drag on regional per capita income until the boll weevil brought it even lower after World War I. In the city a rigid caste system arose which limited those freedmen who did not own their own businesses, teach, or preach, to the most menial of unskilled tasks; dramatically underdeveloped schools helped perpetuate this underemployment for another hundred years.

The major post-war industry was cotton, with a number of mills locating in Macon, and, as was typical in the South, surrounding themselves with villages of small houses for their workers; textiles held a central place in manufacturing until well after World War II. The kaolin industry, developed east of Macon, largely with northern capital, did not get started until around the turn of the century when E. Y. Mallary founded the Georgia Kaolin Company. South of the city farmers bred the "Elberta," which, with the advent of refrigerated railroad cars, brought the peach industry to life. Commercial activities, however, continued to be the mainstay of the local economy; downtown was abuzz every Saturday when the farmers came to town. Naturally, Macon soon became the cultural, educational, entertainment, and medical center of middle Georgia as well.

The City started acquiring the trappings of modern urban life shortly after the war: an expanded water system, sanitary sewers, telephones, electricity, streetcars, paved sidewalks, and, over many years, paved streets. The Board of Public Education was established in 1872, Central City Park developed and the annual state fairs were begun, a hospital opened, and a public library was organized. New citizens emigrated from outlying areas and other southern states and the city also increased its size by annexing its growing suburbs: Vineville (much against its will; the case went all the way to the Supreme Court before the

130 Iobst, ibid., p. 433.

village finally lost its fight to remain independent in 1904), Hugenin Heights, Cherokee Heights, and East and South Macon. By 1910 the population had reached 40,665—more than three times the size of Manitowoc at that time, a proportion it maintains to the present day.

As for religious differences between the two cities, the proportion of Catholics and Protestants in Macon was the reverse of that in Manitowoc: despite the presence of a Jesuit College in Vineville, there were only two Catholic congregations, one white and one black, and seemingly infinite numbers of Baptists and Methodists. Furthermore, religious leaders in both black and white churches tended to exert more political influence in Macon than those in Manitowoc.

When change came to Macon—and it began with World War I but accelerated after Dorothy and Logan Lewis married in 1937—it was spurred by an old Macon tradition. Macon's active volunteer militias had been mainstays of civic and social life since the city's founding. The local units had joined the battle every time the U.S. took up arms, even (despite lingering animosities from the recent fight *with* the federals) the 1898 Spanish American War and a little known 1916 ruckus along the Mexican border. Soldiers for the latter had trained at camps in Macon so it was natural, when America's entry into the "Great War" became obvious, for Macon Chamber of Commerce leaders to aggressively seek military training facilities. Their efforts succeeded in bringing tens of thousands of "Doughboys" and a significant monthly payroll to tented Camp Wheeler in 1917, and the community's hospitable embrace of the soldiers paved the way for the Camp's reactivation in World War II. (The Ocmulgee East Industrial Park and Macon's Downtown Airport are now located on its site.) But the Second World War brought additional installations: a naval ordnance plant, a training center for RAF pilots at Cochran Field, and, most importantly, with the help of Congressman Carl Vinson, the enormous air force base which Maconites secured by purchasing 3,108 acres in Houston County to give to the Department of Defense. That acreage became Robins Air Force Base and the Warner Robins Air Logistics Center, and has grown into the largest industrial complex in the state, employing approximately twenty thousand people and drawing tens of thousands of others to middle Georgia from all over the United States and even foreign countries, in addition to numerous businesses. Thanks to it, the Macon MSA is now Georgia's third largest.

Logan's Life Before His Marriage

Nathaniel Logan Lewis was born just fourteen months after his parents' memorable wedding. An only child, he and they lived with his maternal grandmother Tero Callaway Logan Amos, next door to the home his maternal great-grandmother, Ann Jones Callaway, shared with his great-aunt Annie Callaway, and just a few houses from his paternal grandmother, Mary Jelks Lewis Mallary and her family; his Jelks great-uncles and cousins also lived nearby.

The Callaway and Amos homes sat on a small promontory between Corbin and Callaway streets, sheltered from the nearby thoroughfare by several expansive live oaks reputedly planted from seed in the 1830s by early Vineville resident George Foster Pierce, the Methodist bishop for whom Pierce Avenue is named. In addition to giving the homes a cloistered feeling, the trees, miles inland from their natural habitat, add an exotic note to houses that are reached by short flights of stairs from the road. The two-story Victorian Gothic built by Carleton Callaway and his wife around 1888, is not remarkable architecturally, but gives an impression of size and substance. The home that Tero Amos had designed for her in 1905 is also substantial, but markedly different. Its low façade of dark, Ohio-made bricks behind heavy white Greek columns must have given it quite a modern appearance in the era it was built.

Not much is known of Logan's early life. Presumably he attended the Vineville Public School just up the street, an educational institution for which his great-grandfather Thomas Hardeman had served as trustee for many years before it became part of the Bibb County system.[131] Since both of his grandmothers were staunch Baptists he no doubt attended services every Sunday,[132] at Vineville Baptist, which E. Y. Mallary's father had helped to found; it was located for most of his youth on the corner of Vineville and Lamar,[133] the larger structure on the Pierce Avenue corner not being dedicated until 1925.[134]

Logan's father worked at his step-grandfather's banks, Commercial and Savings and Commercial National, until they were sold in 1914. Then, given the death of John P. Callaway in 1911, who had managed the business affairs[135] of his mother and sisters,[136] it was natural for Nat Lewis, as the only male in the family, to take over that responsibility. Rather than seek other employment, he chose to devote his time to the "extensive realty holdings" belonging to Carlton Callaway's heirs, and courthouse records in Lee, Monroe, and Bibb give evidence of his stewardship. His wife's grandmother, Ann Callaway, petitioned the Court of

---

131 Evans, *Macon Newspaper Clippings*, Vol. III, ibid.,p. 192.
132 Laura Nelle O'Callaghan, Oral Interview.
133 The building now occupied by the Primitive Baptist Church was the original home of Vineville Baptist.
134 Although the Callaways had been affiliated with First Baptist downtown, and its pastor married Tero and John Logan, Vineville's E. B. Carroll officiated at Carlton Callaway's 1900 funeral.
135 A Power of Attorney executed January 31, 1894 designating J. P. Callaway as their agent to manage the properties in Bibb, Dougherty, Lee, and Monroe counties was recorded in Bibb County May 29th 1906, Deed Book 106, folio 575.
136 Carleton Callaway died in 1900; Lula had apparently been married twice but seems to have been estranged from her second husband, J. Murray Whittle, and Annie had never married. Tero, of course, was widowed twice, first when John Logan died in 1885 and again when William B. Amos died in 1895.

Ordinary for him to be named Administrator of the Callaway estate in 1912;[137] when Johnnie's Aunt Lula Whittle died in 1916, her surviving sisters filed a document requesting that he be named to administer that estate also, since her named executor, brother John P. Callaway, had predeceased her.[138] So Lewis's 1915 *City Directory* listing does not include a business affiliation, although in 1917 he is listed as the bookkeeper for Macon Hardwood Lumber Company, and in 1918 he is termed a "farmer." But sadly, in an eerie replay of the early deaths of both his and Johnnie's fathers, Nat Lewis succumbed to pneumonia during the famous flu epidemic that coincided with the end of World War I. He was only thirty-three years old. Logan was ten.

Johnnie Lewis had to take over management of many of the family's business affairs at this point; she petitioned the Ordinary to replace Nat Lewis as administrator of Lula Whittle's estate, and to manage the small estate her husband had left.[139] Her name also began appearing on Lee County indentures in the 1920s, so presumably she took a more active role in managing the family's interests there after her husband's death.

Young Logan, growing up with his widowed mother and a widowed grandmother he adored,[140] next door to his widowed great-grandmother and maiden great-aunt, was doted upon. He "was always the king . . . they gave him everything he wanted." He was good-looking, charming, "dashing" even, but "not a bit cocky—natural," and did not lack for friends: "Everybody that knew Logan, liked him."[141] He had many advantages, ones that he seemed willing to share with playmates: as one who grew up nearby put it "We could all play ball because Logan had a ball."[142]

As had his grandmothers, Logan's mother remarried, in 1922. Interestingly, her new husband was a cousin of her first, and had stood up for him at their 1906 wedding. Julian Strothers Lewis had been born in Albany in 1889, the son of Robert Gallatin Lewis' younger brother Sherrie B. (Sheribiah Butts) Lewis and his wife, Nettie Coley.[143] He attended Albany schools and then Georgia Military Institute in Atlanta before moving to Macon. The 1908 and 1909 city directories show him as a bookkeeper at the bank, Fourth National, which William Minor Lewis, his father's youngest brother, had founded in 1903 before moving to Atlanta. The young businessman may have returned to Albany then, or followed his uncle to Atlanta, since there is no further mention of a Julian Lewis until 1924, when, listed as head of household at his mother-

137 Minutes of Court of Ordinary, Bibb County, Georgia, June Term 1912, Book Y, p. 548, and Return VV, p. 691. E. Y. Mallary signed for his $3,000 bond.
138 Bibb County Court of Ordinary, Minute Book AA, folio 529.
139 Ibid., Minute Book CC, folio 192-3.
140 O'Callaghan, ibid.
141 Ibid.
142 Robert L. McCommon, Oral Interview, February 21, 2003.
143 Obituary, *Macon Telegraph*, January 12, 1942, p. 2A. His father had died when Julian was a baby, in July of 1890, according to the tombstone in Oakview Cemetery cited above.

in-law's home[144] on Vineville Avenue (then numbered 717), he was termed a "peach farmer."[145] In 1925 he is shown as the department manager at the Fourth National Bank, and subsequently as being self-employed in real estate loans and insurance, with an office in what was then known as the Georgia Casualty Building at 516 Mulberry.

Logan Lewis, who called his stepfather "Uncle Julian," was in high school by the time of his mother's remarriage. Copies of *The Lanierian*, the annual put out by graduating classes at Macon's Lanier High School, record an unremarkable secondary school career, one that began co-educationally, at the building on Orange and Forsyth streets in town. Logan was listed as a member of both the freshman and sophomore classes in the 1922 book, and as a corporal in the much-vaunted military program that the Board of Education had instituted in response to America's unpreparedness for World War I, a program whose success led to Lanier's designation as a regional "honor school." His sophomore and junior years saw him fall back to private, however; he regained his freshman rank only as a senior.[146] By that time the boys had moved to a new building in suburban Napier Heights (which the 1925 *Lanierian* termed "the most beautiful school in the South"), leaving the girls behind on Orange Street.[147] Perhaps tellingly, Logan had his senior picture made in civilian clothes rather than his R.O.T.C. uniform. None of the usual activities are listed under that picture, possibly because he failed to turn them in to the yearbook staff since perusal of the books reveals not only his military participation but also membership in the "Question Club." The latter, a social fraternity despite the lack of Greek letters in its name, was a very "in" group, according to a contemporary, peopled with friends that included Herbert "Hub" Birdsey (who lived just a few doors down Vineville and had gone to elementary school with Logan), Sam Corbin, Ham Napier, Dick Jordan, Cliff Anderson, Eugene "Weenie" Killen, and Sanders Walker. The Class Prophet that year foresaw a future in which "Herbert Birdsey, Sam Corbin and Logan Lewis have formed a partnership and are world famed as manufacturers of flour."[148] Designated in the list of superlatives as "Class Baby," Logan's contribution to the senior boys' "Last Will and Testament" reads "We, Logan Lewis and Herbert Birdsey leave our love for each other to Sergeant Catron [a military professor] and George Wimberly." Perhaps most revealing was the quote the yearbook editors chose to put alongside his photograph: "A youth to whom was given, so much of earth, so much of heaven." The boys

144 Johnnie Logan Lewis acquired the home after her mother's 1934 death, and Logan, in turn, acquired it after Johnnie died in 1940.
145 Julian farmed peaches out at the Callaway place near Lorane in Bibb County after he married Johnnie Logan Lewis. Richard Domingos, Oral Interview, February 17, 2004.
146 Military rank, according to friend and contemporary Laura Nelle Anderson O'Callaghan (Interview #2, 2002) had less to do with military skills than academic grades. Interestingly the famed author of *God is My Co-Pilot*, WWII flying ace Robert Lee Scott, Jr., who was a member of Logan's class, only achieved the rank of Sergeant in Lanier's R.O.T.C. program.
147 Among them were Bib Hay, who was a junior, and Laura Nelle Anderson.
148 Birdsey's family already operated Macon's largest flour mill.

wore white pants and dark coats for the graduation exercises held at the Grand Opera House downtown on Mulberry Street, while the girls donned white dresses and carried yellow roses; thanks to the generosity of W. H. Felton, who had pledged a large sum to the fund-raising launched that spring, each graduate received a Stone Mountain Memorial Half Dollar at the ceremony.[149]

After graduation, Logan, like his father, grandfather Lewis, step-grandfather E. Y. Mallary, great-uncle John Callaway, and numerous other Jelks, Mallary, and Callaway relations, matriculated at Mercer University, the college E. Y. Mallary's grandfather had served as president in the 1840s, and of which E. Y. was then a trustee. He earned an A. B. in 1929, having participated in Phi Delta Theta fraternity and the tennis club. His senior photograph in the 1929 yearbook gives the appearance of an arrogantly handsome young man with chiseled features, deep-set, pale eyes, and a full mouth. Driving his four-door LaSalle convertible around town he "cut quite a dashing figure;" the younger brother of a friend compared him to Jay Gatsby: "He was good-looking, athletic, nattily dressed, able to move gracefully in social circles—pretty swish to someone twelve years his junior."[150] An offhand remark made by his mother in the previously-mentioned pencil inventory of her possessions casts some doubt on this description, however; listing a small silver-handled child's cane that went unused by her son she explained "but he was not much of a dude."[151] Another contemporary seconds this impression, remembering him as "quietly elegant, not showy," often choosing to drive an older car rather than the bright yellow, orange-striped LaSalle his grandmother had given him.[152] He was charming, fun to be with (if ungraciously blunt on occasion), but restrained.

It is unclear what Logan did immediately after leaving Mercer. The Macon newspaper's announcement of his engagement[153] reported that "since graduation he has taken an active part in social and civic affairs" of the city, while the Manitowoc newspaper said that he also studied in England.[154] His friend, Laura Nelle Anderson O'Callaghan, recalls his trip to Europe but does not believe it included "study."[155] He had been classified as a student living at his mother's residence in city directories from 1922 through 1930; unfortunately the

---

149 This last came from a 1975 *Macon Telegraph* clipping reporting on the 50th reunion of the class of 1925, on which no other data is visible, which was found in the 1925 *Lanierian* located in the Washington Library Historical and Genealogical Room; other information came from the 1922-25 *Lanierians* located there.
150 John Comer, Oral Interview, October 16, 2002.
151 Ibid.
152 Laura Nelle Anderson O'Callaghan, Oral Interview #3, February 20, 2003. His friends called the car "The Yellow" and regretted that, more often than not, it stayed in the garage.
153 *Macon Telegraph*, June 13, 1937, p 7B.
154 *Manitowoc Herald Times*, June 12, 1937, p. 8
155 Mrs. O'Callaghan acknowledged sharing Logan's lack of interest in academics, remembering that she had once explained it to her mother by saying "It isn't stylish to study." (Interview #2.) The trip to Europe reminded her of a story Logan told on himself: he had tossed a shirt he no longer wanted out of his cabin porthole, only belatedly remembering that he had failed to remove his father's diamond-studded Phi Delta Theta pin beforehand. According to notes in a Bible found in the Lewis home after Mrs. Lewis' death on which his name was inscribed, Logan went to Europe in the summer of 1926 between his freshman and sophomore years at Mercer. The Lewis library produced further evidence of the date, a booklet of photographs entitled "Souvenir Versailles et les Trianons" on which is written, in his own hand, "Logan Lewis, July 4, 1926." Lewis Archives.

Macon library has no directory for 1931 but Mrs. O'Callaghan believes that that may have been when he worked briefly for Macon realtor Thomas Hartley (Jack) Hall.[156] The 1932 city directory described him as a "bookkeeper" and 1934's as a "clerk" at the First National Bank and Trust Co. First National was then the largest bank in the city, claiming capital of $500,000, a surplus of $200,000, and an affiliation with the First National Bank of Atlanta in their city directory advertisement; W. G. Lee was chairman of the board, Marion Liles, president, and Jas. K. Hogan executive vice-president. A number of the young people with whom he socialized were also working at First National,[157] but around 1935 he left to manage the local office of the Atlanta-based Trust Company Bank of Georgia.[158] By 1937, however, the *Directory* shows him as employed at "Logan Lewis and Co" which has a separate listing as "Investment Bankers, Stocks, Bonds and Securities" as well as an ad indicating that the business is located at 605 Georgia Casualty Building, 516 Mulberry Street, the same building in which Julian Lewis' office was located, and the most prominent office building of the era. Working for himself may have been an appropriate choice. Remembering his early career thirty years later Logan twinkled while telling a younger colleague about having gone down to Sea Island for the weekend while he was employed at First National; the weekend stretched into Monday and his boss in the bond department called to ask "Logan, where are you working now?" "In Macon, at First National," he replied. "Well, you were. Until today," the man reportedly responded.[159]

But his family's extensive holdings of real property inevitably directed much of his attention towards land and its management. Laura Nelle Anderson O'Callaghan remembers his driving to Leesburg to collect rents due from tenants there (teasingly reassuring his great-aunt Annie, who sometimes accompanied him, that they were moving at a safe speed by pointing to the half full gas gauge as proof!) The Callaway estate in Vineville stretched from Vineville Avenue all the way to Ingleside Avenue;[160] what is now Callaway Street had been the lane up to the original home place, now 2455 Clayton Street. Subdivision of the property, which had begun when Carlton Callaway moved part of his family from the old home to a lot at the corner of Vineville and Corbin in 1888, and continued with the construction of four brick stores on other Vineville front footage in 1890s, included the development of houses for rent in the 100 block of Callaway during the first decade of the new century. It picked up speed in 1920. Following the

156 Interview #3.
157 Mrs. O'Callaghan was one of them; she also named Sanders Walker, Charles Wasden, and Lora Solomon as employees, recruited in friendly fashion by Marion H. Liles Sr. Ernest Lee, who had married Mary "Tots" Hall, also worked there in those years.
158 Biographical Report filed with the Comptroller of the Currency in connection with the purchase of control of the Farmers National Bank of Monticello, GA, June 4, 1965; in Lewis Archives. Further confirmation of the Trust Company affiliation came from a newspaper ad announcing it found in Crockett Odom's scrapbook, now in the possession of Crockett Rader Sellers.
159 Neal Ham was the younger colleague who recounted this tale Logan told on himself, one of a number of self-deprecating stories reported to this writer. Oral Interview, November 19, 2003.
160 That street was then called "Anola Place."

$1800 sale of a lot on Clayton Street to B. S. Deaver in March of that year,[161] a detailed plat made by H. D. Cutter, C. E., was recorded, which served as a reference for the several dozen lots on Corbin, Callaway, and Clayton that were sold during the decade before the Great Crash.[162]

Who, given the absence of adult males in the family,[163] took the initiative in handling these ventures, as well as oversight of the numerous property management responsibilities in Lee County? It was surely Johnnie, since the plat was drawn several years before she married Julian Lewis. This precedent might well have influenced the manner in which her son regarded his wife's role in future business activities. It's also interesting that the women began involving Logan in the family property at a fairly early age. His grandmother, Tero Amos, and great-aunt, Annie Callaway, gave him one of the Callaway Street lots in 1927 while he was still a Mercer student; the next year they also gave him the lot in Leesburg on which the Bank of Leesburg stood.[164] He had inherited cash and Georgia Kaolin Company stock worth approximately $10,000 from his other grandmother, Mary Jelks Lewis Mallary, in 1926. As his guardian, his mother used those assets to make several loans that were secured by various real estate holdings before he came of age; when the debts failed after the Depression set in, Logan foreclosed in 1934, eventually selling the properties to recoup the loss, although interestingly in one case, to the person he had foreclosed upon.[165]

When Tero died September 17, 1934, Johnnie and Logan were co-executors of her estate. A comparison between the inventory they filed with the Ordinary and the property listed in the 1911 indenture by which the family had bought out John Callaway's widow demonstrates that Carlton Callaway's estate[166] had remained essentially intact over the years, albeit augmented by additions from Lula Whittle's estate and Ann Callaway's interest in the Atlanta property. Together, Tero and her sister, Annie, owned, in addition to the acreage in Vineville, two hundred and twenty-eight acres in north Bibb County near Lorane, several properties in downtown Macon, six hundred twenty-five acres in Monroe County, fourteen hundred thirty-four acres of farmland[167] in Lee County, a dozen or so commercial buildings and several vacant lots in Leesburg, as well as a half interest in one part of the land on which the Keely Building sat near the

161 Bibb County Record Room, Book 248, folio 181.
162 Recorded ibid., in Plat Book 3, folio 39.
163 Annie Callaway had never married; Tero Callaway Logan Amos was twice widowed, and Johnnie Logan Lewis, having been widowed since Nat Lewis' 1918 death, would not remarry for three years after the Cutter plat was drawn.
164 Gifts were recorded in Bibb County in Book 331, folio 547; in Lee County in Book Q, folio 307. The gift in Bibb was Lot #4 of Block One, immediately behind the home he shared with his mother and grandmother.
165 Bibb Record Room, Book 411, folios 85, 377, 665 and 768.
166 Bibb Probate Court, Inventory Book D, pp. 311-317. In 1881 C. B. had deeded his entire estate to his wife and children with a life estate for Ann Callaway and the restriction that if any piece was to be sold all the donees must agree to it; John, who was given power of attorney to manage it (and was only 31 at the time,) was required to seek Court approval for each sale. The tediousness of this procedure is evident in deeds John recorded in Lee County during the 1880s, and in 1894 the property was transferred back to C. B. and re-gifted, eliminating the requirement for court approval. However the siblings did have to act jointly in disposing of any portion of their holdings, which had the effect of keeping the properties together, as well as of increasing the heirs' consciousness of what they owned.
167 While the inventory says 1434 acres, the plat Logan commissioned in 1936 indicates it was 1821 acres. Recorded in Lee County Plat File.

corner of Whitehall and Hunter streets in downtown Atlanta; all told the value of these holdings was estimated at around $150,000. Tero listed most of them individually in her will, specifying that some were to go to Johnnie, some to Logan, and others to the two of them jointly. Two of the Vineville Avenue stores, for example, went to Johnnie, and two to Logan; Johnnie got two-thirds of Tero's half-interest in #92 Whitehall Street, Atlanta, and Logan received one-third. Among the properties to which Logan had exclusive rights were the Lorane acreage in north Bibb County, several lots on Callaway, a 1000-tree pecan grove in Lee County, the bungalow the Callaways used when visiting Lee County, and commercial properties in Leesburg and downtown Macon. In February following Tero's death, Annie Callaway quitclaimed to Logan a piece of the Atlanta Jones property she had apparently inherited singly from her mother, a one-eighth interest in #94 Whitehall Street, the lot adjacent to the one in which she and Tero owned an undivided half-interest. In July she quitclaimed to Johnnie her interest in all of the properties she had held jointly with her sister, recording the same in Bibb, Lee, Monroe, and Fulton counties.

The Atlanta property has a complicated ownership history but was of considerable interest to Logan, even before his grandmother's death; plats showing its configuration and ownership with notes in his hand remained in a file long after his death.[168] The two adjacent lots on Whitehall Street cited above had originally been acquired by Logan's great-great-grandfather, "Cotton John" Jones, in 1869 and 1870, respectively. The one at the corner with Hunter (#94) had a dry goods store in which Atlanta retailer John Keely got his start.[169] Jones left it as a life estate for his widow, Elizabeth Strozier Jones, and that lot was inherited per stirpes by her eight heirs; Ann Callaway's one eighth apparently went to her daughter Annie who quitclaimed it to Logan after Tero's death, but he had already joined with several co-owner cousins to buy a five-eighth's interest from another cousin's widow.[170] Ann Jones Callaway and her nephew, John Pope

168 Lewis Archives.
169 Captain John Keely, an Irish-born dry goods merchant, began his career working in the store run by John Gannon on property owned by John Jones, a lot adjacent to that which Ann Jones Callaway and her nephew John Pope Jones, took as their share of the Jones estate; in 1902 they built a building for the expanding business which became one of the largest in the South. (Walter G. Cooper, *Official History of Fulton County,* 1934 History Commission, Ivan Allen, Chair, reprinted in 1978, pp. 854-5.) During the years in question the corner of Whitehall and Hunter streets was one of the busiest intersections in Atlanta.
170 Elizabeth Strozier Jones died in 1892; in 1896 one of her sons, Enoch Callaway Jones, bought out four of the other heirs, giving him a 5/8ths interest, which was left to his son Edgar Jones in 1916; Otis Jones' share went to his son Robert, and Chandler Jones' to his son Walter. Edgar Jones' larger holding passed to his widow in 1932 who, after going to court to resolve issues connected with settling his estate, sold it to Logan and the other owners in July of 1934, two months before Tero's death. Ann Callaway's 1/8th apparently went to Annie Callaway, who quitclaimed it to Logan in February of 1935, giving him a full 1/3rd interest in that property. After Johnnie's 1940 death he owned a full 1/2 interest in 92 Whitehall. The ownership of these parcels was traced in deeds and wills on file in the Fulton County Courthouse. Record of the original purchase of #94 is in Book O, folio 96-7; for #92 Book L, folio 385. Probate records showing the life estate in #94 for Elizabeth Jones and its descent through her heirs include the estates of John Jones (#3132); Enoch Callaway Jones (#1535); and Edgar C. Jones (#5360). Annie Callaway's quitclaim of her interest in #94 to Logan Lewis is in Book 1548, folio 137, and Logan's and his cousins' purchase from Janie Giles Jones is in Book 1521, folio 473. Ann Callaway's receipt of #92 from her father's estate is in Deed Book W, folio 666, and an indenture relating to the construction of the Keely Building is in Book 164, folios 365-8; the deed of her undivided half interest to her daughters is in Book 827, folio 516. Tero Amos' Will leaving her one quarter to Logan and Johnnie Lewis is on file in Bibb County Probate Court, Will Book J, pp. 74-77; Annie's quitclaim of her interest to her niece Johnnie is in Bibb County's Deed Book 426, folios 191-95, as well as in Fulton County's Book 1560, folio 327. Johnnie Lewis' Will leaving her interest in #92 to her son is in Bibb Probate Court, Will Book K, p. 307. John Keely's purchase of what became #121 Hunter is in Fulton County Deed Book II, folio 83; the City of Atlanta's acquisition of it for tax fi fas is in Book 1506, folio 457, and Logan and his cousins' purchase of it in 1935 is in Deed Book 1550, folios 189 and 191. Copies of these and other documents relating to the Keely Building, including xeroxed Sanborn Maps for 1886, 1899, 1911, and 1931 are in the Lewis Archives.

Jones, received the adjacent lot, #92, as their share of "Cotton John's" estate, and it was this undivided one half interest which Tero Amos and Annie Callaway shared, having inherited it from her. With John Keely's business becoming increasingly successful, a three-story brick building, known as "The Keely Building" had been erected in 1902; it covered not only the two Jones lots, but also another to their east which Keely had purchased himself in 1881. In 1935, after the Keely Company apparently went bankrupt, Logan and the cousins with whom he owned #94 Whitehall also acquired that third lot, which faced Hunter and on which a side entrance to the store was located, known as #121 Hunter. Thus Logan owned a portion of each parcel on which the building sat. The central commercial location of the combined properties provided a good return on their investment.[171] Shortly after the Keely Company went out of business, H. Kessler and Co., another department store, signed a lease that remained in effect until the property was sold in 1965. In addition to the income it provided, Logan used his interest in both land and lease as collateral to raise capital for other business ventures.

With the assets already in his own name and the additional ones inherited from his grandmother, the young businessman had resources to invest in other ventures, and courthouse records document an increase in his real estate activities. In April 1936 he borrowed several thousand dollars from First National and Macon Federal to purchase twenty-four lots on Eldorado Drive in Ingleside Estates, a newly laid out subdivision between Forest Hill Road and Ridge Avenue, as well as several commercial buildings across Vineville Avenue from those the Callaway heirs already owned. Both loans were repaid in the 1940s.[172] He and his Jones cousins also borrowed against the Atlanta property when they acquired the additional lot east and south of those already in the family, so as to own all of the land on which the Keely Building stood.[173] Besides looking after his own business affairs he took increasing responsibility for managing the various components of the Callaway estate, helping to negotiate filling station, grocery store, and turpentine leases, and, as noted above, collecting the rents. He had a plat made of all the Lee County properties in 1936, making it easier to assess and evaluate them. As the Depression deepened and businesses failed, those properties were no longer producing comparable income, which must have been cause for concern and heightened oversight. New federal laws required payment of a tax on Tero's estate and likely there were other expenses associated with its settlement as well. Not surprisingly, some of

171 The Keely Building was just a few steps from Rich's first building, the center of commercial Atlanta in the days when Peachtree north of Five Points was still residential. "You could buy anything on Whitehall Street," according to a popular Atlanta history. In the 1970s, in order to help an area by then flagging in popularity, the seven blocks of Whitehall south of the railroad tracks were re-named Peachtree Street S. W., and Hunter became Martin Luther King Jr. Boulevard.
172 Bibb Superior Court, Book 412, pp. 260, 293 and 351 and Book 432, p. 109 and p. 422.
173 Fulton County Clerk of Court Deed Book II, folio 83.

the 1935 property taxes went unpaid in Fulton, Monroe, and Lee counties. As friend Pink Persons put it "The Callaways were 'land poor,'"[174] without enough cash to meet all of their obligations.[175] It must have been evident to Logan that the properties would have to be further developed so as to increase their yield.

But business was not the only or even the most dominant influence in his life. Always active in leisure pursuits, Logan enjoyed riding gaited horses, keeping a mount at Roland Ellis's stable out near Wimbish and Forest Hill roads, from which he and friends rode far into north Bibb.[176] He may also have ridden at the rural retreat on the Cochran Short Route known as Stone Creek Lodge, jointly owned by the Broadus Willingham and Ralph Birdsey families, both close Vineville friends. In 1934, he joined other enthusiasts to help the Utility Club and the American Legion organize the first major horse show held in Macon in thirty years, serving as Treasurer and chairing the Trophy Committee for the event.[177] He also delighted in flying two-seater planes to St. Simons, trips interrupted by landing on the highway and taxiing up to gasoline stations to refill the small tanks.[178] A big air exposition had drawn 80,000 people to Miller Field in 1929 and a flight school was begun there shortly thereafter.[179] Whether these influences or just the challenge of the new machines motivated him, Logan eventually bought a Stinson 105 that he co-owned with Buford Birdsey.[180] Dove hunting on the large Callaway properties in Lee County was another pastime.

Tennis and golf, however, consumed most of his attention. Both were relatively new sports, becoming increasingly well established via the Macon Racquet Club which maintained a court on Vineville Avenue and hosted a city-wide tournament, and Idle Hour Country Club, which by 1927 boasted a Scottish-born professional and "one of the finest golf courses in the United States."[181] A circle at Christ Church raised money one year by bringing tennis pro "Bitsy" Grant to Macon for a demonstration at Ben O'Neal's court on Vista Circle; the sports pages were full of the exploits of the Georgia golf sensation, Bobby Jones, and even Macon's boxing star W. L. "Young" Stribling, was playing golf. In 1927, while still at Mercer where he was on the tennis team, Logan made it to the final round of the Middle Georgia Tennis Tournament in singles "flashing a brilliant overhead game and consistent hard drives," and partnered with his good friend Ham Napier, in doubles. According to the *Telegraph*

174 Oral Interview, June 11, 2003.
175 In addition to not paying her taxes, it was common knowledge that Johnnie Logan Lewis had outstanding accounts with numerous merchants in town.
176 Betty Hay McCook Curtis, Oral Interview, June 15, 2000.
177 *Macon Telegraph*, May 28, 1934, p. 8, and May 29, 1934, p. 8-9. Dr. W. G. Lee was chairman of the show; Buford Birdsey was among the others involved in bringing "a hundred of the finest horses in the South" to Macon. *Macon Telegraph*, May 30, 1934, p. 7.
178 Robert L. McCommon, Jr., Oral Interview, February 21, 2003.
179 *Macon Telegraph*, April 28, 1929, p. 1A; November 20, 1929, p. 13A.
180 *Macon Telegraph*, "Macon Fly Men," The Georgia Magazine (Sunday supplement), January 26, 1941, p. 3S. It is not known when the plane was purchased.
181 *Macon Telegraph*, April 17, 1927, p. 1 B. A 1925 story on a tournament planned at Idle Hour noted that the course was "considered to be one of the best and prettiest in the southern states" and "second to none in the state" by "eminent golf writers." (*Macon Telegraph*, March 22, 1925, p. 3 B.) Later that spring the club presented a demonstration match featuring famed golf pro Walter Hagen playing amateurs Horace Wright and Watts Gunn and its own Scottish professional Harry Duff, which drew several hundred onlookers. (*Macon Telegraph*, May 2, 1925, p. 6A.)

he "was in top form" showing a "driving game beautiful to behold" although eventually losing to a six-time titleholder.[182] The newspaper's post-tournament analysis said:

> It was known that Lewis when right could play sensational tennis, but nobody in town had ever seen him get right for over one set. The theory was advanced that Lewis was a small match player. In other words, he could completely snow under a player of mediocre ability, but when he came up against a man of his own caliber he was always to be found on the losing side . . . he couldn't play when the sailing was rough and the score against him, only when he was in the lead. He completely blasted these tennis theories when he furnished the two prettiest comebacks and the two biggest upsets of the tournament . . . It is true that Lewis completely blew up after losing the first set . . . but when the time came to rally, he rallied . . . with defeat staring him in the face. Lewis's most important opponent on a tennis court is himself. He is nervous and temperamental and apt to become upset, but of late he has been controlling himself well and his strokes have been nearly perfect.[183]

But the control was intermittent, or perhaps dependent upon the circumstances. Pink Persons, who as a youngster shagged balls for Logan when he played at the Vineville Court, remembers him hurling his tennis racket into the street some years after this news story was written.[184]

In the early '30s, he and friends Eugene "Weenie" Killen and Sanders Walker became young "contenders" in the numerous golf tournaments then sponsored by Idle Hour, other regional country clubs, or the Utility Club (a women's service organization that became the Junior League of Macon in 1937).[185] As with his tennis, however, Logan seemed to make it to the semi-finals or finals without ever winning; a short piece in the *Telegraph* in advance of Idle Hour's 1934 fall tournament opined that he was "not expected to win the medal this week but will offer strong competition." His average score was 80 but, the paper reported, "according to [Idle Hour pro] George Norrie he could easily shoot better than 75 on every round if he played more often." He "has a wonderful match play temperament, say[ing] very little while playing . . . His opponents seem to get hottest when they meet him." [186] As predicted, Logan played "Macon's Number One Golfer" Horace Wright for the Utility Club's mythical southeastern amateur championship that spring, after executing "the biggest upset of the three-day event when he ousted the defending champion

182 *Telegraph* coverage of the tournament is found in papers dated July 7, 1928, p. 11 A; July 8, 1928, p. 1 B; July 11, 1928, p. 10 A; July 13, 1928, p. 11 A; July 17, 1928, p. 9 A; July 18, 1928, p. 11 A; and July 19, 1928, p. 9A.
183 Ibid., July 18, 1928, p. 11A.
184 Oral Interview, June 11, 2003.
185 *Macon Telegraph*, September 3, 1933, p. 6A, among others.
186 May 2, 1934, p. 8A.

Eden Taylor Jr.[187] with a 2 and 1 triumph in the semifinals." In "a bitter battle of long distance tee blows," however, a driving downpour interrupted his three-hole lead, and Wright prevailed.[188]

The Macon Telegraph's engagement announcement described Logan Lewis as "a member of a widely-known and prominently connected Southern family."[189] He was also part of a "very close"[190] set of well-to-do young people who evidenced few ill effects from the Depression and were bent on enjoying each other's company. They got together frequently to make music at each other's houses,[191] to play tennis at the Vineville court, or attend the popular Saturday night dances at Idle Hour.[192] Logan did not reciprocate the home entertainments, rarely bringing friends to his house; while that may have been the preference of his mother and grandmother, it also seemed to reflect his private nature.[193] Nevertheless, he was an active participant in the group's activities.

That "set" often included Bib Hay Anderson, her sister, Betty, who married one of Logan's best friends, Jimmy McCook, and, when she was in town, their friend from the Finch School, Dorothy Vits. According to his third cousin and good buddy Laura Nelle Anderson O'Callaghan, who was also an active participant in that small crowd, Logan had "gone with all the Macon girls," dating one and then another, and he could always be counted on as an escort for out-of-town guests.[194] He had been more particularly involved with another young woman when Dorothy Vits began visiting Macon, and indeed, Dorothy had carried on a flirtation with another Macon swain, one who had pursued her to Manitowoc.[195] But sometime after Betty Hay and Jimmy McCook were married in late 1935 it became apparent to the others in their crowd that Logan had begun to focus exclusively on Dorothy, and that his attentions were not unwelcome.

---

187 Taylor had been a groomsman at his parents' 1906 wedding.
188 *Macon Telegraph,* May 7, 1934, p. 5A.
189 *Macon Telegraph,* June 13, 1937, p. 7B.
190 O'Callaghan Interview #1.
191 In addition to the "Victrola" the group listened to Crockett Odom and Cliff Anderson play the piano. ibid.
192 "At those dances the orchestra never numbered over four pieces and frequently only three, while the small but congenial crowds were kept moving by a whistle blown by a member of the band. At the sound of the whistle all dancers had to change partners . . . . If anything was lacking in ceremony it was made up for in enthusiasm." Winburn Stewart and H. P. Persons Jr., "A Brief History of the Idle Hour Country Club," Club Handbook, 1967, Idle Hour Club, Macon, Ga. Lewis Archives.
193 O'Callaghan Interview #3.
194 O'Callaghan Interview #1.
195 Anderson Interview.

Logan Lewis at age ten in old family photograph. Courtesy Lewis Archives.

Logan Lewis as a senior in high school, from the 1925 *Lanierian*. Photo courtesy of Middle Georgia Archives.

Logan Lewis as a college senior in the 1929 *Cauldron,* the Mercer yearbook. Courtesy of Middle Georgia Archives.

Logan grew up with his mother and grandmother in the above home on the corner of Vineville Avenue and Callaway Street; his great-grandmother and maiden aunt lived next door in the large frame house, left, that his great-grandparents had built in the late 1880s. Both houses still stand.

The Keely Building on the corner of Whitehall and Hunter streets in downtown Atlanta, at right in this 1920s post card photo, proved an important part of Logan's inheritance. Built on property originally purchased by his great-great-grandfather, John Jones, Logan used his interest in both land and lease as collateral to raise capital for numerous other business ventures. Photo from *Atlanta in Vintage Postcards,* Volume I, by Elena Irish Zimmerman, Arcadia Publishing, 1999; used by permission.

This photograph of Logan Lewis on horseback was among Mrs. Lewis's personal affects after her death. Lewis Archives.

Chapter 3

———❖◆❖———

Mr. and Mrs. Lewis
in Macon

Beginning Married Life

Laura Nelle Anderson O'Callaghan remembers that Dorothy Vits spent most of May 1937 in Macon visiting her friend Bib Hay Anderson, and that it was during that month that Logan Lewis' courtship of the stunning young woman from Wisconsin culminated in the decision of the two to marry.[1] But the courting had begun earlier: in one of her weekly "Parties and Personalities" columns for the *Macon Telegraph* the previous January, society writer Blythe McKay reported getting a

> glimpse of attractive 'Do' Vits dashing away early from a bridge game at Mary (Mrs. Vernon) Skinner's to go driving with Logan Lewis . . . . 'Do' was wearing a smart rose colored suede suit with a navy blue sweater, and stopped on the way out to bid farewell to Texas (Mrs. Arthur) Barry, Betty (Mrs. J. W., Jr.) McCook, Sara (Mrs. Allen) Smith, Mary (Mrs. Manley) McWilliams, Margaret (Mrs. Hudnall) Weaver and Mary Bennet (Mrs. Elliott) Dunwody, for she was returning to Wisconsin the next day...[2]

A blurb in "Personal Mention" the previous Wednesday had noted that "Miss Dorothy Vits, who has been a guest of Mr. and Mrs. Halstead Anderson, Stanislaus, has returned to her home in Manitowoc."[3]

Mrs. O'Callaghan's recollection of Dorothy Vits's visit to Macon that May could not be documented by similar "mentions" in the *Telegraph,* but perusal of the sports and social pages demonstrates that it was a busy month. Earlier that spring, the Chamber of Commerce and the Rivoli Riding Club had spearheaded the organization of the Macon Horse Show Association to stage a two-phase competition at Central City Park; Logan Lewis was named General Chairman and Mayor Herbert Smart Honorary Chairman.[4] A special ring was built and lighted, and Junior League members Lora McCord and Rose Kingman took charge of selling the boxes surrounding it to the cream of Macon society. Visitors

1 Oral Interview #2, September 2002.
2 *Macon Telegraph and News,* Sunday, January 10, 1937, p. 2 B.
3 *Macon Telegraph,* January 6, 1937, p. 7 A.
4 *Macon Telegraph and News,* Sunday, March 14, 1937, p. 7A.

and entrants came from Albany, Atlanta, and Columbus as well as Macon, with George Foster of Ft. McPherson serving as Ringmaster.[5] Atlanta 'sportsman' Evan MacDonnell and Atlanta Tuxedo Club President Jim Henry commented favorably on the event, which succeeded in drawing over eight hundred people to both the afternoon and evening shows; *Telegraph* writer Susan Myrick wrote an effusive story about it the following Sunday.[6] Preoccupied as he must have been with the Horse Show on the twenty-first, Logan was also playing in Idle Hour's annual spring golf tournament, winning his matches May 9 and twenty-third but falling to Morris Michael on the thirtieth.[7] Meanwhile the Macon Home Show, at which "the magnificent organ recitals of Mr. Crockett Odom proved to be one of the most popular attractions," brought more than 5000 to its exhibitions at the City Auditorium before closing on the twenty-second.[8] The pool at Idle Hour opened that weekend, and many of the horse show guests stayed in town to attend the Saturday night dance there. The multitude of social activities doubtless provided numerous opportunities for the couple to pursue their courtship.

Johnnie Lewis learned of her son's intentions when he scratched on her bedroom window late one night to request the heirloom diamond ring that had been set aside for his betrothed.[9] On June 13 the *Macon Telegraph* told the rest of the city: "Of wide social interest is the announcement made today by Dr. and Mrs. Albert J. Vits of Manitowoc, Wis., of the engagement of their daughter, Dorothy Ann, to Mr. N. Logan Lewis of Macon. Miss Vits, daughter of a widely known manufacturer, is a social leader in Manitowoc and in Los Angeles, Cal., where her family spends the winters. . . . The wedding . . . will take place in Manitowoc in July."[10]

On that same day Dr. and Mrs. Vits hosted an "at home" in Manitowoc to announce the engagement to their friends there. Unfortunately the groom could not be introduced in person; he was in Macon with his mother who had suffered a serious heart attack. Mrs. Lewis' precarious health also prevented her and her husband from travelling north for the July 22 nuptials, although a number of Macon people went to wish the groom well. Eugene ("Weenie") Killen "motored" up with his buddy, and then drove Logan's car back to Macon so that the newlyweds could honeymoon in the wedding gift from the bride's parents:[11] a shiny five-passenger gray Buick Roadmaster convertible with leather seats.[12] Driving north together were Betty and Jimmy McCook, Laura Nelle

5 Ibid., May 21, 1937, p. 1 A, and 3 B.
6 *The Macon Telegraph*, Saturday, May 22, 1937, p. 1 A, and *Macon Telegraph and News*, May 23, 1937, p. 2 A.
7 Ibid., May 10, 1937, p. 6A; May 24, 1937, p. 7A, and May 31, 1937, p. 6A)
8 Ibid., May 22, 1937, p. 8 A.
9 O'Callaghan Interview #2. Johnnie Lewis told her this story when Mrs. O'Callaghan dropped by 717 Vineville after returning from Manitowoc to share details following the wedding. Dorothy "had very long, exotic fingers," Mrs. O'Callaghan remembers, and the large, three-diamond ring "looked beautiful on her." Interview #3.
10 "Vits-Lewis Engagement Announced Here Today," June 13, 1937, p. 7 B.
11 O'Callaghan Interview #1, September 2000.
12 John Comer, Oral Interview, October 2, 2002.

Anderson, and Crockett Odom, who stopped at Chicago's Palmer House on the way home where they heard Eddie Duchin perform the night his son Peter was born.[13] Emily and Sanders Walker also drove, planning to take advantage of Wisconsin's many lakes by scheduling a fishing trip following the festivities. Mr. and Mrs. Broadus E. Willingham Jr., lifelong friends of Johnnie Logan Lewis,[14] who served as her representatives at the event, and the Ernest Lees (accompanied by Mrs. Lee's aunt and sister), journeyed by train. Marion Liles, president of the bank for which Logan had worked just out of college, and his wife, Mary, went to Wisconsin,[15] as did Dorothy's classmate, Mary Jane Hermann, of Covington, Kentucky,[16] and other friends from Atlanta. Bib Hay Anderson and her husband, Andy, however, awaiting the arrival of their first baby, had to remain in Macon.

According to Mrs. O'Callaghan the Maconites were in for a treat. "You think about *southern* hospitality!" she exclaimed. "Well, they left us in the shade[17]. . . They shamed us they were just so nice."[18] The Vitses, she explained, "were kind of the royal family up there" and that is the way they treated their guests.[19] Their hosts put them up at the family-owned Manitowoc Hotel on North 8th Street, and they had barely unpacked their bags upon arriving Monday afternoon when they were escorted to the Walter Hamilton home where Mr. and Mrs. Hamilton entertained fifty for cocktails and a buffet supper.[20] Tuesday afternoon Mrs. Edward Hamilton and Mrs. Wistar Ambler of New York, who was visiting her parents, Mr. and Mrs. Lyman Nash, next door neighbors of the Vitses, gave a tea. That night Mr. and Mrs. Walter J. Brand of Sheboygan gave a dinner at their summer home near that of the Vitses at Elkhart Lake; Miss Margaret Reiss, also of Sheboygan, gave a luncheon at the lake Wednesday. Wednesday evening the Vitses hosted the bridal dinner at their home on Michigan Avenue; guests were feted by an array of delicacies prepared by the caterers Anne Vits had imported from Milwaukee, and amused at having their fortunes told by a costumed gypsy.[21] Betty Hay McCook Curtis remembers Dorothy as "just the most gracious thing you've ever seen, just loving everybody having come to the wedding." In addition to the parties, the Maconites enjoyed sampling a bit of local culture when they stopped by a tavern (reportedly one frequented by Al Capone) and joined in singing German songs; unfamiliar as that was, it was apparently less foreign to the Southerners than being waited upon by white servants.

13 Betty Hay McCook Curtis Interview #1, June 15, 2000.
14 Mrs. Willingham was the former Rosalie Mallary, daughter of Frank Lorraine Mallary and step-cousin to Nat Lewis; she had served as a junior attendant at the Logan-Lewis wedding in 1906. Both Willinghams had grown up in Vineville, Broadus Willingham Sr. having built the large brick, columned home on the Avenue (now numbered 2048) while constructing his cotton factory just back of it, across the Macon and Western Railroad track. The Willinghams and the Lewises were so close that, as Betty Curtis put it in a June 24, 2003 interview "Mr. Broadus thought he *birthed* Logan."
15 "Friends to Attend Vits-Lewis Wedding Party Next Thursday," *Macon Telegraph*, July 17, 1937, p. 5.
16 *Manitowoc Herald Times*, Tuesday, July 20, 1937, p. 6.
17 Interview #2.
18 Interview #3.
19 Interview #1.
20 *Manitowoc Herald Times*, ibid.
21 O'Callaghan Interview #1.

Dorothy Vits was a devout Catholic while her fiancé had been raised in a Baptist family that took its religion seriously.[22] Not surprisingly, their decision to marry outside their own faiths in that pre-Vatican II era raised a few eyebrows, including those of the church fathers in Manitowoc. As his friends began making plans to go Wisconsin, the groom had phoned Laura Nelle to alert her that non-Catholics would not be able to attend the exchange of vows, which was to be restricted to the bridal party and members of the immediate families.[23] With none of Logan's family able to be present, Broadus Willingham, whose wife Rosalie's close friendship with his mother had made him almost an uncle to the young man, was his only attendant. Abby's wife, Florence, was Dorothy's only attendant. The ceremony was conducted by the Rev. E. A. Radey in the rectory at Holy Innocents Church on Waldo Road at 11:30 a.m. Immediately afterwards a wedding breakfast for twenty-four close family members and the out of town guests was served in the Vits dining room. It was an impressive setting: a sparkling crystal chandelier hung from an ornate ceiling medallion above a long table covered with "low plateaus of gardenias and valley lilies" and accented by two seven-candle crystal candelabras. All "the appointments" were of white or silver, with the only note of color being the groom's cake which was decorated with clusters of glaceed fruits. Dorothy wore a "white Rodier ensemble"[24] of rough crepe with a matching turban; her three-quarters length-matching coat was banded with silver fox and she carried purple-centered white orchids.

That afternoon at four o'clock Dr. and Mrs. Vits hosted a reception for additional friends and extended family. Their fourteen-room home, situated well back from the road on an expansive property occupying no less than seven city lots,[25] was one of the largest and most elegantly furnished in the city.[26] Built in 1860 and added on to several times over the years, its most prominent feature is a two-story white portico with four slender columns supporting a pediment ornamented by a fanlight and dental work. Two wings extend unevenly on either side, the wider one having an exposed brick lower story with a large bay window that gives a Midwestern feel to the Greek design elements. The front door, featuring another fanlight, as well sidelights flanked by two substantial carriage lamps, opens onto the west end of the portico, balancing the different-sized wings.[27] The Vitses were well known for their lavish entertaining, and their daughter's

22 Tero Amos had been among the founders of the Vineville Baptist Church, and E. Y. Mallary's father, Rollin D., had been its first pastor. Logan, while not as overtly religious as his fiancee, had read the Bible from beginning to end during his late teens, recording when he began and finished each section of the leather-bound, gold-monogrammed King James version that had been a gift from his mother in 1919. There is a note on the page following her inscription in Logan's hand that says, "Finished the first time January 15, 1928." (Now in the Lewis Archives.) While respecting each other's beliefs, the couple adhered to separate faiths until Logan Lewis converted to Catholicism just before his death.
23 O'Callaghan Interview #1.
24 "Miss Vits and Mr. Lewis Are Married Thursday," *Macon Telegraph*, July 23, 1937, p. 1 B. Rodier, long a household name in France for its nineteenth century textiles, began producing fabric influenced by twentieth century art movements, including art deco and cubism, in the 1920s and '30s, evolving into a fashion house of worldwide repute.
25 According to a letter from Jane Protz to Dorothy Lewis dated July 12, 1992; now in Lewis Archives.
26 John Spindler, Oral Interview, October 2000.
27 This description taken from mid-century photographs in a scrapbook belonging to Michael Place, Manitowoc.

wedding was no exception. The public rooms beyond the spacious entrance hall were filled with "a profusion of roses and delphinium, while palms and tall vases of lilies served as a background for the receiving party in the drawing room." Elaborate refreshments were served in the garden. For the reception the bride was again strikingly attired, this time in a heavy, white, crinkle satin empire gown with "an ornament of brilliants in the center of the bodice from which white silk fringe fell to the floor; an orchid halo adorned her dark hair." Anne Vits wore a gown of heavy black crepe while Rose Willingham was dressed in black chiffon with a jacket of white Swiss embroidery, and Flo Vits wore black taffeta with a tunic of white Swiss embroidery.[28]

After the festivities the bride and groom toured Canada and New York in the Buick Roadmaster, and spent a few days in Charleston where they purchased a pastel by Charleston artist Elizabeth O'Neil Verner.[29] When they returned to Macon they set up housekeeping in a brick cottage at 204 Corbin Avenue (one block north of the Lewis and Callaway homes on Vineville) that had been a gift from the groom's mother.[30] But the celebrating was far from over. Their friends threw a host of parties to honor the couple: Laura Nelle Anderson invited thirty young people to a buffet supper on the porch of her family's home in Shirley Hills, after which the group attended the dance at Idle Hour Club;[31] Mrs. Hugh Hardin, a second cousin who had been a member of Johnnie Lewis's wedding party in 1906, and her husband hosted an informal barbecue to introduce members of the "younger married contingent in Macon" to a like group from Forsyth;[32] and Emily and Sanders Walker gave a small dinner party at their home on High Street.[33] Perhaps the most elaborate party, termed by the *Telegraph* "one of the most beautiful social events of the late summer," was the tea given by Mrs. Parks Lee Hay and her daughters Bib Hay Anderson and Betty Hay McCook at the Hay home on Georgia Avenue. "The three hostesses and the honoree received the guests in the long drawing room" which was banked with giant dahlias and vari-colored gladioli. The new Mrs. Lewis wore a gown of black chiffon, the skirt very full, the waist formed of white Swiss embroidery," a corsage of gardenias and valley lilies, and an orchid in her hair. Mrs. Hay's gown was gold satin, Mrs. Anderson's blue lace, and Mrs. McCook's white chiffon.

28 *Macon Telegraph*, July 23, 1937, p. 1 B. Interestingly, the *Manitowoc Herald Times* (July 27, 1937, p. 6) report of the wedding said that Anna Vits wore a gown of steel blue and white printed chiffon to the reception, but the other costumes described alongside Mrs. Vits' were those that both the *Telegraph* and Laura Nelle Anderson O'Callaghan said were worn to the ceremony rather than the reception. The two papers used separate photographs that nevertheless appear to have been taken at the same time and in the same place: the terrace steps at the Vits home after the principals returned from the church rectory. (*Manitowoc Herald Times*, Saturday, July 24, 1937, p. 8, and the *Macon Telegraph*, "Dorothy Vits Becomes Bride of Logan Lewis of Macon," Sunday, August 15 p. 5B,) Apparently the southern paper's description of the costumes is correct. *The Herald Times* also noted that the bride changed into an imported black crepe suit with a bolero jacket accompanied by a black velvet monk's cap, for her wedding trip.
29 O'Callaghan Interview # 3.
30 Logan and Johnnie had inherited a half interest in the house, previously used as rental property, from Tero, and Annie Callaway had deeded her half to Johnnie in 1935. When her son became engaged, Johnnie quitclaimed her three-quarters interest in him in a deed that was recorded the day after his engagement was announced in the newspaper, making him the owner "in fee simple."
31 "Recent Bride Honor Guest at Party Here," *Macon Telegraph*, August 22, 1937, p. B5.
32 "Mr. and Mrs. Hardin Are Hosts For Mr. and Mrs. Logan Lewis," ibid., August 27, 1937, p. 4 B.
33 "Mr. and Mrs. Lewis Will Be Honored," ibid., August 31, 1937, p. 6.

Assisting in serving and entertaining were Mrs. Herbert Birdsey, Mrs. Vernon Skinner, Mrs. Roy Crockett, Mrs. William C. Turpin Jr., Mrs. Parks Lee Hay Jr., Mrs. Sanders Walker, Miss Laura Nelle Anderson, Mrs. Allen Smith, Mrs. Elliott Dunwody Jr., Mrs. Joseph R. Clisby, Mrs. Robert McCord Jr., and Mrs. Ernest Lee. About two hundred and fifty guests attended, including the mother of the groom.[34]

The liveliest party was the barbecue that Crockett Odom and Ed Everett threw at Cedar Crest, the country home of Everett's parents near the Callaway place at Lorane. The young bachelors decided to take a pictorial approach to inviting some hundred-plus Macon, Atlanta, Fort Valley, and Montezuma friends, using a bar, a bee, and a Chinaman's que to convey the nature of the event, and a child in a tub with a cake of soap next to it to signify the day of the week on which it would be held. Much to their amusement, the guests responded in kind, giving Blythe McKay a whole column's worth of material for "Parties and Personalities." Herbert and Cynthia Birdsey, for example, sent a card with a large "D" followed by a light bulb and then a teddy bear, to explain that they were "de-light-ted" to attend, and signed their names by drawing two little birds named "Hub" and "Cyn" followed by an eye. Steve Popper wrote his reply, but then cut it into pieces, mailing half to Ed and half to Crockett. The responses were so clever, in fact, that the hosts decided to offer a prize for the best one, recruiting a set of disinterested judges to make an impartial selection. Art and Texas Barry were the lucky winners—of a live baby goat.[35]

No sooner had these events ended than another round of teas, luncheons, and dinner parties began to honor Anne Vits who came to Macon in early October to spend a few days with her daughter and new son-in-law.[36] The very next week the William Elliott Dunwodys hosted their annual anniversary dance at Idle Hour for two hundred friends "in the married and debutante sets;" Dorothy turned heads in "a handsome gown of white crepe satin simply fashioned, the low cut décolletage finished with an ornament of pearls and gold beads from which deep white fringe fell to the hem of the skirt."[37] Elliott Jr.'s wife, Mary Bennet, who had a talent and interest in music and theater, soon became a dear friend.

Thus was Dorothy Vits, or "Do" as she was most frequently called, welcomed to Macon, where indeed she had already made a great many friends, having begun to visit Bib Hay in the late twenties. Naturally there were a

---

34"Mrs. Lewis Honored at Beautiful Tea Here," ibid., August 25, 1937, p. 5. This story gives an after-the-fact description of the party; a story on Sunday, August 22 (p. 1 B), "Mrs. N. L. Lewis To Be Honored At Tea Tuesday," previewed the August 24 event and mentioned Johnnie Lewis' expected presence.
35 "Messrs. Odom, Everettt To Be Barbecue Hosts," ibid., September 2, 1937, p. 6, and "Parties and Personalities," Sunday, September 12, 1937, p. 8 B.
36 "Parties and Personalities," ibid., October 5, 1937, p. 7 B.
37 Ibid., October 10, 1937 and October 12, 1937, p. 5. The description suggests that this may have been the gown Dorothy wore to her Manitowoc wedding reception.

few reservations about the Yankee who had picked off the city's most eligible bachelor, and it probably didn't help that she exuded glamour and fashion. Mrs. O'Callaghan describes the new Mrs. Lewis as "gorgeous, stunning, with beautiful skin" and "having great style; she knew how to dress." When Macon women were "still in dresses and frocks, she was wearing suits; she even had one with pants! We were in awe of her."[38] Her religion, in any event, would have set her apart. None of the friends with whom Logan had grown up were Catholic, and those with whom she and her husband socialized attended various Protestant churches; indeed many local Catholics still felt the sting of discrimination.

Yet by most accounts Dorothy was not discomfited to leave Manitowoc for Macon. Actually, she had not spent a great deal of time in her native city as an adult, a fact that cousin Jane Protz explained by noting that she had few "peers" there. Statistics from contemporary city directories[39] give a hint of the differences between the two cities. Physically they were about the same size, but Macon had a larger population, 54,000 as compared to Manitowoc's 25,000. That was reflected in the larger school enrollment (17,154 as compared to 6,150) and numbers of churches (115 as compared to 17 in Manitowoc), but there were so few Macon students in parochial schools that no note was made of them, while the Manitowoc Directory reports that 1800 children, more than thirty per cent of the total student population, attended eight parochial schools; also there were only two Catholic Churches in Macon, as compared to five in the much smaller Manitowoc. Macon's postal receipts were larger ($353,153 cf. $163,916), it had more telephones (10,276 cf. 5,650), and it was served by four railroads and eight hotels with 1150 rooms to Manitowoc's two railroads, two hotels and 250 rooms. But Manitowoc had three libraries with a total of 40,400 volumes as compared to Macon's two libraries that contained only 30,000 volumes. It also had a higher proportion of hospital beds per capita, more paved streets, and an assessed valuation of $42,000,000 as compared to Macon's $40,000,000. Not surprisingly, Macon's tax rate was substantially less as well. While the directories do not break down the population by race, the biggest demographic variance was the substantial percentage of African Americans in Macon. The most dramatic difference between the two cities however, may have been the one that appealed to the Wisconsinite the most: the weather. "It never got warm up there, even on the Fourth of July," Mrs. Curtis avowed; "Dorothy loved the Macon climate."[40]

38 Interview #1.
39 The data cited came from Wright's 1938 *Manitowoc City and County Directory* and Polk's 1937 *Macon City Directory*, R. L. Polk Company, Birmingham, AL. The Historical and Genealogical Room at Washington Memorial Library in Macon does not have a 1938 directory, and the 1938 Directory was the only one available at the Library of Congress, but they are close enough in date to be comparable.
40 Interview #1, June 15, 2000.

Despite some awkwardness[41] the new bride settled into the life of a young Macon matron. Dutifully, if not enthusiastically, she joined the Junior League in the fall of 1939, taking part in a provisional course that covered "social work and adult delinquency, recreation and leisure time, health and community planning," as well as Junior League projects such as "arts programs, children's theater, and the Well Baby Clinic;" the group took field trips to the Bibb Mill Villages, state and federal housing projects, and the Appleton Church Home.[42] She took a leave from her League activities when Johnnie Logan Lewis died in March of the next year,[43] during which she and Logan sold the house on Corbin Avenue and moved into the old family home at 717 Vineville. Dorothy was busy for months arranging an estate sale of some of Johnnie Lewis's things, and altering the décor of the home so as to leave her own imprint, including, thanks to Betty Hay McCook, the installation of a brass Victorian chandelier which had originally hung in the double drawing rooms at the Hay home. But in November she was on hand to help friends Emily Walker, Mary Liles, Tots Lee, and Rose Kingman stage a dance honoring the new Junior League Provisionals, with the table decorations being her particular responsibility. That year, also, drawing on her postgraduate apprenticeship in New York, she gave technical advice to the Children's Theater Committee. Perhaps her most extensive effort for the League came after the war when she chaired a fashion show presented in conjunction with Davison's Department Store at the Walter Little Room in the Dempsey Hotel, raising a remarkable $430.

She also joined the Masqueraders, a women's social organization whose sole purpose was to present an annual ball at which the women wore identical costumes while their husbands came in black tie, the ladies revealing their identities at midnight. When it was Dorothy's turn to chair the dance she selected "Surrealism" as her theme, a rather more exotic choice than was typical, as was her plan to use a case in which stylish footwear was displayed as a decorative element.[44] Like, and perhaps because of, her mother, she had

41 According to both Mrs. Curtis and Mrs. O'Callaghan, Dorothy was uncomfortable around black household servants, and unlike her contemporaries, did not employ regular domestic help, keeping her own house and doing her own cooking. "They ate out a lot," Mrs. Curtis added, smiling. Her lack of interest in food preparation is further documented by the fact that there were only four cookbooks in her kitchen after her death, all dating from the 1930s, and one of them dealt primarily with cocktail recipes; a crossword puzzle dictionary rounded out that shelf. A small softbound pamphlet titled "Favorite Recipes of the Macon Junior League" which appears to date from the late '30s or early '40s was found in the library and includes submissions from nearly all her contemporaries, but not Dorothy, although some recipes are marked as though having been followed. A large drawer, however, full of dress and costume patterns in Dorothy's size, and a sewing machine in the pantry, indicated that she made use of the sewing skills she acquired at Finch. Numerous garden catalogs and newspaper clippings were also found. More of the kitchen shelf space, however, was taken up with the Annual Reports of companies in which she owned stock.
42 Dorothy Lewis' League career was followed in yearbooks, newsletters, and minute books on file at Junior League of Macon headquarters, 2055 Vineville Avenue, Macon, Georgia. Minutes of a November 1939 Board Meeting, for example, mention the reporting of a note from Mrs. Logan Lewis asking to be excused from a Provisional Meeting which she had inadvertently forgotten to atten□
was not recorded. Her primary activities, beside planning and executing social events, were Children's Theatre Committee and work with the League's thrift shop, known as the Bargain Box.
43 Among the memorabilia in the Lewis home was the 1940-41 yearbook of the Mary Hammond Washington Chapter of the Daughters of the American Revolution, which had been dedicated to Johnnie's memory. She was a member of the Chapter's Board, and President of the Chapter, as well as a member of the State Board, during much of the 1930s. Now in the Lewis Archives.
44 O'Callaghan Interview #2.

a natural flair for entertaining, although it was not often drawn upon; Mrs. O'Callaghan remembers a time she'd served pistachio ice cream in a huge silver bowl, and another when she used a champagne fountain for a Georgia Bank party at Idle Hour. Once when helping with a luncheon she came in after the tables had been set to add crisp cards on which the menu had been printed, a sophisticated touch new to Macon at that time. In later years she lunched with a group of friends who called themselves the "Wednesday Widows" because their husbands didn't come home for the midday meal that day, eating at a civic club meeting instead. Still, Pink Persons remembers that "she didn't do 'lady things,'" like playing bridge or belonging to a sewing club, the sorts of activities that were typical for her social set in those days. "She was all the time doing something with the nuns, the Sisters," Persons notes, referring to the Sisters of Mercy who had a convent in Macon and ran Mount de Sales School.

    Her religion was an important part of Dorothy Lewis's life. She impressed the young people with whom the Lewises frolicked during trips to the Georgia coast, because no matter how late they had been out on Saturday night, Dorothy never missed going to mass on Sunday mornings. In Macon she was a loyal[45] communicant at St. Joseph's Catholic Church, the larger of Macon's two Catholic congregations, though she occasionally attended the other, St. Peter Claver, located in an inner city neighborhood, which had been founded to serve African Americans. Priests for both were provided by members of the Society of Jesus, an arrangement that dated from the era in which the New Orleans Province of the Society had trained candidates for their order at St. Stanislaus College at the northwest end of Vineville. While the college had burned in 1921 and was not rebuilt, the Jesuits still staffed several Georgia congregations, and Jesuit influence is credited[46] with the design and construction of St. Joseph's, an imposing Neo-Gothic, Romanesque structure at the crest of one of the hills rimming the original city of Macon. Dorothy Lewis admired it very much.[47] The church's cruciform basilica, clad in red brick with marble trim, surmounts twenty-seven marble steps and is framed by two bell towers that rise over two hundred feet. Three marble Gothic arches lead to double oak doors that open into a "striking interior" which, wrote one of its priests, "gives worshippers an immediate sense of the Presence of God."[48] A magnificent one-thousand-pipe organ, three altars, and a pulpit of Italian-quarried Carrara marble, plus more than sixty German-made stained glass windows, including the twenty-two foot-diameter rose window that graces

---

45 According to longtime members of St. Joseph's she attended the 6:30 a.m. Mass every day during Lent, on the first Fridays of the month, and on numerous other occasions.
46 Brother Cornelius Otten, a native Dutchman who became a master builder and worked closely with several architects on the construction of a number of churches, served as the chief architect-contractor when St. Joseph's was built in two phases, from 1889-1892 and 1900-1903. Sister Mary Sheridan, *History of Saint Joseph's Parish*, 2001, (independently published), pp. 58-65.
47 James Berg, Oral Interview, December 11, 2002.
48 Father John Cuddy, *A Tour of St. Joseph's Catholic Church*, December, 1978. This mimeographed brochure was found in Mrs. Lewis' home after her death; now in Lewis Archives.

the front façade, are only the most prominent of the many decorative elements. When the church was dedicated, the *Macon Telegraph* described its architecture as "frozen music."[49] In addition to her frequent worship, Dorothy worked with the Altar Society, both sewing and maintaining the linens used in services, as well as taking charge of arranging the altar area on such special occasions as Holy Week.[50]

Logan continued to be a strong competitor in local golf contests, though after beating Morris Michael to get into the finals he lost Idle Hour's 1938 spring tournament; he won an overtime match in the next fall, but lost in a subsequent round.[51] In describing the style of the "young businessman," the *Telegraph* praised his "long carries from the tee" and his putting, but acknowledged that he was "temperamental."[52] Logan was still known to throw a club, or a racket, on occasion. There were also horse shows and flying and trips to the coast or to Lee County to hunt to amuse the young couple.

Logan's business activities do not appear to have involved his wife much early in their marriage, perhaps because most of them pertained to properties owned jointly with his mother. Before describing those activities, however, a curious aside is worth mentioning: the single story most enjoyed, if frequency of repetition is any measure, by Maconites interviewed during the research for this book (almost none of whom had heard it firsthand), was Anne Vits's remark during the wedding festivities, that she was "so glad Do was marrying a poor boy." In amusement that anyone would think of Logan Lewis as a "poor boy," as well, perhaps, in awe at the apparent comparative size of the Vits wealth such a comment suggests, no one telling the tale seemed to wonder why Mrs. Vits should desire a husband without means for a daughter used to living in style and luxury. From this distance one is curious as to whether Mrs. Vits was referring to the fact that her new son-in-law did not have a salaried job, to the poor performance of some of the stocks he purchased in the mid-thirties,[53] to unpaid property taxes in several counties, or to the thousands of dollars of indebtedness he had incurred in mortgaging the properties his grandmother had left him. Whatever lay behind the remark, which may, in any event, be apocryphal, Logan Lewis was interested in making money and he used the resources of his family— both the real assets and the cumulative experience of their management—to make more of it.

His prior employment at First National and running the local office of the Trust Company, coupled with the way he advertised "Logan Lewis

---

49 Quoted in Sheridan, ibid., p. 64.
50 After examining a set of notes in Dorothy's hand found in her kitchen after her death, former St. Joseph's pastor Monsignor John Cuddy said they reflected arrangements for services during a pre-Vatican II Holy Week. Oral Interview, March 15, 2004. Now in Lewis Archives. The back of another envelope was inscribed with measurements of the altar, indicating that she had sewn the curtain over the tabernacle where the consecrated host is kept.
51 *Macon Telegraph and News*, June 12, 1938; p. 8 A, June 13, 1938, p. 7 A; October 13, 1939, p. 9 A; October 16, 1939, p. 6 A; October 23, 1939, p. 7 A.
42 June 12, 1938, p. 8 A.
53 A number of certificates for worthless holdings were found in the Lewis files after Dorothy Lewis' death; they include 625 shares of Alma Lincoln Mining Company and 220 shares of Bruce Consolidated Mining Company, both Colorado firms. Now in Lewis Archives.

Investments" in the City Directory—"Investment Bankers, Stocks, Bonds and Securities"—might lead one to assume a concentration on financial services. But in what may have been a natural consequence of his grandmother's death coupled with his mother's continued illness, he appears to have been primarily involved in real estate. Moving his office to 813 Vineville, one of the buildings Tero had left specifically to him, he began developing the last segment of the old Callaway estate in Vineville. This more rolling part of the property had been referred to as "Callaway Grove" in City Directory street listings through the twenties and thirties, and it remained enough of a "wilderness" that the Boy Scouts frequently had their camp-outs there.[54] In 1935 S. R. Shi Jr. and Joe Thomas had divided it into lots closely following the plan done by H. D. Cutter in 1920,[55] but in 1938 Logan decided to change their scheme. Recognizing that the road bordering the back side of the property (termed "Anola" on old plats) would become an artery connecting Riverside Drive and downtown with the fast-growing section known as "Ingleside," he chose not to site homes there; instead, the front footage along what is now appropriately called Ingleside Avenue was reserved for later commercial or multi-family use.[56] The other change he made was primarily aesthetic. Rather than extending Callaway Street straight from Clayton, parallel to Corbin Avenue to the east and Buford Place to the west, with a short additional street (shown on the Shi-Thomas plat as "Bancroft") made possible by the greater width at the north end of the property, he decided to "spiral" it—that is, to put a curve in it. The change eliminated the extra street and reduced the number of lots by one-third.

But in addition to lowering the density there was a complication to the latter alteration. Since the lots in the first block of Callaway and along Corbin had been sold according to the 1920 "straight street" plan, property owners who had bought under it had to sign off on any change, and at least one used his signature as a bargaining tool to get the developer to add curbs and sidewalks as well as to pay the cost of paving of the first block.[57] Believing that the increased attractiveness of his revised plan would make the new lots easier to sell, Logan acquiesced, laboriously obtaining more than three dozen quitclaims from the property owners and their mortgage-holders to put the issue to rest. Naturally, with fewer of them, the new lots in what was to be known as "Callaway Estates" were a bit larger than the earlier ones;[58] in addition restrictive covenants intended

54 Albert P. Reichert, Oral Interview, April 23, 2003.
55 The 1935 Plat, never recorded, was found in the Lewis files after Dorothy Lewis' death and is now in the Lewis Archives; the 1920 Plat is recorded in Plat Book 3, Folio 39, Bibb County Record Room.
56 James W. McCook III, son of Logan's good friend Jimmy McCook, recalls going by the corner which was later sold for the Ingleside C & S branch bank, to pick up Logan's hunting dogs, which were kept by a householder there, as a child. (The men usually went down to the Callaway place in Lee County to hunt, but the dogs were kept in Macon; Bob Kingman and Sanders Walker also kept their dogs there.) Oral Interview, February 5, 2004. Logan held the Ingleside front footage until after the war, when he sold the piece next to the old Buford property to Inglewood Apartments; he appeared at a 1948 Planning and Zoning meeting to assert that the corner should be zoned commercial but did not sell it to C & S until 1956.
57 Cubbedge Snow Jr., Oral Interview, June 30, 2000. Cubbedge Snow Sr. led the effort to ensure that the property owners in the first block got these previously unscheduled improvements.
58 There were ninety-nine under the new drawing done by R. W. Cowan with changes by W. Branan, Jr., recorded in Plat Book 9, Folio 141, Bibb County Record Room, rather than the one hundred thirty-eight shown on the Shi-Thomas plat.

"to assure [Callaway Estates'] development as an exclusive residential section" were attached to their sale.[59] Because the new design featured a gentle bend in the street and property lines were not drawn at exact right angles, the homes seem to nestle into the sheltering slopes, which made the new subdivision one of the prettiest in Vineville. The curbs and sidewalks added in the first block, however, either because of the extra expense, or because they did not match the more rural layout, were omitted from the second and third.

Sales began in the fall of 1938, some to businessmen like Sanders Walker, Jimmy McCook, and R. A. Bowen, who undertook to construct homes for sale on them, others to individuals who planned to build their own residences. Logan, too, built "spec" houses on several lots after Johnnie Logan Lewis quitclaimed her interest in them so that he could use the property as collateral against loans from First National or J. W. McCook Lumber Co., "satisfying" the debts when the houses sold. In addition to the single-family homes Logan was developing, once his mother deeded her interest in them to him in 1939, he mortgaged lots 22 and 23 of Block One, property immediately behind the old Callaway home (and not covered by the Callaway Estates covenants), in order to build a four-unit apartment house.[60]

Deed records in both Bibb and Lee counties indicate that Johnnie Lewis's death in March 1940 was followed by an increase in Logan's real estate activities not unlike the one after Tero's demise six years earlier. Cognizant of changing living patterns whereby people increasingly drove to shop rather than walking to a neighborhood grocery store, he made plans to tear down the four small brick stores fronting Vineville Avenue that his great grandfather had built in order to replace them with two much larger ones. He filled those commodious new spaces by securing long-term leases with the Great Atlantic and Pacific Tea Company and Lane Drug stores. His great-aunt, Annie Callaway, quitclaimed any interest she might appear to have had in those properties (she had deeded them to Johnnie in 1935 but reaffirmed that intention in separate deeds naming Johnnie's heir) and the new stores opened the next year.[61] Pink Persons, who at twelve began work at the nearby Vineville Drug Company, remembers that Logan's new store "was just the epitome, the finest grocery store in Macon, Georgia."

Logan also sold off parts of other family properties: eighty-three acres in the Howard District to M. J. Witman and the Walnut Street property that had been Lula Whittle's, to C.C. Harrold. The original Callaway home at 301 (now

59 The covenants included such specifics as setting the distance from the street and the minimum size and value of homes, a requirement for advance design approval, and limiting construction to single-family residences. The covenants also prohibited non-Caucasians unless they were servants; the further subdivision of any lot; outbuildings, septic tanks or cess pools; placards or advertising, etc. Recorded in Book 455, folio 452, Bibb County Clerk of Court.
60 Recorded in Book 448, folio 368, ibid.
61 Annie Callaway to Logan Lewis recorded in Book 474, folio 258; Deeds to Secure Debt and Leases recorded in Book 481, folio 491, Book 484, folio 729, and Book 492, folio 179, Bibb County Clerk of Court.

2455) Clayton Street, the charming cottage in which Tero Callaway had married John Logan in 1885, and which had been occupied intermittently by Lula Callaway Whittle after the rest of her family moved up to Vineville Avenue, and rented since her 1916 death, was sold to A. A. Drake in November of 1940.[62] In Lee County he negotiated the $27,500 sale of both the agricultural and commercial properties (excepting only "that certain house occupied by Logan Lewis," presumably the hunting lodge) to the Cannon Peanut Company.[63] With the building in which he managed his business (813 Vineville) about to be torn down to make room for the new grocery store, Logan moved his office again, into the new Bankers Insurance Building built by P. L. Hay on Cherry Street. There "Lewis & Co." handled "Investments, Stocks, Bonds, Real Estate and Insurance" according to an ad in the 1942 *City Directory* which listed two associates, Alex Cliett and Buford Mathis, in addition to the firm's principal. The alphabetical listing in the directory also credits him with having an interest in the France Granite Company on Vineville Avenue, apparently one acquired through the default on a loan.[64] But by the time that directory was in circulation Lewis & Co.'s principal had left to defend his country.

A shadow had fallen over the pleasantries of Macon life when war broke out in Europe in 1939. On September 2, reported the *Telegraph,*

> Cries of 'Extra' rent the morning stillness of an inherently peaceful community as youthful couriers again bore tidings of a world gone mad after twenty-one years of fitful peace. Not since the Lindbergh baby was found in a New Jersey wilderness . . . had an extra sold so well . . . . All night long and through the early morning hours news of the impending disaster crackled across the wires of the world and into the *Telegraph* office. . . . Citizens discussed the situation in their homes, at their work, [and] at the soda fountains over their morning or afternoon 'cokes.'[65]

The next year Logan Lewis joined other private plane owners in organizing the Bibb County Home Defense Corps Flying Squadron whose work paralleled the duties of the National Guard; realizing that additional facilities were needed for the maintenance and operation of their craft, given the commercial and military demands on Herbert Smart Airport, they built a new field on W. P. Montgomery's farm down near Tuft Springs.[66]

Laura Nelle O'Callaghan's brother, Peyton Anderson, a naval reserve officer in public relations, was called up about that time, but it wasn't until

---

62 Sales are recorded in Book 489, folio 505 (Howard), Book 489, folio 414 (Walnut Street), and Book 478, folio 360 (Lots 1, 2, and 3, Block Three, Callaway Estate). A. A. Drake bought an additional lot, number 4, behind the original three on which the cottage sits, in April of 1941 (Book 489, folio 71.) The house at 301 Clayton had been damaged by fire January 7, 1938; Logan and the insurance company were unable to agree on the extent of that damage so that an umpire had to be appointed by the Ordinary to settle the issue. (Minute Book OO, p. 193-5, Bibb County Probate Court.)
63 Clerk of Court, Lee County, Book V, folios 517, 524-29.
64 Clerk of Court, Bibb County, Book 489, folios 274 and 275-6.
65 Frank Hawkins, p. 1 A.
66 *Macon Telegraph*, September 29, 1941, p. 5A.

Pearl Harbor that Logan and his friends put aside their affairs to join the military. They were not alone. According to historian Kenneth Coleman "some 320,000 men and women, approximately one of every ten people in the state, served in the armed forces," during World War II, "an impressive number given the fact that the inductee rejection rate in Georgia was considerably higher than the national average."[67] With Peyton's help,[68] Logan obtained a naval commission (Lt. J.G.) and by early March 1942 he had reported to the Sixth Naval District Headquarters in Charleston, S. C., assigned to the office of Naval officer procurement.[69] Dorothy joined him there for the few months before he went on to Norfolk, where she also visited[70] while he trained with the crew of LST 397.[71] Later she worked at Warner Robins for a time during his absence, something which, according to her friend Betty Hay McCook Curtis, she felt to be her "patriotic duty." While it is not clear what she did, Mrs. Curtis' son, Jimmy, who remembers having gone out to the base to see her, believes that "like 'Rosie the Riveter,' she was a worker—working on planes."[72] City directory listings for 1943-45 simply read "USA" after her husband's name in the space in which occupation is usually listed, and following the custom of the day, there is no occupation listed for the lady of the house. She was able to meet him in various ports, from time to time, but they also endured lengthy separations.

Before he left Logan executed a power of attorney in which the First National Bank was given complete authority to manage his business affairs "to all intents and purposes as I might do or could do if I were personally present" with the only exceptions the making of "gifts or voluntary conveyances" or entering "into any contract of suretyship."[73] While he did not mention involving his wife in either a direct or a consulting role, she witnessed a 1944 quitclaim in which Annie Callaway affirmed that her 1935 deed to Johnnie Lewis had been executed under the terms of Lula Whittle's will, removing any possible cloud on titles then held by Logan, which indicates that Dorothy was taking some part in her husband's business.[74] A. J. Vits had begun transferring Mirro stock to his daughter in 1940,[75] when he put five hundred shares in her name. In 1941, perhaps in concern for her income while her husband was away, he gave her fifteen hundred more, and in 1944, another one hundred fifty, for a total of twenty-one hundred fifty shares. These shares were then valued at $11,714.61, and with A. G. M. C. usually paying dividends of $1.00 per share in those years,

---

67 Kenneth Coleman, ed., *A History of Georgia*, 1991, UGA Press, Athens, p. 339.
68 O'Callaghan Interview #2.
69 *Macon Telegraph*, March 13, 1942, p. 11. This notice includes an official U. S. Navy photo of a smiling Logan looking very sharp in uniform.
70 Betty Curtis recalls Dorothy spending the night with her and Jimmy upon her return to Macon, recounting her confusion in driving on the large highways in the vicinity of the bases she visited. She preferred driving however, because she did not like to fly. Interview #2.
71 LST stands for Landing Ship Tank, a decidedly unglamorous part of the Navy.
72 McCook interview. Junior League records indicate she was excused from responsibility for doing placement in the spring of 1942 "because of absence from the city" and from meeting attendance in November of that year because she "had been working." Both Jane Protz and Laura Nelle O'Callaghan recall that she worked at Warner Robins, but did not know what she did there.
73 Recorded in Book 496, folio 35, Bibb County Clerk of Court.
74 Recorded in Book 524, folios 160-1, ibid.
75 A history of Dorothy's ownership of what was by then Newell Companies was prepared in 1984; the document is now part of the Lewis Archives.

produced an annual return of several thousand dollars.[76]

Buck Melton, a younger Maconite who joined the Navy after Logan but also served on an LST, gave a good description of the craft and their use in his 2004 memoir, *Closing Arguments*.[77] Derisively nicknamed 'Large Slow Targets,' the ships were "designed to carry large cargoes of tanks, rolling artillery, trucks, [and] heavy tractors . . . all manner of equipment needed to fight a war . . . . It was the mission of the LST . . . to make high speed (ten knot) controlled crashes on 'landing beaches.'" Three hundred twenty-three feet long, fifty-three feet wide and weighing three thousand tons, "with less than powerful engines, huge freeboard sides, and no keel at all . . . they were terribly hard to handle." Still, unlike several destroyers that were lost in the Pacific, "they managed to stay afloat. . . . The interior of the ship consisted of a huge 'tank' deck, over two hundred feet long and about forty feet wide." In order to accommodate speedy off-loading, the bow consisted of two massive doors which were swung open by heavy cables just prior to the "landing" on the beach, at which point "a huge and very heavy steel ramp was quickly lowered between the open doors," allowing the equipment to move out, albeit sometimes through shallow waters, to dry ground.

LST 397 was sent to the Pacific theater in the winter of 1943. Something of Logan's experience can be gleaned from an annotated copy of the LST's log kept by a crewmember and circulated to his former shipmates in 1986. Don Connell prefaced his narrative: "The LST was not the warship most of us envisioned boarding. It was odd looking with its long deck . . . [had] few guns, and [it was] very slow (ten knots). However, all of us who served aboard can look back with pride knowing the LSTs got the job done efficiently and effectively in the amphibious and island hopping warfare that was the battle plan in the Pacific."[78] Ted Andrews, another crewmember, contributed a more colorful, doggerel description:

> Now 397 ain't a fighting ship,
> She doesn't move along at a hell of a clip.
> She's a light green shade, not a bad looking Job,
> But it just ain't the thing for a sea going gob.
> She carries a crew of 66 all told
> With every man knowing his goal
> They'll do as they're told and they'll fight for Uncle Sam,
> But they're a mean bunch of guys that don't give a damn . . . .

Despite his lack of seagoing experience, Logan's leadership skills made

76 Annual Reports of Earnings from *The New York Times,* November 29, 1940, p. 31, col. 7; December 2, 1941, p. 35, col. 6; November 28, 1942, p. 20, col. 1; November 21, 1943, Section III, p. 8, col. 3. Earnings per share in 1942 were actually $.85.
77 Buckner F. Melton, Sr., *Closing Arguments, A Memoir,* Mercer University Press, 2004, pp. 24-36.
78 Xerox copy mailed to Dorothy Lewis in 1993, found in the original envelope in her bedroom desk after her death, now in Lewis Archives.

him captain of this "mean bunch." Connell's account proves those skills were tested: "In February 1943 we sailed up the Atlantic coast to New York for supplies and dropped anchor in the Hudson River. . . . While trying to dock at Pier 54 Capt. Lewis and 397 crashed into the wooden pier and smashed it all to hell." Various Maconites reported hearing of similar mishaps that Logan himself reported in later years: finding the 397 out in front of the ship it was supposed to be following to the South Pacific when a fog lifted, for example.[79] But there was much to be praised about the 397 as well, as the log's author makes clear: "The success of any ship is certainly in the hands of its crew and although we came from all parts of the country and different backgrounds without any sea or ship experiences, we learned fast, worked together . . . and got the job assigned to us 'well done.'" It had been so cold in New York the men "had to sleep under [their] mattresses," a chilling that they might have recalled with wonder when they reached their final destination. After the ship was finally supplied, LST 397 joined a convoy of forty vessels March 9 that steamed to Cuba, through the Panama Canal, and then west to New Caledonia with a stop in Bora Bora; at one point they sailed for almost three weeks without seeing land. From there it was north to New Hebrides and then to Guadalcanal where they were part of the effort to take Japanese airbases in the Solomon Islands, running supplies in support of amphibious assaults. The log gives a vivid description of what awaited them:

> June 15th, 1943. Arrived at Guadalcanal. What a reception! About 140 Jap planes came over. All the ships were racing all over the Bay or channel trying to escape strafing and bombs. 'Flak' from the ship's guns flooded the sky; there was a dogfight between our planes and the Japs [that] lasted about three-quarters of an hour. About three American ships sank, one of them LST 340, our sister ship. About ten American ships damaged. Japs lost sixty-eight planes.

While that was "the last big Jap air raid at the Canal" the fighting in the Solomons went on for months, and then it was on to the Philippines. The crew took what precautions they could:

> Several times we would load hundreds of fifty-five gallon drums of aviation gas on our top deck. We didn't like this because if we got hit by shellfire, torpedo or bomb we would be an inferno. If we heard the "Tokyo Express" or air raid coming . . . we would roll them off into the water hoping they would drift to shore. No use losing ship and gasoline if we were hit.

They were fortunate:

> Looking back, the Lord certainly must have been with us. We had a lot

---

79 Giles O'Neal reported hearing Logan tell that story on himself in the early sixties. Oral Interview, April 12, 2003.

of close calls. We didn't have enough guns to protect us against surface ships or antiaircraft guns to protect us against planes. . . . Most of the destroyers that were with us throughout the Solomon campaign were sunk later on . . . mostly by 'kamikaze' planes. It was sad to see a lot of these old friends . . . disappear beneath the waves.

Logan Lewis had become a Lt. Commander by the end of his three and one half years of service, winning seven battle stars and a unit commendation for the Philippine operations, as well as a Bronze Star. The latter was presented at the Naval Ordnance Plant in Macon on December 6, 1945. Signed by Admiral R. K. Turner, commander of the amphibious forces, U.S. Pacific Fleet, the citation, which covered action that took place after that described above, read:

> For heroic service in connection with operations against the enemy as operations officer on the staff of the commander of a flotilla of tank landing ships from September 1944 to August 1945, during the assault and capture of Palau, Leyte, Lingayen Gulf and Okinawa Shima. Throughout these operations he displayed outstanding skill and leadership by maintaining complete and accurate records, and ably supervising the numerous functions of his department. On January 10, 1945, when the flagship was attacked and damaged by enemy suicide boats, he, demonstrating great courage and determination, efficiently directed the movements of the other vessels and informed them of enemy tactics to be expected. With keen foresight, sound judgment and profound devotion to duty, he contributed materially to the success of these operations. His conduct throughout distinguished him among those performing duties of the same character.[80]

In a cover letter to Dorothy Lewis that accompanied the copy of the log which he sent her in 1993, Don Connell wrote "I knew your husband very well; I was on the bridge with him for eight or nine hours a day. He was a fine officer, well liked and respected by all crew members. He was firm but fair. He saw to it that everyone did their job and worked as a team for the betterment of all.[81]

It cannot have been easy for Dorothy Lewis to wait at home while her husband faced such challenges. But he returned safely at last, and like millions of others, the Lewises set about picking up the pieces of their lives.[82]

---

80 *Macon Telegraph*, December 6, 1945, p. 12 A.
81 Cover letter with materials on LST 397, ibid. This writer attempted to contact Mr. Connell at the phone number included in his letter to Mrs. Lewis, but was told he had died some years earlier.
82 It is likely that his wife made a scrapbook of his experiences in the Navy; an empty book whose pages were crammed with the fragments of dozens of pasted-in telegrams and photographs, almost all of which had been torn out, was found in a closet off Mrs. Lewis' bedroom after her death. Only three items, all of which indicated that it had been a repository for memorabilia, remained: a tag for a package or luggage addressed to Mrs. Logan Lewis at 717 Vineville Avenue, Macon, that had been shipped from Panama on March 23 (year unclear); a blue ticket marked "Amphibious Force Training Base, Officers Mess, November, 1942, No. 394, with most holes punched out; and a printed envelope with a return address of Leyte, P.I. addressed to Messrs. Go Singco Sons & Co., Manila, P.I., with a purple stamp reading "First Day Cover, First Regular Victory Stamps, sold in reopened post offices in the liberated Philippines, January 19, 1945," with the stamp affixed and postmarked as of that date. Lewis Archives.

Post War Years

Things were different after the war. While social Macon remained closely knit and restricted, the city was changing: the air base at Warner Robins had brought many newcomers to the area,[83] and the postwar construction of branch plants of such national firms as Armstrong Cork and Inland Container brought even more. Jobs opened up and the commercial climate improved, bringing new financial opportunities; Georgians were enjoying more affluence than ever before in their history as manufacturing jobs surpassed those in agriculture in the 1950 census.[84] On the other hand, on a personal level, Logan's stepfather, "Uncle Julian" Lewis had died just before he left for the Navy, and his great-aunt Annie Callaway died while he was in the South Pacific;[85] a maiden aunt, his father's younger sister "Jelksie" Lewis, having "always been recognized by her family and friends as peculiar and eccentric," became unable to care for herself and was finally diagnosed, at age fifty-five, as "paranoid," and, penniless, was committed to the State Hospital at Milledgeville.[86] Several friends from the old crowd had moved away, and the attention of many of the others was increasingly absorbed by the raising of young families.[87] Inevitably, the Lewises' recreational and business lives took a different turn.

As the only surviving heir to the Callaway estate, Logan Lewis, a young man with substantial assets, found himself in a position to launch a number of business projects. Dorothy too, had assets of her own.[88] In addition to managing the old properties, Logan sought new opportunities, and a number of the projects he undertook were developed with his wife's money and in her name. While the extent of Dorothy's role in these activities cannot be known, she signed the deeds and notes and she must have been aware of what was being done and the rationale behind it. In any event, as noted above, she eschewed the usual volunteer activities. In 1947, after a year working on the Junior League's Thrift Shop and successfully staging the fashion show fundraiser she, as had her

---

83 There were more training facilities in Georgia than any other state except Texas. (Coleman, ibid.) One of those who came was Jane Protz' husband Bill who was at the base several times during the war, and visited with Dorothy on those occasions. Oral Interview, September 2000.
84 Coleman, ibid.
85 Aunt Annie had been ill for several years according to her obituary; in support of their absent buddy, Crockett Odom, Jimmy McCook, Charles Newton, D.S. Wagnon, B.E. Willingham, and R.C. Souder served as pallbearers. *Macon Telegraph*, December 28, 1944, p. 3A.
86 Neuropsychiatric Examination Report on Miss Mary Jelks Lewis, May 13, 1946, by J. R. Shannon Mays, M.D., Mary Jelks Lewis File, Lewis Archives. Letters in the file indicate that Logan had been helping Jelksie with her affairs for some years, experiencing increasing difficulties as her paranoia increased. He made sure, for example, that she signed papers acknowledging her agreement to holdings and actions. After her commitment he sent periodic checks for deposit on her account at the hospital and served as contact and consenter when medical procedures became necessary.
87 Dorothy and Logan Lewis did not have any children. According to those who knew them well Logan would have welcomed progeny while Dorothy was considered less child-receptive. The wording of A.J. Vits' will and Logan's actions regarding property he inherited from his grandmother indicate that they knew either in advance or early in their marriage that children would not be part of it, possibly owing to an injury Dorothy had suffered while riding horseback. Several friends believe they had considered adopting, but certainly by the time James Berg designed their home in Country Club Estates in the early fifties, children were not expected.
88 She may have had other securities besides the A.G.M.C. stock noted above. Dave Jeffords recalls her having once told him of complaining to her mother once that "all the other girls at school had portfolios," and presumably such a shortfall would have been rectified.

---

friend Betty Hay McCook, resigned from the Junior League. The Lewises began to socialize more with their new business associates than the old friends with whom Logan had grown up.

One of those was Pink Persons, some fifteen years younger, who had "always" known Logan, having been raised in the Vineville neighborhood. Pink was by then working at Murphey, Taylor and Ellis, a local real estate firm, and Logan became a client; they soon moved from acquaintanceship to friendship to partnership, embarking on an increasing number of business ventures together.[89] For the next twenty years they talked daily, often meeting for coffee at the Dempsey Hotel with an informal group of businessmen that included Bib Hay's husband, Andy Anderson, among others.

Something that didn't change after the war was Logan's interest in golf and in the well being of the Idle Hour Club where he played. Membership at Idle Hour had dropped severely during the Depression, with Maitland Solomon, who had acquired a majority of the club's stock from members experiencing financial strain, assuming responsibility for managing its affairs. Even in those years Logan exerted some leadership, having been elected treasurer in 1935, working as head of the swimming pool and entertainment committees,[90] and serving with Solomon and Peyton Jones as one of three trustee/directors in the late thirties.[91] But following the war, according to a club history, "as members returned from service they felt a desire to return the club to the direction of the membership as a whole. After a 1946 golf game, Sanders Walker, Bob Kingman, and Logan Lewis were sitting in the bar discussing club operations with Mr. Solomon" when the older man agreed to relinquish his interest for $75,000. The three quickly accepted, each agreeing to underwrite one-third of a $500, 60-day option. New directors were appointed who recruited new members, additional funds were raised by selling $1,000 "Club Notes," and plans were made and implemented to remodel and expand the run-down facilities.[92] "Mrs. Logan Lewis, Mrs. Halstead Anderson, and Mrs. Angus Birdsey" undertook the job of redecoration, using dramatic colors such as puce, with fashionable white accents to give a bright new appearance to the interior of the familiar English Tudor-style structure.[93] Bob Kingman served as president for the next two years, and Logan served for the two years after that, as well as taking on another term in 1954.

Co-decorator Kit Birdsey was one of Macon's preeminent hostesses, one with whom Dorothy later labored on behalf of the Macon Community Concert Association. In the 1950s the group presented a four-concert season of

89 Oral Interview #2.
90 Chamber of Commerce Scrapbook, 1935, Box 7, Chamber of Commerce Collection, Middle Georgia Archives, Washington Memorial Library.
91 *Macon Telegraph*, May 29, 1938, p. 10 B.
92 Winburn Stewart and H. P. Persons, Jr., "A Brief History of the Idle Hour Country Club," Club Handbook, 1967, Idle Hour Club, Macon, Ga. Prepared in conjunction with the opening of a new clubhouse; Lewis Archives.
93 O'Callaghan Oral Interview #3. The Tudor structure was razed and replaced in the 1960s.

nationally renowned artists that included the likes of Rise Stevens, Isaac Stern, and Hilde Gueden, often sponsoring elegant post-concert parties for the visiting artists at which Maconites in evening clothes dined on delicacies in the company of some of the most talented musicians of the day. Prominent among them were those at the Birdsey home, and it was at one such party that the popular ladies magazine *McCall's* sent a crew to do a photo spread. Mrs. Logan Lewis, chair of that year's membership drive, is pictured receiving "a steaming cup" of Mrs. Birdsey's "renowned oyster bisque" as Elliott Dunwody Jr. and Stanley Elkan smile in the background.[94]

Meanwhile, Logan's passion for cars had blossomed into an absorbing hobby; he spent months working on his first acquisition in the garage behind his Vineville Avenue home. At different times he owned two 1939 Jaguar roadsters, a 1952 Jag, a 1954 two-liter Maserati[95] and two Rolls Royces, a 1925 Silver Ghost, and a 1933 wooden-sided wagon, the "shooting brake." The Lewises bought one of the Jags in California and drove it back to Macon. They purchased the Rolls wagon on a 1959 trip to England, but the Silver Ghost was found in terrible shape in Ned Willingham's pecan orchard; with mechanic Joe Ward helping to manufacture the parts needed, Logan completely restored it.[96] He and Dorothy went to old car rallies in Barnesville and Indian Springs, and eventually began showing and racing the sports cars at tracks all over the South—Sebring and Gainesville, Florida; Tuskegee, Alabama; the Carolinas, and Virginia. The gentlemanly genre emphasized competition and camaraderie more than winning, but was involved enough to require a pit crew, albeit one made up of friends like Jimmy McCook and Pink Persons rather than hired help, and Dorothy pumped gas when she wasn't driving herself. According to Pink they "headed out to races most every weekend." Logan, he said "was like another man when he was racing, he loved it so much." Then he guffawed at the memory of his friend, in a fit of his famous temper, yanking the fan belt from under the hood of the Silver Ghost in frustration when the vintage vehicle sputtered on the way to an antique car show in Orlando. "Now Logan," Pink recalls telling him, "All my life I've known that Lake City, Florida, was famous for its supply of Rolls Royce fan belts." Logan had to produce a goodly supply of greenbacks in order to charm a truck driver into fashioning a replacement out of a leather belt so as to salvage the trip.

---

94 Information drawn from the Stanley and Rosalyn Elkan Collection in process at the Middle Georgia Archives.
95 It is unclear where Logan got the Maserati but according to Arlan Ettinger, President of Guernsey's Auction House in New York City, who purchased it from Mrs. Lewis in 1989, it is a fabulous vehicle with a glamorous history. Manufactured to exacting standards and used by the firm as an exhibition vehicle, it had been driven by the famous Argentine race driver Manuel Fangio. After Ettinger acquired it he raced it himself, accepting an invitation from the Pebble Beach Automotive Concourse where it won a trophy as the best racecar in America. Oral Interview, July 18, 2003.
96 Comer interview.

Sometimes they went even further. Betty Curtis remembers races in Nassau, where Finch classmate Betty Collins, lived, for which she, Jimmy, and Dorothy drove in one car to Miami while Logan and Joe Ward towed the racing car with another, crossing to the island by boat. Dorothy also raced on occasion; Persons and Mrs. Curtis recall her driving both the 1939 Jag and the Maserati in the days when General Curtis Lemay allowed racing on the track at Hunter Field in Savannah.[97] Those times, another friend remembers Dorothy telling him in her later years, "were some of the best of her life;" she "loved racing cars."[98] The Lewises bought stock in the RoadAmerica racetrack at Elkhart Lake, Wisconsin, where the Vits summer home was located, and raced there. But the racing came to an end after a tragedy in Gainesville: a brother of Veazy Rainwater, a well-to-do Chattanoogan and "great friend" of Logan's on the circuit, was killed during a race. Logan told Joe Ward that his racing days were over, though he held on to the cars.[99] Dorothy kept the Maserati for more than twenty years after Logan's death and still had both the Rolls Royces, and the RoadAmerica stock, when she died.

By the end of 1946 almost all the vacant residential lots in Callaway Estates section of the old Callaway property, as well as those in the earlier developed portions, had been sold, with C. R. Rader buying most of those remaining. Logan had also sold the rest of the acreage in the Howard District to Andrew Miller in 1943 and the six hundred acres of land in Monroe County to M. J. Witman in 1944. But a clause in Tero's will cast a cloud over his title to the properties inherited from his grandmother: it specified that should her grandson die without heirs any property not disposed of before his death was to be sold for the benefit of Vineville Baptist Church (one half), Mercer University (one fourth), and Georgia Baptist Orphanage in Hapeville (one fourth). Having obtained a legal analysis which concluded that "the interest of the charitable institutions at best is uncertain, contingent and remote,"[100] but nevertheless concerned at the implication of this clause for Dorothy's survivorship, Logan took two actions in 1947.[101] In February, he made a gift of $2,000 to cover the contingent interest of the Church under Tero Amos's will, following which the Vineville trustees (among them Broadus Willingham Jr.) quitclaimed any possible interest.[102] Then in June he deeded to Dorothy a part of what was left of the Vineville assets, specifically the store at the far end of the A & P that was at that time and for many years after

---

97 William P. Simmons Jr. also reported seeing Dorothy drive at a race in Danville, Virginia, while he was in college. Oral Interview, May 11, 2002.
98 Thurman Willis, Interview #2.
99 Persons interview #3.
100 Letter from C. Baxter Jones to Logan Lewis dated January 15, 1946 now in the Lewis Archives. Like Laura Nelle Anderson O'Callaghan, Baxter Jones was a distant Hardeman cousin.
101 These actions indicate that the Lewises knew at this time that they would not have children.
102 Original in Lewis Archives; recorded in Book 555, folio 206, Bibb County Clerk of Court.

occupied by a pastry shop.[103]

Logan retained Lots 1, 2, 3, 4, 22, and 23 in Block One (the Callaway house at 707 Vineville which had by this time been turned into apartments, the apartment house behind it, and the house at 717 Vineville in which he and Dorothy were living) as well as Lots 1, 2 and 3 of Block Two (the A & P and Lane Drug Store, and the corner filling station.) Part of the property behind the houses on Carlton Way, which fronted on Ingleside Avenue, was sold to Inglewood Apartments in 1947, with the corner lot held for later commercial development.

Its owner was clearly husbanding that resource. At that time the City of Macon was establishing a new mechanism for zoning, having passed an ordinance which essentially locked existing land use in place and created a Planning and Zoning Commission to review requested changes (previously such issues had come before Mayor and Council). About this time Logan took a public position against a plan to permit commercial buildings on Ingleside Avenue between Rogers and Corbin that left his property (just on the other side of Corbin) residential. At an early Commission meeting he went on record as being opposed to the approval of a single petition before the whole area in which it was located was zoned.[104] Probably as a result of that stand the Commission then voted to recommend to City Council that all lots facing or abutting Ingleside from Inglewood Apartments to Rogers Avenue be zoned to allow commercial structures.

Given his increasing real estate activity, that was not Logan's last encounter with the Commission. In 1954 he sought Baxter Jones' advice on whether tearing down the filling station at the corner of Callaway and Vineville to accommodate the A & P's desire for additional parking would foreclose his ever rebuilding it, given the de-facto nature of zoning in that area. Some ten years later he expressed his frustration to the tax assessors when valuation of a vacant lot Dorothy owned on Callaway increased from $650 to $1000, writing: "I would be hesitant to take up your valuable time to present my argument regarding this: but for your information, this lot at this particular time is of little value as it is impossible for me to put it to any use due to the attitude of the Macon-Bibb County Zoning Commission."[105]

His business interests were not confined to the Callaway properties, however. In 1948 Logan joined forces with local real estate developer Charles E. Nash to incorporate Parkside, a firm for "buying, selling, renting, leasing, subleasing and developing real estate, personalty and property of all kinds; erecting and constructing buildings, stores and houses" etc., for which 100 shares of stock were issued at a value of $100. The two parties brought different assets to

---

103 Recorded ibid., in Book 555, folio 522.
104 Carbon copy certified by J. E. Ferguson, Secretary, to be a true copy of the Minutes of the Planning and Zoning Commission, January 24, 1949 found in the Lewis files after Mrs. Lewis' death; Lewis Archives.
105 Carbon copy of letter to Board of Tax Assessors dated March 18, 1963, ibid.

the partnership: Nash had a lease from the Baconsfield Park Board of Managers for land on the Emery Highway which was then sub-leased to Parkside; Logan had capital for the construction of a Colonial Foods store which was ready for occupancy the next year in what was known as Baconsfield Center. That business connection was short-lived, however, as Logan sold or transferred all his stock in Parkside in 1950.[106] The year before, when the Securities and Exchange Commission ordered the Georgia Power Company to divest itself of the municipal bus system Logan had joined a "syndicate"[107] of twenty-four Macon businessmen who purchased the system for $230,000 in a deal brokered by investor Frank Peeples. Linton Baggs, who had operated a bus service between Macon and Warner Robins during World War II, was named President, and Logan Lewis treasurer of what became known as the Bibb Transit Company.

Several of Logan's increased business activities in the late '40s were in Dorothy's name and accomplished with her assets. In August of 1949 she purchased a seven-acre tract between Ingleside and Forest avenues with frontage on Riverside Drive, from the Blanton Winship estate. Under Logan's supervision, ten homesites were carved out of the property, and sold over the next few years, several to contractor William H. Jones who erected spec houses on them. The frontage on Riverside was under lease to Henry K. Burns who built the Alpine Lodge on it; that last parcel was finally sold to Burns in 1959. In addition to the piece of Callaway property Logan deeded to her, Dorothy purchased a house and lot on the west side of Callaway Street directly behind the small shopping center.

Real estate was not the only way in which Dorothy invested her assets, however. She also bought and sold securities, primarily large cap, blue chip type stocks, but additionally some local issues such as Security Life and Bibb Transit. Her father may have offered suggestions as to these purchases, as several of them were also equities bought in Anne Vits's name, and her husband was probably involved as well since from 1955 forward the ledger entries recording her activities are made in the handwriting of his clerical assistant. She kept accounts at several brokerages and balanced her portfolio by adding bonds, primarily municipal, hence tax-free, paper. Detailed ledgers include, beginning in 1956, a capital account in Dorothy's name, into which additions and subtractions were made at year-end. Her husband bought and sold securities too, often the same ones, but was more heavily invested in real property.

The regard in which Logan had come to be held in the business community became apparent when a committee composed of E. A. Worm Jr., Ed Everett Jr., William A. Fickling, Albert S. Hatcher, C. O. McAfee, and J. V. (Buncie)

106 Per release signed by Charles E. Nash October 23, 1950.
107 *Macon Telegraph*, April 27, 1949, p. 1A; May 4, 1949, p. 3A; and June 1, 1949, p. 1A. Others were J. D. Stetson Coleman, A. P. Boone, A.M. Phillips, J. NeVille Birch, Campbell Jones, Edward M. Lowe, I. Berry, J. R. Maddux, R. W. Mass, Bertram Maxwell Jr., A.M. Peeler, Morris Michael Jr., C. O. McAfee, Robert A. Bowen, S. B. Clay, Leo Huckabee, B. Sanders Walker, W. A. Fickling, K. W. Dunwody, and W. Elliott Dunwody.

Skinner called on him to request that he chair the newly reorganized Community Chest fund drive in the fall of 1953. "Of course it's an honor to be selected by . . . such representative citizens as are serving on the Chest executive committee, and to follow two outstanding leaders such as Bill O'Shaughnessey and Buncie Skinner as general campaign chairman," the *Telegraph* quoted Logan as saying. "I feel privileged to follow in their footsteps. Much has been accomplished by the Macon Community Chest in the past two years. I trust that I will be able to make a contribution by my services to its continued success. I hope that every worker and all those who have served the Chest so well in the past two years will accept the challenge with me."[108] A particular challenge he had in mind was to speed up the work: "I would like to see an objective this year to complete the campaign in three weeks. I believe it can be done with the concerted effort of everybody." One of the approximately 1500 people who helped was his wife: Dorothy served as vice chair of the Women's Division. Sanders Walker and Art Barry filled other top spots. From the vantage point of the twenty-first century 1953's goal seems surprisingly modest—$191,000—but it supported eleven agencies. Publicity plans included posters and displays in store windows, menu stickers in restaurants, and, in a particularly telling indication of a bygone era "local dairymen will dress up their milk bottles with special 'chest' dollars on the morning the drive officially begins."[109] Baxter Jones' son, Frank, who helped by invigorating the Professional Division that year, recalls that Logan exhibited "the same bulldog tenacity that he later gave to the Georgia Bank,"[110] with the result that the campaign broke records for both funds raised and the time spent raising them. It brought in $199,049, or 104.1 per cent of goal, going "over" in every division—and, per its chairman's other objective, it did so in two fewer days than any previous campaign.[111] Logan continued to serve on the charity's board as increasingly ambitious goals were set ($303,000, a fifty per cent increase, in 1955[112]) and the organization changed its name to the United Givers Fund. In 1956 he became president of the Board of Directors; the plaque awarded at the end of his term read "for aggressive leadership and faithful service."[113]

In addition to the satisfaction of having performed a significant service for his community, Logan came into contact with Community Chest stenographer Anne J. Bryant. He must have been impressed because the 1955 City Directory listed a change of employment for Mrs. Bryant: secretary to N. Logan Lewis, whose office was briefly on Cotton Avenue and then at the First National Bank. Mrs. Bryant later worked out of the Georgia Bank, which, according to one of

108 *Macon Telegraph*, Sunday, March 29, 1953, p. 1A.
109 Ibid., Friday, October 2, 1953, p. 5, and Saturday, October 3, 1953, p. 8A.
110 Oral Interview, November 11, 2003.
111 *Macon Telegraph*, Tuesday, November 24, 1953, p. 1A.
112 Ibid., November 24, 1955, p. 1A. Sanders Walker was chair that year.
113 1956 United Givers Fund Award of Merit Plaque found in Lewis home after Mrs. Lewis' death. Lewis Archives.

its vice presidents,[114] also tried to hire her; she preferred, however, to assist the Lewises oversee their multiple business interests, typing correspondence and keeping extensive hand-written ledgers. The relationship continued until Logan's death and after; Mrs. Bryant was a part time bookkeeper for Dorothy Lewis until 1976.

While Dorothy and Logan went to Manitowoc most Christmases and often in the summer as well, the Vitses rarely came south. In a peculiar coincidence, however, thirty students from Manitowoc visited Macon in the spring of 1952 in what was believed to be the first inter-state high school exchange program ever attempted. While its origin apparently had nothing to do with Dorothy's being a native of that city, her connection must have added to the enormous interest in it. Bibb School Superintendent Mark Smith and his counterpart, Angus B. Rothwell of Manitowoc, had hatched the idea at an educator's convention in Atlantic City, and Dr. Smith brought it before the Board of Education in January. Despite reservations about its legality, it was approved. Superintendent Rothwell was quoted in the *Telegraph* as having said that he "believed his pupils will obtain, among other things, a first-hand view of the Southern Negro problem" but the Board was advised that given the prohibition against "mingling the races in the schools" it would necessarily be an all-white exchange.[115] The Macon students went to Manitowoc in February, and their Manitowoc hosts returned the visit in March, a trip that took twenty-six hours by train. News coverage was extensive[116] and included a January 17 interview with Dorothy Lewis as to what the students might expect from a Manitowoc winter. "Snow usually starts falling in October and stays on the ground until March," said the lady who loved the Macon climate, and "usually the temperature hovers around 14 below." But cold weather did not shut down the city's social life: "There's never a lack of things to do. The school kids can hire a runner, get a gang together and go for a long sleigh ride through the frozen countryside. Bobsledding is another popular sport and the high school used to have a ski jump right on the school grounds." The local fire department could be depended upon to flood the baseball diamonds for seasonal ice rinks. "Almost every child in Manitowoc learns to skate as soon as he learns to walk. Ice hockey is played there like baseball is in the South." Since the school is right on the lake Maconites would be able to look out the windows and see icebergs floating. "Everyone lives in ski clothes and boots. The students go to school in them and the girls never wear dresses but . . . warm ski pants and boots. . . . it's a most colorful thing." After skiing or skating parties, kids congregate at a

114 Neal Ham, Oral Interview #2.
115 *Macon Telegraph*, "Student Swapping Plan is Approved," January 11, 1952, p. 1A.
116 No less than fifty-two stories are listed in the *Telegraph*'s index, most of them on page 1, and there was additional coverage in the *Macon News*.

local drugstore. "I mean the old-fashioned kind," she added; "The places that make their own candy and ice cream."[117] Then too, there would be new foods. "Bratwurst," Mrs. Lewis said, "is to Manitowoc what frankfurters are to Macon. . . It is a very highly seasoned food."

Every day that the Macon students were away one of the girls selected for the trip, Harriet Fincher (later Mrs. Donald Comer), filed a dispatch to report their experiences.[118] In addition to winter sports, numerous parties—and a few classes at the co-educational high school—they toured the Manitowoc shipbuilding company, Rahr's Malting, and of course, the Aluminum Goods Manufacturing Company, which gave each student an aluminum frying pan. Blizzards, basketball games, and learning the polka were also on the busy schedule. The next month arriving Manitowoc students were greeted at Terminal Station by an estimated ten thousand Maconites, a brass band, scores of flying Confederate banners, and the American Legion box car which ferried them to the City Auditorium where a color guard, the Mayor and other dignitaries presided over opening ceremonies that included stirring renditions of "Dixie" and "On Wisconsin."[119] The Manitowocans sported unique name tags: small aluminum frying pans courtesy of the Aluminum Goods Manufacturing Company, just the sort of novelty item in which Henry Vits's firm had specialized early in its history. The tags gave the students an opportunity to tell their hosts that A.G.M.C. was "the biggest such company in the world, you know." The company also provided double boilers and cookbooks for each student to present to their Macon hosts. One of the young people, "stocky" George Vits, grandson of Dorothy's cousin Albert L. Vits, told Rotarians that he found "Macon schools . . . swell but Manitowoc has it all over Macon with co-education."[120] The whirlwind of tours and parties ended on Saturday, March 23, with a tea dance from 4-7 p.m. at Idle Hour Country Club hosted by Mr. and Mrs. N. Logan Lewis. The next year, cognizant of the extensive preparation and execution required by the dual visit—at a time in which it was faced with a $2.2 million school expansion program—the school system dropped the swap and it was never repeated.

In remembering her friend, Betty Curtis noted that she "loved Dorothy because she was herself; she was opinionated, but had thought things through" unlike others who spoke too quickly. One of the things Dorothy Lewis, a lifelong subscriber to the *Chicago Tribune*,[121] was opinionated about was politics, and

---

117 She was doubtless referring to Beerntsen's Candies on N. 8th Street, a Manitowoc soda fountain-candy shop renowned for its traditional treats.
118 Mrs. Comer shared the scrapbook she kept of her odyssey, which contained not only her stories, but numerous mementoes. She and Sherry Schleunes, with whom she was paired for the exchange (staying in each other's homes during their time in the other's city), continued the friendship they formed during the swapped visits for many years.
119 Jim Chapman, "Huge Macon Crowd Shouts Welcome to Manitowocans," *Macon Telegraph,* March 18, 1952, p. 1A.
120 Jim Chapman, "Manitowoc Youths See Lanier Drill and Visit Local Industrial Plants," ibid., March 20, 1952, p. 1A.
121 *The Tribune,* still under the control of Robert McCormick in the middle part of the century when Dorothy Lewis began reading it, was staunchly Republican; after the pioneering editor Clayton Kirkpatrick took the reins in 1969 it came to be seen as much more objective. "Milestones," *Time,* July 5, 2004, p. 20.

her opinions were quite conservative. She joined the semi-secret John Birch Society[122] soon after its 1958 founding, acknowledging that fact to *Macon News* reporter George Doss, in contrast to the others he interviewed who refused comment. She was "a member of the 'home chapter,'" she said, but she could tell him nothing about the local unit: "I just can't tell you a thing because I don't know."[123] She was not hesitant in sharing her opinions with others. "If she had a cause, she was vocal about it," said cousin Jane Protz, who was one of those to whom Dorothy sent materials.[124]

In the spring of 1961 she weighed in on the heated public discussion that followed a controversial Bibb County Grand Jury investigation into the Foreign Policy Association's Great Decisions Program, a series of study groups sponsored locally by the Macon Council on World Affairs. In a letter to the editor titled "How To Get Information on Communist Activities" she wrote, "Because the following information has been requested by many patriotic Macon Americans, it is my hope that you will print this letter." She went on to describe various House Un-American Activities Committee and Senate Internal Security Subcommittee publications "concerning the film 'Operation Abolition'"[125] (showings of which had been riling Middle Georgia audiences for several weeks), as well as ones "for the Business Man . . . the Medical Man," and "for all Patriotic Americans." Without further comment she concluded "Remember when ordering to give full title of the report, the date and name of the committee. Make check payable to Supt. of Documents, Government Printing Office, Washington, D.C. Allow two weeks for delivery."[126]

122 Named for a Macon native who had nothing to do with the group but whom Birch founder Robert Welch thought was "probably the first American casualty in that third world war between Communists and the ever-shrinking free world," the Society adopted an authoritarian structure in its stand for "less government, more individual responsibility and a better world." (Barbara Bundschu, United Press International, "John Birch Society Aims, Methods Stir Controversy," *Macon Telegraph*, March 3, 1961, p. 1A.) Welch's belief that President Eisenhower, his brother Milton, Secretary of State John Foster Dulles and his brother Allen (head of the C. I. A.) were members of the Communist underground, and that "the exposure of such persons, even through 'mean and dirty' techniques" was necessary "to shock Americans awake in time to save themselves" struck a chord in post-McCarthy, post-atomic-secrets-stolen-by-the-Soviets, America. "The danger is almost entirely internal," Welch was quoted as saying, "from Communist influences right in our midst and treason right in our government." He viewed the twentieth century "trend toward 'collectivism' not simply as a mistake, but as a sinister conspiracy to change the economic and political structure of the United States so that it . . . [might] be merged with the Soviet Union without a fight." To those who disagreed with him he was a "marvelously gifted demagogue . . . driven by an almost wild fear of a persistent and pervasive sort." To his admirers, the controversy about the Society "was set off by a Communist paper in California," and "a complete disclosure . . . of all the facts gathered by Robert Welch would obviously deal the Communists a blow from which they might not recover." (George Doss, "Publication by Mercer Sophomore Comes to Defense of Ultra-Rightist Birch Society," *Macon News*, April 27, 1961, clipping from John Birch Society File, Middle Georgia Archives, Washington Memorial Library.) The Society was still decrying the influence of the Council on Foreign Relations (whose "goal of a socialist world government looms ever more ominously on the horizon") and warning of the Communist threat in 1990s literature found in Dorothy's kitchen after her death: John F. McManus, "Is the Cold War Over?"
123 George Doss, "John Birch Society Has One Or More Chapters In Macon," *Macon News*, March 22, 1961, and "Birchers in Macon Still Aren't Talking," *Macon News*, April 13, 1961, clippings from John Birch Society File, ibid. Dorothy Lewis likely had some sort of a relationship with Birch's parents, who lived near Macon; the warmth but formality of it is indicated by the inscription in a small book entitled *Beside Still Waters, Daily Devotionals and Bible Study* found in the Lewis library in 2002: "To Mrs. N. Logan Lewis in memory of Mr. Lewis, the George S. Birches, May 26, 1966." The date was the day after Logan's death.
124 Oral interview, March 20, 2004.
125 This controversial film, produced by Fulton Lewis III, son of a conservative radio personality, purported to show Communist infiltration and manipulation of a student demonstration against the House Un-American Activities Committee in San Francisco. Maconites Henry K. Burns and Alvin Koplin, having seen the film at a Seminar on American Strategy conducted by the Third Army at Fort Benning, concluded, Burns wrote in a letter to the *Telegraph* published March 14, 1961, that "that the affair was much more serious than we had thought from reading press reports, and that we should obtain this film at our expense and show it to as many people . . . as possible." The film showings and the Grand Jury investigation of the Foreign Policy Association were separate situations but dealt with the same issues-how America should respond to the Communist threat.
126 Forum of Reader Opinion, *Macon Telegraph*, March 16, 1961, p. 4A.

The week before she had taken out a quarter page ad on the last page of the *Telegraph*'s front section that had gone into considerable detail.[127] Under an eye-catching 36 pt. boldface headline, "Communist Calendar of Conquest of the United States of America," she had written "Most Americans who are informed on Communism feel our Republic is now in great danger. Our survival as a free Republic depends on our ability to openly combat Communism with knowledge and established facts." She then quoted F.B.I. Director J. Edgar Hoover's *Masters of Deceit* and, at length, a report of the Cardinal Mindszenty Foundation of St. Louis[128] on the Communist Master Plan for 1961. "One of the most frightening facts in the report . . . is this: 'The date for the surrender of the United States to world Communism was set for 1973 by Josef Stalin . . . and Mao Tse-tung . . . at their last meeting.'" After setting out thirteen points of the plan she continued:

> You, the reader, might ask 'how is it possible that such a system, long since rejected scientifically and now proved erroneous by experience, could spread so rapidly in all parts of the world?' The explanation lies in the fact that too few persons have been able to grasp the nature of Communism. Since 1937 over 800,000 more human beings have been locked behind the Iron Curtain. It is tragically true that these people did not recognize Communism under its numerous disguises until it was too late. For those readers desiring to become better informed Americans, contact the Cardinal Mindszenty Foundation . . . [to order] or the Superintendent of Documents, Government Printing Office [a list followed.]
>
> This information has been compiled and published by the undersigned hoping it will render a public service. Mrs. Dorothy V. Lewis

At the bottom of the ad large type proclaimed: "WE ARE A REPUBLIC! NOT A DEMOCRACY!" followed, in smaller type, by "Let's Keep It That Way!"

The Lewises also became involved in the Committee of 150, a local group organized to counter the Communist threat, with Logan agreeing to join its Advisory Board. "The object of the corporation shall be to acquaint the citizens of our community with the dangers of Socialism and Communism, socialistic and communistic influence and socialistic and communistic infiltration by all legal means and methods," read an excerpt from its bylaws printed on its letterhead.[129] A paperback collection of articles published by Edgar C. Bundy and the National

127 March 8, 1961, p. 14 A.
128 Founded in 1958 by a Catholic missionary expelled from China by the Communists, the Foundation is named for Cardinal Joseph Mindszenty, a Hungarian prelate who was jailed by the secret police after the Communists took over Hungary in 1948; during the 1956 uprising he found refuge in the American Embassy in Budapest where he remained for fifteen years. According to its website the Foundation "is a worldwide, non-profit educational organization which offers reliable information on the nature, propaganda and goals of atheistic Communism." Its purpose is "to build and defend the Catholic Faith, to strengthen and sustain family life, and to work for freedom for all under God." The CMF may be a point where Dorothy Lewis' strong religious faith and her political convictions came together. A first edition of Jozsef Cardinal Mindszenty Memoirs was on her bookshelf in 2002.
129 An example of the letterhead can be seen in two letters from Mrs. William W. Chichester (who was chairman of the organization) to Charles J. Bloch dated July 7 and July 16, 1964 in Box 28, Folder 122 of the Charles J. Bloch Papers, 1932-1971, Middle Georgia Archives at Washington Memorial Library. In addition to Logan Lewis the Advisory Board included Bloch, Henry K. Burns Jr., Kenneth W. Dunwody, William A. Fickling Sr., Charles C. Hertwig, Robert A. McCord Jr., Wallace Miller Jr., Robert Train, B. Sanders Walker, and B. E. Willingham Jr.

Laymen's Council of the Church League of America—the organization that provided much of the information used to attack the Foreign Policy Association before Macon and Atlanta grand juries—in the Lewis library was inscribed "Please return to Mrs. Dorothy Lewis," implying it had been frequently lent.[130] Other materials remaining in the house indicate that she read widely among conservative publications such as those of Western Islands Press and the Birch Society, and was interested in the message of Fatima, a village in Portugal where the Virgin Mary had appeared to children in 1917 to urge the saying of prayers and the consecration of Russia by the Pope in order to defeat Communism.

It was natural for a couple with such strong opinions to be involved in electoral politics. After World War II the Republican Party had increased its inroads into the solid South; Elbert Tuttle of Atlanta traveled the state speaking out in favor of a two-party system in the late forties, and Eisenhower's success in 1952—after twenty years of Democratic presidents—brought new life to a small group that was at the time bi-racial. A number of people with whom the Lewises socialized and did business were becoming active at the local level, among them Eden Taylor Jr., Sewell Elliott, the Ed Mallarys, and Frank Jones; Anne Bryant was 1966 President of the Republican Women's Federation and her husband Wallace (who had also served on an LST during World War II) won election to the Georgia House of Representatives as a Republican.[131] Dorothy and Logan Lewis, while remaining mostly behind the scenes, and not newcomers to GOP activism, became enthusiastic members of this movement, participation documented by records of the local party now in the Middle Georgia Archives. Minutes of the March 24, 1956, Bibb GOP convention, for example, note that Logan had been elected treasurer, named a delegate to the Sixth District Convention, and served on the nominations committee. Perhaps the most intriguing item in the collection, however, is a copy of a letter from Logan to William Miller, then Chairman of the Republican National Committee (later the vice-presidential candidate on the Goldwater ticket), in January 1964, in anticipation of the summer convention. Drafted at a time when party leaders still exercised considerable control over the nomination, it gives great insight into its author's political ideology and history:

> Many of us in this area have diligently supported the Republican candidates in national elections, thinking that the conservative element in the Republican Party would eventually prevail. Contrary to this, however, the liberal wing apparently is gaining control with alarming speed.

130 Now in Lewis Archives.
131 Anne Bryant summed up the philosophy shared by members of the party at this time in a 1965 letter to the editor: "Early last year it became quite clear to the people of Bibb County, and the whole State of Georgia, that the Republican Party stood for the principles that they believed in. As a result, organization by the Republican Party was simply a matter of bringing together over a period of a few months before Election Day those people who believe that this great nation of ours was built on a belief in God, human dignity, individual responsibility, and limited government." From Mrs. Wallace L. Bryant, "Forum of Public Opinion," *Macon Telegraph*, November 27, 1965, p. 4A.

I ask your indulgence while I review briefly my association with the Republican Party in my area. When General Eisenhower's opponent in the Convention was Senator Taft, I was most enthusiastic when Eisenhower was nominated. I felt that next to Mr. Taft, who I did not think could be elected, General Eisenhower was the best man for the office. A very small group, including the writer, worked long and hard, primarily to raise money which was tendered to the Republican Party. Although Eisenhower's first term in office was very disappointing, I still, with reluctance, worked and supported him as best I could the second time he ran. His second term was even more disappointing.

With even more reluctance, we worked very hard in Mr. Nixon's behalf, primarily for the purpose of defeating the late President Kennedy. Prior to these elections, for your information, I voted for and supported Dewey and not once did I vote for or support the late President Roosevelt. Granted, my open support of these candidates probably did not benefit them, it is nevertheless true that I was responsible for and personally solicited a large percentage of the money raised in my area for the support of General Eisenhower and Mr. Nixon. It is also true that if the Republican Party nominates any candidate other than Senator Goldwater, or someone equally as conservative, you have lost the support of the writer and many others in Macon and Bibb County. It is time for the Republicans to offer for election a conservative candidate. Otherwise, you will lose the support of the independent and dissatisfied voters in the South, regardless of what you hear to the contrary.

As stated, so that you may be sure of the authenticity and sincerity of my remarks, I am taking the liberty of naming the following references: Senators Richard B. Russell and Herman Talmadge, The Chase-Manhattan Bank of New York, The Chemical Bank New York Trust Company, and your well-known local and state-wide Republican leaders.[132]

Whatever Miller's response to this plea, Barry Goldwater did indeed capture the nomination in 1964. His candidacy precipitated what a paper titled "History of the Bibb County Republican Party" called "the biggest political upheaval of the century," because it led to an almost complete sweep of local GOP candidates, an astonishing feat in a part of the country in which victory in the Democratic primary was tantamount to victory in the general election.[133]

132 Dated January 31, 1964, the copy sent to Draft Goldwater-leaders G. Paul Jones and J. W. Adams is in the Correspondence file of Collections of Bibb County Republican Party, Acc No 79-03, Middle Georgia Archives in the Genealogical and Historical Room, Washington Memorial Library.
133 Ibid. A "Proposed Bibb County Republican Platform County Convention, March 15, 1966" in the same folder spells out the party's core values and principles, ones with which the Lewises would clearly have identified: "Trusting in God from whose bounty come all the blessings of life . . . we reaffirm our belief in these basic concepts . . . that this is a God-fearing nation based on moral government . . . the capitalistic system, where a man may invest his money in the economy . . . with the right to earn a profit, and never be harassed or coerced by his government . . . the rights of the individual, as set forth in the Bill of Rights and the Constitution of the United States . . . the initiative of the individual to do for himself . . . fair taxation . . . balanced budgets . . ." The extent of the Lewises' support for Barry Goldwater can be inferred by the extensive memorabilia from that campaign still in the Lewis home after Mrs. Lewis's death in

Dorothy Lewis' name was on the lists of the ladies working at the polls and taking office duty at Republican headquarters—a compilation that reads like a "Who's Who" of socially prominent Maconites. Minutes of Executive Committee meetings during 1964 and '65 make clear that Logan continued to raise money for the party as well as to recruit candidates, despite a "feeling among old line [i.e. pre-1964] workers that they had been shoved aside in the enthusiasm of the Goldwater Republicans." Secretary J. H. Brenner wrote that following "a spirited and encouraging discussion . . . with party loyalty the golden theme" those at the meeting agreed that the talents and labor of all were sorely needed in the important work ahead.

Oliver Bateman, who was a GOP State Senator from 1964-74 and Republican activist during those years, remembers admiring Dorothy's "strong opinions. She was one of the most articulate people I've ever known; she wrote beautifully." Shunning public attention, however, she rarely put her thoughts into published form. Since he was then traveling all over middle Georgia on business and political matters, Bateman says he told her "I can find people who would love to have your abilities and would be honored to sign their names to your words." The next morning there was a stack of letters in his mailbox, and he thereafter made a habit of carrying such pieces in his vehicle to show the like-minded as he moved around the state, people who would re-type and send in the letters without making any changes at all. "She was a very private person who preferred to remain behind the scenes," Bateman said, but she obviously felt strongly about issues.[134]

Whatever else Dorothy Lewis was involved in, nothing was more central to her life than her Catholic faith. In addition to her frequent attendance at daily Mass she, like her mother, kept a prie-dieu under a wall-mounted crucifix and rosary in her bedroom for private prayers. Her work with the Altar Society at St. Joseph's has already been mentioned;[135] she was also supportive financially: the thank you notes in her desk testify to gifts to a number of religious orders. A 1962 letter from Monsignor Andrew McDonald, Chancellor of the Diocese of Savannah, thanked her for contributing two silver chalices, apparently to be used for any church he selected: "This is a noble and beautiful expression of love for the Holy Sacrifice of the Mass. . . . The chalices arrived today. They are very beautiful." Though Logan was less active with his church, Betty Curtis remembers attending a service at Vineville Baptist with both Logan and Dorothy to commemorate a similar gift he made at about the same time, and a 1950 letter in his files details his concern about plans for building an addition to the church.[136]

While Logan was involved in a number of real estate projects in the

2002.
134 Oliver C. Bateman, Phone Interview, April 2003.
135 Sketches of the altars and measurements for linens were still in her kitchen after her death.

early 1950s, the development of the old Lamar property out near Idle Hour into the upscale subdivision Country Club Estates became the largest. The project was one that the five Lamar heirs had begun in the forties, but after a decade of miniscule progress Henry Lamar, who was in the automobile business with Pink Persons' father, told Pink that he and his sisters had decided to sell the land. Pink thought it an ideal opportunity because "wherever I'd been during the War, I saw that the number one residential section in any city was always around the country club."[137]   Logan agreed to "take a part," attorney Sewell Elliott, who lived next door to Pink, and his wife, Mary Grace Elliott, took a part, and the Lamars took a part. In January of 1953 each of the five heirs sold Dorothy Lewis and Mary Elliott an undivided 1/20th interest in the property, and Eden Taylor Persons and her father-in-law H. P. Persons Sr. undivided 1/40th interests, retaining a 1/20th interest for themselves.[138] The next year Logan, Pink Jr., Sewell, and Henry J. Lamar IV sought a charter for the Idle Hour Development Co., for the purpose "of pecuniary gain and profit" in the business of buying, selling, leasing, subdividing, and improving real estate; the corporation had 10,000 shares of stock at $10 per share and capital of $30,000. Logan was president of the firm, Pink vice-president and secretary, and Sewell the attorney; each owned 7500 shares and the five Lamar heirs, who sold their remaining 1/20 interest in the property to IHDC, purchased the remaining 25 percent.[139] The wives then sold their interests in the property to the company and the development began.[140]

Despite its promise, the undertaking was venturesome because it was so far—seven miles—from "town," quite a bit beyond most residential development at the time. As Pink remembers "Everybody said it was in the country. My father-in-law, Mr. Taylor, told me, 'Son, you just bit off more than you can chew. It ain't gon' go over; it's too far out.'"[141] Indeed it did take more than thirty years to sell all of the original 200 acres plus adjoining parcels purchased from Mrs. Warren Roberts, another member of the Lamar family, and Tom Standard. An advantage to the property, however, was that the road to Idle Hour's clubhouse, and to the few lots that the Lamars had sold in the early '40s, was already in place, so that sales of the lots on existing streets funded the further development. In 1954, IHDC hired Atlanta and Forsyth landscape architect John Hoffman to lay out roadways on the remaining acreage.[142] "I don't like straight roads" Logan told the man, and he did not draw any.[143] A number of lots were purchased by people providing their own house plans;[144] Logan and Pink bought others on which to

136 Logan Lewis to the Board of Deacons, October 27, 1950, Lewis Archives.
137 Interview #2.
138 Bibb County Clerk of Court, Book 653, folios 529, 532, 535, 538, and 541.
139 Ibid., Petition for Charter, Book 10, folio 676.
140 Ibid., Book 275, folio 273.
141 Persons interview #2.
142 Drawing on file in Bibb County Clerk of Court Plat Book 26, p. 38.
143 Persons interview #2.
144 A set of covenants, based on those drawn up by the Lamars in 1942, protected the neighborhood from inappropriate development, and lot-owners were required to have their plans approved by the company. Recorded in Book 478, folio 322 and Book 675, folio

construct spec houses, probably twenty-five or thirty of them. Pink amusedly remembers one Logan built using an old set of drawings originally done for Broadus Willingham, which, unlike contemporary designs, had only two bathrooms for its five bedrooms. Initially quite time-consuming, the project was less demanding once it got off the ground; lots were offered in several phases, with most of the Forsyth Road front footage, as the Callaway land fronting Ingleside had been, reserved for later commercial use.

Given Logan's immersion in the development of Country Club Estates and his devotion to Idle Hour Club, it seemed appropriate that he and Dorothy decided to build a home there.[145] In 1954 Dorothy bought lots eight and nine of Block B, property immediately adjacent to the golf course's fourteenth green, while in 1955 Logan bought nearby Lot 4 from Hiram Manning, acreage that included a small brown house John McCord had used for a country retreat in anticipation of later living in the area before selling it to Manning.[146] The Lewises asked architect Ed Ferguson to draw plans for their home, but since his area of expertise was Georgian Colonial, he assigned the commission to associate James Berg. "I could tell from the start that they didn't want an ordinary house," Berg recalls.[147] Producing the drawings took six months. While Logan initiated the process, his role in it was limited to excitement about one of the city's first "heat pump" furnaces (a great improvement over the one burning coal on Vineville Avenue), and making sure his wife would have what she wanted; it was Dorothy who determined the house's character. It was to have an "old world," European feel, and not to "look new." Berg was never given a budget and obviously children were not a consideration; what he designed was an elegant, eclectic home for a mature couple.

Positioned on a rise very close to the green (Berg's warning about errant balls notwithstanding) the house was approached by a long semi-circular driveway. Berg said that "Mrs. Lewis made it clear that she wanted to be able to ride up and get out of a car under cover, not in the rear but at the front door," so a substantial porte cochere centered the front façade. She also wanted the garage to open to the back of the house, and its interior to be fully finished rather than simply "roughed in." Given their interest in collecting automobiles, space was allocated for four, and in addition, a detached workshop in which the vehicles could be worked on and restored, anchored the opposite end of the home. Most details of the interior finishes, however, were left for Dorothy to work out with contractor Chris Sheridan, since Berg did not supervise

270, Bibb County Clerk of Court.
145 They must have thought about dividing the Vineville Avenue home into apartments while Logan was still in the South Pacific, an indication that they did not plan to live there permanently, since plans for such a conversion, drawn by architect Ella Mae Ellis League and dated 1942, were found in Mrs. Lewis' files after her death. According to Betty Curtis they had also considered property on Riverside Drive that was high enough to look over the Ocmulgee (Interview #2.)
146 Recorded in Book 682, folio 229, and Book 719, folio 20, Bibb County Clerk of Court.
147 Berg Interview, ibid..

construction. Laura Nelle O'Callaghan remembers asking Kit Birdsey if she were going to help Dorothy decorate: "You know Dorothy doesn't need any help," was the reply. The house was designed to suit their particular needs, Dorothy told Mrs. O'Callaghan: "There's a room for Logan, a room for me, place for the cars."[148]

While the house did not have a large number of rooms, those it had were of generous dimensions and elegantly appointed. Marble steps under the porte cochere led to carved teak double doors that opened into an arched teak entryway beyond which lay a spacious foyer with a marble floor and tray ceiling. Mrs. Lewis had asked Berg to measure two large Italian sconces before designing the space in which she planned to put them. They and the antlers of two exotic animals, marble sculptures on pedestals, and Oriental rugs added distinction to the architectural features, and set the tone for the rest of the house. (Many of these pieces were apparently purchased at Rich's Connoisseur Shop in Atlanta during one of the many shopping trips Dorothy Lewis made with Betty Curtis; "We did love to shop!" Mrs. Curtis said.[149]) Tall double doors opposite the front entrance opened into the drawing room; at fifty by twenty-eight feet, with a twelve-foot tray ceiling, it was large enough to make the grand piano look inconspicuous. A white marble fireplace with brass fittings set in the middle of the far wall was flanked by rows of built-in teak bookcases with grille-front doors and marble topped cabinets that contained hundreds of books, many handed down from Logan's parents, grandparents, and great aunts and uncles. An elaborate chandelier hanging from a medallion in the center of the room, damask-covered walls, and a plethora of antique, mostly French furnishings, fulfilled the expectations evoked by the foyer.[150]

The dining room featured more intimate proportions with a table to accommodate eight, a graceful crystal chandelier, complimenting sconces and the crystal candelabra from the Michigan Avenue house in Manitowoc. It had a tile floor but the huge kitchen, in a choice that Berg remembers as most unusual in that era, was originally hardwood with Oriental scatter rugs. An Emil Holzhauer painting was displayed on the wall between two of the three sinks; monogrammed linen hand towels hung from rings nearby;[151] paintings and ceramics depicting chickens, and a brightly colored clown ornamented the walls of a hall leading to a large walk-in pantry and a larger laundry, beyond which was the garage.

The bedroom wing was at the opposite end of the house. It had generous walk-in closets, his and her bathrooms with marble fixtures,[152]

148 Interview #3.
149 Interview #2.
150 This description comes from viewing and photographing the house in late 2002 following Mrs. Lewis' death, and reviewing a set of plans with her notes found in the pantry; plans and photographs now in Lewis Archives.
151 These were likely done by Dorothy herself; monogram patterns with the "D" "V" and "L" cut out were found in the kitchen.
152 Berg believes it to have been the first time he was ever asked to do an all-marble bathroom.

chandeliers and similarly distinctive furnishings. It is a measure of Mrs. Lewis' penchant for privacy that Berg, acknowledging that she had never mentioned it specifically, nevertheless had the impression that his client wanted the house "to recall her home in Manitowoc, especially its interior character," and indeed Anne Vits gave her daughter a number of pieces in 1955 as the house was being planned and built.[153] But the style of house was not at all like Dorothy's childhood home, and most of the contents were selected and purchased by Dorothy Lewis herself, giving full range to her highly regarded taste and sense of style. It was, Betty Curtis affirms, "Dorothy's house." Logan's interest was apparently confined to the then new and innovative heat pump furnace. The Lewises moved into it in July of 1956.[154]

The next year Pink and Eden Persons, who had bought a group of three lots across the street, completed their Georgian style home and took up residence at 440 Old Club Road. Their proximity must have been handy for Logan who, despite owning numerous automobiles, frequently found himself without one in working order; on those days he caught the seven-mile ride downtown with his friend and neighbor. It was on one of those trips to town that Pink broached a sensitive subject. Eden, pregnant with their fourth child, had suggested that, should it be a boy, it would be nice to name him after Logan, and the prospective father had been assigned to make sure that suited the honoree. When his explanation of the idea was greeted by silence, Pink began to have second thoughts. But as Logan opened the door to get out he turned and "with fifty cent tears on each cheek said, 'Tell Eden I'd be honored.' " As it happened, the baby was a girl, born very early in the morning. Logan was unperturbed. Arriving at the hospital shortly after four a.m., he foreclosed any further consideration by saying "I've always thought that 'Logan' would be a perfect name for a girl."[155]

Idle Hour Development Company consumed much of his attention in the mid-fifties, but there were other business affairs on Logan's agenda. He negotiated a new lease with the A & P on Vineville, agreeing to tear down the filling station which had been at the corner of Callaway and Vineville since the late 1920s in order to make more room for parking. He was also involved in Dorothy's 1953 purchase of a house on Hemlock Street, which was developed into a medical office building before being sold in 1955,[156] and in her 1954 purchase of the piece of property at the corner of Riverside Drive and Pierce Avenue discussed in detail below. He sold 717 Vineville to Robert McCommon

153 This gift was one of those itemized in Anne Vits U.S. Estate Tax Return, filed in 1968. Anne M. Vits Estate File, Lewis Archives.
154 Biographical Report filed with the Comptroller of the Currency in connection with the purchase of control of the Farmers National Bank of Monticello, GA, June 4, 1965; Lewis Archives.
155 This being one of Mr. Persons' favorite stories, he told it in each interview.
156 Bibb County Clerk of Court; the purchase, borrowing against, and sale of the property are recorded in Book 661, folio 60; Book 686, folio 281; Book 677, folio 671; Book 685, folio 516; Book 697, folio 495; Book 709, folio 692 and 695.

Jr., and talked him into buying 707, Annie Callaway's home that had been turned into apartments, as well as the apartment house he had built immediately behind it on Corbin Avenue.[157] The *City Directory* in this period consistently listed him as Treasurer of the Bibb Transit Co., and in the earlier years, put his office at 377 Cotton Avenue, the headquarters of Odom Realty Co., by then being managed by his friend, Crockett. Later he rented an office in the First National Bank Building on the corner of Cherry and Second.

Dorothy Lewis too, was increasingly involved in real estate. A. J. Vits, still the President of the Aluminum Goods Manufacturing Company at 84, had died in January 1955. That year Anne Vits made a substantial cash gift[158] to both Dorothy and her brother Abby, an amount comparable to what Dorothy paid for the 2.009-acre tract of land fronting Riverside Drive at North Pierce Avenue in 1956. The property was not developed immediately, but held, perhaps due to uncertainty about the direction of the area. In 1963 a small shopping center anchored by a Piggly Wiggly grocery store[159] opened on Pierce, diagonally across Riverside from the North Pierce land, and Pink, who negotiated that lease and had been listed as a witness on Dorothy's deed, had apparently sketched plans for a similar development on her parcel. It was not to be. That great legacy of the Eisenhower administration, the interstate highway system, was also in the planning stages, and as fate would have it, the Lewis property was condemned by the State Highway Department of Georgia for I-75, leading to a lengthy fight which did not conclude until 1968.[160]

Based on an appraisal by J. A. Leggett, the State offered the Lewises $59,850, which they believed inadequate and declined. After a hearing before a Special Master in October of 1963 they were awarded $68,750, which they also found unsatisfactory, Logan having testified that its value was $100,000. Nevertheless, it was the State which appealed that price, winning at trial the following February when a jury dropped the amount to $52,000. Frank Jones, who tried the case, believes news stories about some owners "taking advantage of the state"[161] by requesting unreasonable profits for their property contributed to the negative result, but there were other factors at work as well. Opposing counsel, cross-examining Pink Persons about his $91,000 appraisal, managed to impeach his opinion, establishing the realtor's ties to the Lewises by asking the location of his home (across the street from Logan and Dorothy's) and bringing out that one of his children had been named for Logan.[162] That was a

157 Robert L. McCommon Jr., Oral Interview, February 21, 2003.
158 Anne M. Vits Estate Tax Return, ibid.
159 The rebuilt stores on this site in 2003 were Blockbuster Video, Aunt Zelda's Furniture, and Eckerd's Drug.
160 A thick file containing correspondence between Frank Jones, attorney for the Lewises, and Logan, as well as copies of his correspondence with other litigants and briefs filed in the case, was found with Mrs. Lewis' business records in a cabinet in the pantry off the kitchen, after her death. Now in Lewis Archives.
161 Interview.
162 The various stages of the litigation are summarized in a letter proposing a settlement from Frank Jones to T. Reese Watkins, attorney for the State Highway Department, dated February 12, 1965, a copy of which was found in file described above. Description of the cross-examination came from interview with Pink Persons, June 11, 2003.

sidebar, however, since presiding judge Oscar Long disallowed Pink's testimony because it was based on the value of the Piggly Wiggly lease, rather than a sale of property. Jones used that ruling, as well as Judge Long's jury charge placing the burden of proof on the condemnee rather than the condemnor (which was the plaintiff in this case), to win a new trial from the Court of Appeals, a decision that broke new legal ground in Georgia. Efforts to obtain a settlement at that point failed, and despite Logan's reluctance to endure the invasion of privacy another trial would involve, preparations for such were put in place, though various postponements kept it from ever happening. After four more years of offers, counter-offers, and changing attorneys for the State, in a testament to the Lewises' perseverance, the case was finally settled for $61,000. Toward the end of that period Jones was informed that Jack Hall, a Macon realtor well known for making extremely conservative appraisals, had put a $50,000 value on the land early on, so that even when the State was ready to settle on a higher figure, the federal government was not. "It was not like Logan or Do not to resist when not being given fair recompense," Pink Persons notes.[163]

In 1958 Anne Vits made another gift to each of her children, stock valued at approximately $75,000.[164] Coincidentally or not, on May 6, 1958, Dorothy purchased a 4.58-acre tract of land between the Gray Highway and Old Clinton Road in east Macon from Colonial Stores for $50,470, with the intention of developing the Town and Country Shopping Center. She signed the first two leases, with Colonial and Chichester's Pharmacy, that same day. Shortly thereafter she obtained a $150,000 loan from Macon Federal and contracted with Henry Clark of Clark-Wincey to construct the center; it opened in 1959. A fairly extensive file in Mrs. Lewis' records demonstrates that Logan, assisted by Anne Bryant, handled the numerous logistics for this business venture from his Cotton Avenue office, but it is clear from notes in her hand on the papers that Dorothy took an active interest in it.[165] The center opened with only two properties but soon added a dentist, cleaners, and doctor's office; in 1966 a substantial expansion added a bookstore, ladies apparel shop, florist, beauty salon, barber, shoe repair, and laundromat.

At about the same time the Lewises began assembling, with Murphey, Taylor and Ellis' help and in Dorothy's name, a group of properties on Pio Nono Avenue that would become Cherokee Heights Shopping Center.[166] Pink Persons, who brokered these transactions, recalled that the Kroger Company—expected

163 Ibid.
164 The gift is noted in numerous places in the Lewis business records; a letter from attorney Pat Clark to Dorothy and Abby dated October 10, 1958, indicates that Dorothy planned to sell hers since she had begun trying to determine its basis even before her mother transferred it. The stock had been purchased in 1945, and experienced several splits as well as a spin-off into another firm.
165 Found after Mrs. Lewis' death with other of the Lewises' business records in cabinet described above; now in Lewis Archives.
166 A number of legal documents and some correspondence pertaining to the purchase of these properties were found in a file with other Lewis business records noted above; public record of the sales are in the Bibb County Record Room, Book 812 folios 301, 306, 407, 573 and 251, and Book 810 folio 736.

to be the anchor tenant—considered it a prime location.[167] That was probably an important motivator since obtaining the various components was a tedious process involving six separately owned parcels. One of them, which Murphey, Taylor and Ellis purchased for later resale to Dorothy, had belonged to a woman who died intestate leaving multiple heirs at law; its purchase necessitated thirteen quitclaims, several from out of state, and a guardian to protect the interests of eight minor children. In addition, the primary heir had half a dozen fi fas lodged against him which also had to be settled before the property could be transferred. Another of the parcels was part of an estate which the terms of the will required the executrix to keep together; a long-term lease was negotiated and executed for that lot. Still another part of the proposed area had to be acquired from the City of Macon. Nevertheless, the pieces came together in 1959 and construction began early in 1960, again by H. J. Clark of Clark Wincey General Contractors. The Center, managed by Murphey, Taylor and Ellis' Bill McCowen,[168] opened late that year. In addition to Kroger's, it contained Head's Variety Store, Statesman Piano and Organ, Dixon's Drugs, Murray Biscuit Co., The Playpen, Econowash, Crescent Sno-White Cleaners, McDaniel's Barber Shop, dentist Dr. Bradley Askew, and Wilsie Kostedt, a beauty salon.

It's impossible to know how much of these business activities, if any, were initiated or guided by Dorothy Lewis. All of the correspondence concerning the management and operation of Cherokee Heights, like that pertaining to east Macon's Town and Country, was written and signed by Logan. Although he sometimes makes note of needing to consult his wife before finalizing a decision, even allowing for the customs of the day by which a wife would be expected to place her affairs in the hands of her husband, he appears to be directing what those decisions will be.[169] Frank Jones never had any reason to think that it was not Logan making the decisions, even when the property under consideration had been purchased in her name. Still, Dorothy was clearly aware of what was being done with her resources and, presumably, why. And she must have felt increasingly knowledgeable in business affairs. For whatever reason, her father had not named her one of the three trustees of the trust established under his will, specifying Anne, Abby, and First Wisconsin Trust, with Abby commissioned to vote the stock shares.[170] When her mother resigned her trusteeship, Dorothy wrote the bank managing the estate to ask that she be added in her place; unfortunately, as the lawyer who drew the will responded

167 Interview #2.
168 McCowen, who had purchased his home at 500 Old Club Road just down the street from the Lewises before the formation of Idle Hour Development Company, also managed rental of the small brown house at 441 Old Club for Logan, and later Dorothy Lewis.
169 In a February 10, 1965, letter to realtor David Thornton, for example, he wrote "I have not yet had an opportunity to talk to Dorothy with reference to the Pio Nono lot but I expect to do so before the end of the week." But in the next paragraph the only pronoun used is the first person: "It is doubtful that *I* will put a price on it so *I* suggest that if your people have a definite interest that you submit to *me* a net bid. . . . *I* am of the opinion that *I* would be more interested in a sale than a lease but *I* would be glad to entertain both." (Italics added.) Lewis Archives.
170 Will of Albert J. Vits, 1951, Albert J. Vits Estate File, Lewis Archives.

several months later, the terms of the will did not permit successor trustees, which effectively left her brother and the bank in charge of matters that were of vital interest to her.[171] She did ask questions however, as the letters from the trust officer and lawyer in the estate file reveal, exhibiting an increasing interest in how the estate was being managed, and occasionally correcting things they had said.[172] She also suggested that she join Abby as an attorney-in-fact after her mother had executed a power of attorney naming only her brother, which Anne agreed to do.[173]

As noted above, a ledger of her holdings reveals that she had begun to buy and sell stock soon after World War II; these activities increased markedly in the early fifties, and continued at a fairly brisk pace. She bought and sold from several brokerages and in the custom of the time, kept her stock certificates in her safe deposit box. Pink Persons remembers that she consulted a friend of her father's, Rawson G. Lizars, of Ardmore, Pennsylvania, who apparently had an interest in a brokerage in Chicago.[174] Mr. Lizars was also Chairman of the Board of Certain-teed Products, a substantial building products firm in which A. J. Vits had invested heavily on his wife's behalf; that put him in a good position to advise Dorothy on her basis in the shares of that stock which her mother eventually transferred to her and Abby.[175] Interestingly, it was Dorothy, rather than her brother, who seems to have gotten on top of the complexities. A copy of a letter to Abby in the file reads:

> Logan tells me that when he was in Manitowoc at Christmas he discussed briefly with you the cost to us of the Bestwall and Certain-teed stock . . . . He thinks that you stated that you had ascertained a cost of $39 on the Bestwall, which was furnished you by a stockbroker. Walter Clark's letter dated October 10, 1958 to you and me states that according to his figures, which were taken from various records, that the cost of 2607 shares of Certain-teed was an average of $7.93 per share; and although no record could be found of the additional shares, it must be assumed that it was approximately the same as most of the Certain-teed was purchased during this period. If this is the case, according to the enclosed formula . . . furnished by Certain-teed at the time of the spin-off, I figure the cost of the Certain-teed to be $2.83 and the cost of Bestwall $15.30.[176]

171 David G. Owen to Dorothy Lewis, November 23, 1964, and Walter J. "Pat" Clark to Dorothy Lewis, January 28, 1965, Anne Vits Estate File, ibid.
172 For example: "Dorothy correctly pointed out that my December 26 letter incorrectly listed the number of shares of Pepsi-Cola Inc. It shows 4,090 shares, which should have been 7,090. . . . Since the value as listed is correct even though the number of shares is not, it has no effect on the proposals." Donald Buzard to Mrs. Logan Lewis and Albert J. Vits, Jr., January 3, 1968, ibid.
173 Pat Clark to Mrs. Logan Lewis and Mr. Albert J. Vits, Jr., March 3, 1964, ibid.
174 Oral Interview, August 6, 2004.
175 Rawson G. Lizars to Dorothy Vits Lewis, October 17, 1958, Stock Gift File, Lewis Archives; this letter refers to hers of September 9th of that year requesting his help in determining her cost. Lizars enclosed flame-tinged ledger sheets detailing the original stock purchases that had fortuitously escaped a fire in his office.
176 The letter is missing date, salutation and signature, but is clearly to Abby; from content and provenance it appears to have been written in 1961.

Clearly Dorothy was interested in what was being done with her money. Logan further obtained an opinion from Charles Cork, the tax specialist at Frank Jones's firm, that the cost of the gift tax paid by Anne Vits could be added to the basis.

While all this was happening in Macon, the Lewises took an extended trip to Europe in 1959. They sailed April 20 on the R.M.S. Mauritania,[177] stopping in Paris but spending most of their time motoring in England and Germany. They visited Cologne, Frankfurt, Heidelberg, and Weisbaden, traveling down the Rhine by boat, a treat for the former naval officer.[178] At the resort town of Baden-Baden, Dorothy bought a remarkable diamond and ruby broach from Hulse Jeweler, the invoice for which was still in her bedroom desk when she died;[179] she also purchased various porcelains on that trip.[180] Logan played golf at famous St. Andrews in Scotland, and they acquired another Rolls Royce (the "Shooting Brake") that they had shipped to New York and drove to Macon at the end of their journey.

It was sometime after the Lewises' return that Eugene Chambliss, a tall, dignified African American began working for them as a handyman/gardener. Many years later Chambliss described the origins of his employment to Mrs. Lewis's trust officer, Dave Jeffords.[181] He had been leaving Idle Hour Club on foot one afternoon, he said, going home despondent after having been fired, when Logan Lewis pulled up next to him and inquired as to what had happened and where he was headed. Upon hearing Chambliss's story he gestured towards his car and told him to "Get in," whereupon they drove to 455 Old Club Road: "You've got to work somewhere," Logan said. Which Gene did, doing whatever needed doing in yard or house until his death in 2001, long past his eightieth birthday. In addition to giving Chambliss a job, papers in Mrs. Lewis's files show that the Lewises helped him and his wife, Virginia, buy and insure a home on Bayne Street, and acquire and insure a truck.[182] The Lewises, according to Pink Persons, "treated Gene like a member of the family" and he gave them his complete devotion in return. Other neighbors remember his gentle demeanor, friendly nature, and positive outlook.[183] Dorothy Lewis, who had never before employed household help, was often seen riding as a passenger in Gene's truck.

177 A small leather-bound book titled "My Trip" found in Mrs. Lewis' desk was marked "Sailed April 20, 1959" but had no other entries; a photograph of the Lewises also found in her desk, is stamped "Taken aboard the R. M. S. Mauritania."
178 Guidebooks from that journey were still in the house after Dorothy Lewis' death: the *1959 AAA Motoring Abroad Travel Guide to Europe, Heidelberg, An English Guide, Historic Houses and Castles in Great Britain and Northern Ireland, 1959 edition, and Travel Tips . . . BRITAIN,* 1958 edition, Trans World Airlines. Lewis Archives. Betty Curtis recalled Logan's pleasure in the boat trip.
179 Lewis Archives.
180 A letter pertaining to its shipment was also found in Dorothy's desk after her death.
181 Interview #2, February 24, 2003.
182 In a letter dated September 4, 1964, Logan wrote to Sam Lamback at Home Federal making reference to a home recently purchased by Virginia Chambliss and saying "You will doubtless recall that this is the loan I asked you to make." He had apparently earlier negotiated with another lender to reduce the size of Chambliss' indebtedness and used the Home Federal loan to consolidate and organize her payments; the folder also contains correspondence indicating that he arranged insurance for the home, and the Georgia Bank loan repayment schedule on a 1965 Chevrolet pick up. Lewis Archives.
183 Mary Anne Berg Richardson, Oral Interview, September 21, 2005. Ms. Richardson and her husband lived in the "little brown house" for several years in the late 1970s.

The Lewises' generosity was not limited to those in their employ. Dorothy's gifts to her church have been noted above; in 1963 she gave two hundred shares of Certain-teed to Mt. De Sales School for its library. According to financial records remaining in the Lewis home after her death, her husband's contributions went not only to the United Givers Fund and Vineville Baptist, but to several other churches, including St. Joseph's, and to civic/charitable organizations like the YMCA and Red Cross; in 1965, he gave $525 to the Macon Independent School Board for Stratford Academy. Neal Ham, who later worked with Logan at the Georgia Bank, believes "there were not many people who did as many things for other people as Logan Lewis."[184] In 1961, he accepted chairmanship of the committee to launch the first fund drive for ALSAC, Aiding Leukemia Stricken American Children, in connection with the visit to Macon from entertainer Danny Thomas,[185] and a few years later he joined a group of businessmen seeking to increase opportunities for youth recreation.[186] Usually he didn't want his generosity to be known, however, once going to some lengths to conceal from Ham that the several thousand dollars in cash he had asked him to deposit to a customer's account one morning before dashing off to lunch was actually his gift to a family whose academically gifted daughter would otherwise have been unable to attend college. On other occasions his help consisted of unsecured loans to friends and colleagues, loans that tided them over a rough spot or enabled them to meet an otherwise unobtainable objective. Not only did he not require collateral for these "back pocket loans,"[187] he sometimes signed documents attesting that as "second mortgagee" the bank holding a first mortgage had prior rights to such collateral as there might be.[188]

It is not surprising that a man in the habit of making loans should eventually find himself in the banking business.

184 Oral Interview, November 19, 2003.
185 "Logan Lewis Accepts Post," *Macon Telegraph*, March 17, 1961, p. 14 A.
186 "Fifty Years Ago Today-A Macon civic workers committee met to plan a city youth center," *Macon Telegraph*, March 24, 2005, p. 9B.
187 Herbert M. (Buddy) Ponder Oral Interview, July 10, 2000.
188 Several of these documents were found in a file together in Mrs. Lewis' business records. Lewis Archives.

Crockett Odom took this snapshot of
Dorothy on the day of her wedding in the
yard of her parents' Manitowoc home;
she is wearing the Rodier ensemble she
chose for the ceremony. Photo courtesy
of Crockett Rader Sellers.

Johnnie Logan Lewis deeded her interest
in this Corbin Avenue home to her son
on the day his engagement to Dorothy
Vits was announced; he and his bride
settled there upon their return from their
honeymoon.

This 1939 photograph of shotgun-toting
Dorothy Lewis, probably taken on a
hunting trip to the Callaway retreat in Lee
County, was found in Mrs. Lewis' kitchen
after her death. Lewis Archives.

Newly commissioned naval officer Logan Lewis poses with Peyton Anderson's daughters Katherine (l) and Deyerle (r) in Charleston, in 1942. Photo courtesy of Laura Nelle O'Callaghan.

In another photo from Crockett Odom's scrapbook, Logan and Dorothy Lewis are shown with Odom (r), Jimmy McCook (l), and McCook's sons Jimmy and Tommy, during Logan's January 1944 leave from duty in the South Pacific. Courtesy of Crockett Rader Sellers.

A. J. and Anne Vits, Abby and Do, in the Vits's 1304 Michigan Avenue home. This portrait is one of a series of photographs taken on what was likely the Vits' fiftieth wedding anniversary, in 1952, three years before A.J.'s death. Courtesy of Michael Place.

In another of the series, Mr. and Mrs. Vits pose in their well-appointed dining room on what was clearly intended to be a festive occasion. Courtesy of Michael Place.

In this photograph taken by Fons Ianelli for a spread in *McCall's* magazine, Dorothy accepts a cup of the hostess's "renowned oyster bisque" from Kit Birdsey at a Macon Concert Association party in the early 1950s. Elliott Dunwody, Jr., Stanley Elkan, and Rosalind Elkan are in the background. Courtesy of Middle Georgia Archives, Washington Memorial Library, Macon, Ga.

Both Lewises loved cars. Above, before and after shots of the 1925 Rolls Royce Silver Ghost that Logan, with Joe Ward's help, restored after retrieving it from Ned Willingham's pecan orchard in Byron. Jack Thomas, who also coveted the car, took the "before" picture; Drinnon took the "after" to accompany a 1954 *Telegraph and News* story on the "Old Car Craze" (Gertrude Trawick, July 25, p. 9). While the Lewises allowed the car to be featured, they were not, as was their wont, identified as the owners, and the Albert Glass Jr., children, were pictured with it. According to the story, the eighteen-foot long car would have cost $18,000 when new. Courtesy Jack Thomas (above) and Middle Georgia Archives, Washington Memorial Library, Macon, Ga. (below).

Opposite: "Racing days," Dorothy Lewis told a friend late in life, were her happiest. In the top picture she is getting set to race the 1939 Jaguar SS100 roadster; in the middle Logan poses with his prized 1953 Fantuzzi-bodied Maserati A6GCS; in the bottom picture Betty and Jimmy McCook (l) and Dorothy and Logan (r) relax between races under a tarpaulin draped across the trailer used to tow the cars. Lewis Archives.

These photos of the James Berg-designed Lewis home at 455 Old Club Road, taken after Mrs. Lewis' death, show the broad expanse of lawn and unusually windowless facade. Above left is a glimpse of the foyer with one of the "Italian sconces"; at right, the prie deux in Mrs. Lewis's bedroom.

Dorothy and Logan Lewis pose on board the R.M.S. Mauritania on their 1959 trip to Europe. Lewis Archives.

These 1965 Drinnon photos were most likely made for the renewal of passports. Courtesy of Middle Georgia Archives, Washington Memorial Library, Macon, Ga.

Chapter 4

———◆×◆———

Banking Becomes
a Mission

The Georgia Bank

It was cold in Macon on March 8, 1960; there had been an ice storm the week before and snow and sleet would cover the ground from Atlanta to Augusta the next day. Up in New Hampshire (which is what Georgia must have felt like), John Fitzgerald Kennedy was about to get the presidential election off to a dramatic start by winning the nation's first primary; in Washington D. C. a 157 hour-41 minute filibuster over a civil rights measure was coming to an end. Closer to home the Committee on Schools headed by Atlanta banker John A. Sibley was taking testimony from witnesses across the state in order to advise the legislature on how to respond to school integration orders. Locally, Bibb sheriff's deputies had raided a still a few miles north of town, after which they arrested the operator of a construction company for bootlegging.[1]

That Tuesday evening, as they often did, Do and Logan Lewis, Eden and Pink Persons, and Mary and Frank Peeples went to dinner together at Idle Hour. Perhaps the couples discussed some of the news noted above, but nothing captured their imagination like an offhand comment Persons made. "For want of something to say," remembers Pink, "I asked, 'Did ya'll see that article in the *Macon News* this afternoon about the C & S Bank buying out Rad Turner?'" That question, apparently, was "like lighting a Roman candle" under the table.

In a front-page story *The News* had reported on separate meetings during which directors of the two financial institutions had recommended a merger. Such a combination, said C & S Executive Vice President Ralph Eubanks and City Bank and Trust Chairman T. Rad Turner, would enable the banks "to keep pace with the tremendous economic growth of Macon and Middle Georgia."[2] Turner also pledged that "City Bank and Trust customers . . . will continue to receive the same personal attention" as always, plus they will enjoy "the advantages of the services and facilities of the larger combined bank." All City Bank employees

1 *The Macon News,* Tuesday, March 8, 1960, p. 1 A.
2 Ibid.

were to remain in their same jobs at the familiar Cotton Avenue and Cherry Street location, but join the C & S pension plan. Two and one-third shares of C & S stock would be exchanged for each share of City Bank and Trust stock, increasing the number of area C & S stockholders from 265 to 315. Those stockholders would then own more than 80,000 shares having a value of $3.5 million. Such details, however, were not of particular interest to the group gathered around the table at Idle Hour.

What caught their attention was this: with First National owned by the Atlanta-based Trust Company, C & S run by Mills B. Lane from Savannah and Atlanta, and City Bank and Trust now merger-ed out of independent existence, Macon no longer had a locally owned bank. An opportunity had opened: "Meet me at my office at 8 o'clock in the morning," Logan is said to have told the men.[3]

Once assembled the next day, the three men made lists of prospects who would be invited to purchase no more than $25,000 each in stock, and set another meeting for the following Monday. The plan to launch a new local bank was well received; no one turned them down. Perhaps they weren't given much choice: Laura Nelle O'Callaghan said Logan insisted that she and her husband borrow, if need be, to make their commitment.[4] By the time the instigators reconvened they had raised nearly half a million dollars; sales went so well, in fact, that they delayed the cutoff until Wednesday. When they met in Linton Baggs's office for the third time, their capital pledges totaled over $1 million from individuals and corporations.

News of the venture was announced on the front page of *The Macon Telegraph* on March 19, less than two weeks after the *News* had first broken the City Bank/C & S merger story. According to the *Telegraph,* some seventy-five "business and professional men" had met to name a steering committee "to secure a state charter and attend to other necessary matters." Serving were Halstead T. ("Andy") Anderson, Linton D. Baggs, J. Neville Birch, Joe Timberlake, Logan Lewis, John Marbut, William A. Snow, Ed M. Lowe, and Dr. Milford Hatcher.[5] The bank as yet had neither name nor location, but its deposits would be covered by the Federal Deposit Insurance Corporation. The steering committee was to apply for a charter immediately, even before an organizational meeting tentatively set for the following week, and Cubbedge Snow was chosen to handle legal affairs. "There has been such a tremendous interest in the formation of the bank," the newspaper quoted the group's leaders as saying, "that it is contemplated the capital stock might be increased over the million dollars

---

3 Henry P. ("Pink") Persons, Jr., Oral Interview #1, June 14, 2000. Mr. Persons is fond of telling this story and repeated it in essentially the same form when interviewed again (#2) June 16, 2003.
4 She also said it was one of the best investments she'd ever made. Interview #3.
5 "New Bank Slated Here," *Macon Telegraph*, March 19, 1960, p. 1A.

subscribed." A board of directors was to be elected by the stockholders, which would then appoint the bank's officers.

There were other housekeeping details to be addressed. Logan told Pink Persons that he planned to refinance his outstanding C & S loans at Fulton National Bank in Atlanta.[6] That bank's president, Gordon Jones, was a good friend; Fulton National also agreed to finance the purchases of would-be stockholders who lacked liquid assets to invest, and it would eventually become a correspondent[7] for the fledgling operation. (The two banks continued to have a close working relationship until Fulton National, by that time doing business as Bank South, acquired the Macon institution in the 1980s.)

Logan Lewis was no stranger to banking, having begun his business career at First National in the early 1930s. Furthermore, thanks to his and Dorothy's multiple real estate transactions, he had been a frequent customer of multiple financial institutions. In addition, he had served on the local board of the C & S Bank in Macon since 1956, a position he resigned as the Georgia Bank was being organized due to the conflict of interest.[8] Actually, his service on the Macon C & S board, which was essentially an advisory board, may explain his interest in organizing a locally owned bank. "We weren't directors—we were rubber stampers,"[9] he told one of the young bankers later hired to help run the new enterprise. Logan had become increasingly convinced that "a bank should be owned by people in the area it served so that the master of the bank is the community in which it is located," the associate remembers. Having seen that "the primary interest of the chain banks was in the community in which they were headquartered. . . . He felt like Macon was never going to grow until we had a strong, community-owned bank." For a long time he had wanted to start an independent bank in Macon.

An episode from the mid-fifties likely fueled this conviction. At that point in time conservative, Depression-era laws restricted both the organization

---

6 Interview #2. Pink said he also refinanced his loans with Fulton.
7 Because their capitalization limits the amounts of loans banks can make, they invite "participation" by another, larger institution, when a customer needs a loan exceeding the authorized size. This is particularly important for new banks since they naturally have lower capitalization. In Georgia Bank's case, its initial stock sale yielded $1,300,000 of which $812,500 was set aside for capitalization ($325,000 for surplus and $162,500 for undivided profits); that meant that any loan over $81,250 had to be sold in part to another, correspondent bank. (April 5, 1960, letter from Logan Lewis to Subscribers, Dr. Milford Hatcher Collection, Middle Georgia Archives, Washington Memorial Library.) Interestingly, another letter in the same file reveals an early wrinkle in the relationship between the two banks. From Cubbedge Snow to Gordon Jones on April 9 it reads: "Logan Lewis is sitting at my desk as I dictate this. We are most appreciative of your kindness yesterday afternoon, but we are quite distressed by that part of the Associated Press story in this morning's *Macon Telegraph* to the effect that the announcement was made by Mr. Hixon of your bank, who had helped prepare the papers for the application." (The story referred to reported on Georgia Bank's charter request to the Georgia Secretary of State; "New Macon Bank Applies for Charter," *Macon Telegraph*, April 9, 1960, p. 7 A.) Snow's letter went on: "This language would certainly cause others to infer that our bank had formed an alignment with the Fulton National. As you probably know, several other banks have been extremely gracious to us, and Mr. Lewis has made it perfectly clear to all of them that the choice of correspondent banks would be the decision of the Directors and Executive Officers. I am sure that you and the others at the Fulton to whom we have talked understood this." The letter shows that copies of the reproof were sent to First National, Macon, Georgia, Railroad Bank, Augusta, and Directors of the Georgia Bank.
8 John Comer, who served on that C & S board with Logan, remembers him dropping by his office, which, like Logan's was on the fourth floor of the First National Bank Building, to tell him about the formation of the new bank. He sensed a diffidence in Logan on that occasion and believes it came from concern that he, Comer—who was also a cousin of Mills Lane—would consider Logan disloyal. Oral Interview, October 2, 2002.
9 Neal Ham, Oral Interview, November 19, 2003.

of new financial institutions and the addition of branches to existing ones; there had not been a single bank formed in Macon since 1931. Historically, of course, the South had always had fewer banks than other regions of the country; its rural nature and dependence on a single crop led farmers to rely on cotton factors and merchants for credit, using their crops for collateral. The collapse of farm prices after World War I and the invasion of the boll weevil had brought the Depression to Georgia a decade early, so that between 1914 and the early thirties nearly half Georgia's banks failed.[10] When the economy picked up in the Eisenhower era, however, the lack of available credit was squeezing business expansion.

In 1955 Logan Lewis had been part of a group of Macon businessmen[11] who petitioned the Georgia State Banking Department and the Federal Deposit Insurance Corporation to charter a new bank which was to be located on the corner of Ingleside and Corbin avenues, the last parcel of the original C. B. Callaway property where Logan was still keeping his hunting dogs. In its petition the group pointed out that despite Macon's growth over the previous decade (from 57,000 to over 75,000 people), the city still had fewer banks than cities of comparable size. In addition to its population growth, Macon's industrial payrolls had increased from $26.3 million to more than $57.6 million and industrial jobs had more than doubled, from 8,400 to 18,400. Retail sales had risen from $53 million to more than $121.9 million. The number of telephones, electric meters, motor vehicles, and the size of effective buying income had also all doubled—even as the city itself had expanded from approximately eight square miles to more than 14 square miles. The metropolitan area's population numbered 152,000. Yet there had been no new bank since 1931, and there were none outside the downtown area. The solution these men proposed was a new bank, modestly capitalized at $100,000 with a $50,000 surplus and $25,000 undivided profits;[12] it would affiliate with the statewide C & S banking system in order to draw on its tools in credit, installment lending, checking, savings, industrial development, personnel benefits, public relations, and other services. Despite this beneficial affiliation, the new bank would be a separately chartered state bank known as the Citizens and Southern Macon Bank. An architect had begun drawing plans.

Alas, the state supervisor of banks declined to approve the proposal, not because Macon did not need a new bank, but because he was not convinced that the venture would be a separate institution. (Ralph Eubanks was to be

---

10 Kenneth Coleman, ed., *A History of Georgia*, 1991, UGA Press, Athens, p. 266.
11 Others were John D. Comer, Albert S. Hatcher Jr., Hamilton Holt, Henry J. Lamar IV, R. A. McCord Jr., John M. McElrath, Robert Train, W. C. Turpin, T. Irving Denmark, and Ralph Eubanks. "Group Planning New Bank Here," *Macon Telegraph*, August 7, 1955, p. 1A.
12 Just how modest this capitalization was is apparent from the comparison to the capitalization of First National Bank that advertised having capital of $500,000 and surplus of $200,000 in the 1932 City Directory.

president and Walter Chew vice president, even as they kept their original positions at the C & S bank downtown.) While the Atlanta bureaucrat apparently failed to return phone calls from the petitioners,[13] he sent a lengthy statement to *The Telegraph* expressing his belief that the "requirements . . . prescribed by statute" had not been met. He doubted that "the proposed bank would have a profitable operation without being materially subsidized by the Citizens and Southern Holding Company," and, he pointed out, "Macon, due to the existing branch banking laws is prevented from having branch banks." He suggested that the parties seek clarification of the statutory rules at the upcoming session of the Georgia General Assembly.[14] The organizing group later went to court to get the unfavorable ruling overturned, but before the case was resolved the legislature did indeed change the law, enabling C & S to establish a branch in Ingleside on the very site selected for the "new" bank, after which First National and City Bank and Trust also announced plans for branches.[15] Then, just as things seemed to be getting sorted out, an Atlanta stockholder of C & S, believing that the bank's expansion would lose money and damage his stock, filed suit in Chatham Superior Court claiming that the law under which the branch was to be opened was unconstitutional.

While this brouhaha did not prevent Logan from selling the afore-mentioned property in August of 1955,[16] it clearly demonstrated the frustration of having decisions that substantially impacted Macon's business climate made so far outside the city limits. And it doubtless helped Logan Lewis to see the value of locally owned and managed banks. C & S's 1960 purchase of City Bank four years later finally gave him a chance to put his principles into practice.

Thanks to an unusually complete set of records that one of its original directors, Dr. Milford Hatcher, not only maintained but donated to the Middle Georgia Archives (now in the Genealogical and Historical Room at the Washington Memorial Library), it is possible to trace the early history of the bank spawned by the C & S-City Bank merger in some detail. On March 22, three days after the news story announcing formation of the enterprise, Logan Lewis, who had been elected Chairman of the Steering Committee, sent a mimeographed letter to all subscribers requesting that they return an attached form with personal information needed by law. He included another form giving them a chance to indicate their preference among three proposed names. Regrettably, Dr. Hatcher did not retain a copy of the sheets he returned, so the

---

13 "Denial of Bank Charter Held Disservice to City," *Macon Telegraph*, November 3, 1955, p. 1A.
14 "New Bank Permit Denied by State," *Macon Telegraph*, November 1, 1955, p. 1A.
15 "Way Opened for Macon Branch Banking," *Macon Telegraph*, February 18, 1956, p. 1A; "Branch Proposed by First National," *Macon Telegraph*, March 9, 1956, p. 1A; "City Bank and Trust Co. Maps Expansion Program," *Macon Telegraph*, April 10, 1956, p. 1 A; "C & S to Erect $250,000 Branch," *Macon Telegraph*, April 17, 1956, p. 1A.
16 Bibb County Clerk of Court, Book 713, folio 413. C & S bought only about forty per cent of the parcel Logan owned on that corner at that time, however; the remaining sixty per cent was purchased in October 1956. Book 741, folio 424; plats are recorded in Plat Book 23, folio 238 and Plat Book 16, folios 53 and 67.

other suggested names are unknown. On April 1, Cubbedge Snow wrote the proposed directors requesting the financial statements that had to be filed with the Superintendent of Banks and the F.D.I.C., and asking for remittal of their portions of the $100,000 that had to accompany the filing of the charter in order to secure trust powers. On the fifth, Logan wrote the subscribers again to inform them that the Directors had determined a sale price of $20 per share for the stock, with $12.50 to be allocated as capital and $7.50 as surplus and undivided profits. He had intended, he said, for them to have this information "before it broke in the press, but Peyton Anderson offered to give us a good story and a good position if we gave the *News* the story this afternoon."

Indeed, in a page one, above-the-fold article that afternoon, the *News* reported that stockholders had decided to call the new financial institution the Georgia Bank and Trust Company. A few days later the bank made front page news again: Logan Lewis had been named permanent chairman of the board; Ernest Lee, a twenty-five year resident of Macon, a vice president of the First National Bank where he and Logan had worked together in the early 1930s (and who, with his wife Tots had attended the Lewises' Manitowoc wedding), had been named president.[17] "We are especially delighted that Mr. Lee has accepted the presidency," the new Chairman announced, "not only because of his experience and well-known capabilities but because it is most appropriate that a local independent bank should have as its president a man whose entire business life has been identified with Macon and Middle Georgia."[18]

Frank Jones, who was not directly involved in the bank's formation,[19] but played "intensely competitive" tennis with Logan and Pink several times a month during those years, saw Logan's strong commitment to developing a community bank as a natural extension of his earlier work for the United Givers Fund: while he recognized a good business opportunity he also deeply believed that a locally owned bank would lead to growth for the city. That conviction, Jones believes, accounted for his becoming "the moving spirit" behind organizing the new financial institution. Other members of the newly formed board, many of whom were longtime business and social colleagues of Logan's, were Halstead T. Anderson, J. Neville Birch, Robert A. Bowen, Nat A. Hardin, Milford B. Hatcher, S. Bert Kinard, Henry B. Matthews, Lee T. Newton, Harry M. Schwartz, Chris R. Sheridan, William A. Snow, and Joe E. Timberlake. Two hundred forty-one stockholders had subscribed $1.3 million in capital stock.[20] Don W. Gordon, "a Buckeye from Ohio"[21] who had been in the automobile business and a director

17 Mrs. Lee was ill when this announcement was made, and died May 10, 1960. *Macon Telegraph*, May 11, 1960, p. 15A.
18 "Lee Elected Head of New Bank Here," *Macon Telegraph*, April 30, 1960, p. 1A; see also "Ernest Lee Heads New Macon Bank," *Macon News*, April 29, 1960, p. 1A.
19 Jones handled many of Logan's legal affairs, but his firm, Jones, Sparks, Cork and Miller, represented the First National Bank, an affiliate of the Trust Company of Georgia, a conflict of interest which prevented his participation in the project. Oral Interview, November 11, 2003.
20 "Georgia Bank Sets Opening This Morning," *Macon Telegraph*, Friday, July 1, 1960, p. 14A.
21 So-called by his wife, Lucy Gordon. Oral Interview, January 24, 2004. Don Gordon was an experienced businessman in his forties and, like Logan, had served in the South Pacific during World War II. Mrs. Gordon is a native of Atlanta.

of his hometown bank before moving south in 1958 to become vice president of the Hubert State Bank in Athens, Georgia, was hired as vice president and cashier. Miss Margery M. Pate, who, like Lee had formerly been with First National, was to be assistant cashier.

While the March *Telegraph* story had quoted the organizers' optimistic belief that "several desirable possibilities are available" for housing the new bank, Pink Persons found that locating space was a challenge; building downtown had not caught up with increasing demand and every inch of office space was already rented. Having purchased the larger quarters next door that were then occupied by S & S Cafeteria, Macon Federal Savings and Loan Association was planning to vacate its vault-equipped, Greek Revival home at 341 Third Street, but it was waiting on remodeling and did not expect to be out until early 1961.[22] The four-man committee of directors charged with finding a site ("Messrs. Anderson, Baggs, Snow and myself," Logan wrote to the stockholders) went on and signed an agreement with the S & L anyway, but an interim space was needed if the bank, as anticipated, were to open as soon as the organizational hurdles had been cleared. The best that could be had in the short time frame allotted was the old Crane Building, a converted warehouse that later became the Macon Rescue Mission, at the corner of Broadway and Poplar. "Fortunately [it] has a vault which will meet insurance requirements," Logan told the stockholders.[23]

Undaunted by their unlikely location, the directors worked hard to get ready for the opening, lining up depositors and heralding the day with a full-page ad in the *Telegraph*: "Welcome to the Georgia Bank and Trust Company Opening" the advertisement blared in large, bold-faced type. "Home Owned-Home Managed" it bragged. "If you want a banking connection which is more than just a 'safe place to put your money,' one that takes a genuine interest in you and your personal and business plans, we invite you to come and join us in building a better Macon, Bibb County and Middle Georgia . . . You'll like our way of doing business because our attitude is one of service. We want your business and will do everything we can to deserve it."

But that didn't end the sales pitch. Some background seemed appropriate and the copy continued: "Organized by a substantial group of local people who have recognized the need for an independent, locally-owned and operated Macon bank, the Georgia Bank and Trust Company provides friendly and experienced management plus a staff of home folks to serve you with

22 "New Local Bank Selects Name, Acquires Site," *Macon News,* April 5, 1960, p. 1 A.
23 April 5, 1960, Logan Lewis to Georgia Bank Subscribers, Hatcher Collection, ibid. Logan wrote again on June 9 to tell stockholders that the application for a charter had been approved by the Superintendent of Banks but that the business permit could not be issued until all of the $1.3 million subscribed capital had been paid in; therefore he urged them to send in their checks "as promptly as possible after the receipt of this letter." At that point renovations of the temporary quarters were more than fifty per cent complete, office equipment and forms had been ordered for a pre-July 1 arrival, and "We believe that the prospects for the success of our bank are brighter than ever."

efficiency and a sincere appreciation for your business." Should that not be persuasive enough, the ad went on: "Local acceptance of Georgia Bank and Trust Company has been evidenced by the prompt and enthusiastic support of the more than two hundred outstanding business and professional leaders and local citizens who are stockholders. No single stockholder owns more than two percent of the total stock." Down the side of the page ran a list of all of the services to be offered—and just in case potential customers needed help in finding their way to the new facility—a drawing of the building occupied a prominent position at the top.[24]

In a news story that morning Chamber of Commerce President Albert S. Hatcher Jr. extended a welcome to the new business, noting that the quick subscription of stock was an "expression of confidence" in the venture. Macon Area Development Commission Chair E. A. Worm, called the new bank "a good omen for our future growth."[25]

The opening had been set for the first day of the month, which happened to be the Friday before the Fourth of July weekend. If cold weather had characterized the night on which the idea for the bank was hatched, the thermometer overcompensated the day it opened for business. Temperatures going into the weekend had set a seasonal record, and they did not break, reaching a sweltering 97 degrees.[26] Nevertheless, the bank stayed open until 6 p.m. that Friday and was open from 9:15 to 1 p.m. on Saturday, after which it planned to cut back to "regular banking hours."[27] Thanks to the advance efforts of its directors, who had targeted the small firms with whom each of them did business as they recruited customers, over $2 million in deposits were rung up on the first day. On Sunday the bank ran a prominent half page ad with a large "THANK YOU MACON!" announcing the size of first day deposits followed by "We are truly appreciative of your heart-warming confidence and support of the Georgia Bank & Trust Co."[28]

As soon as the old Macon Federal headquarters on Third Street became available in February 1961, the bank moved there.[29] It had twelve employees.

It was a propitious time to launch such an enterprise. The post-war economic climate was increasingly vibrant, and banking laws that had been tightened in the years following the numerous Depression-era failures, were

24 *Macon Telegraph*, Friday, July 1, 1960, p. 16.
25 "Georgia Bank Sets Opening This Morning," ibid.
26 Don Gordon's wife Lucy recalled the unrelenting heat, and did not think that the bank was air-conditioned at that time. Oral Interview, January 24, 2004.
27 In an era when most banks closed at 2:00 p.m., Georgia Bank made a point of better serving its customers by maintaining longer hours, a factor one director believes contributed to its success. James W. McCook, III, Oral Interview, February 5, 2003.
28 *Macon Telegraph*, Sunday, July 3, 1960, p. 3A.
29 "One of the few early bank buildings to have survived," according to preservationist Maryel Battin, 341 Third Street had been a bank since at least 1838 when the Bank of Hawkinsville was located in it. Now known as the Hogue Harvey Building, it won several historic preservation awards after its recent restoration for law offices. Other financial institutions which operated behind its stone Greek Revival façade included the Merchants Bank in 1846, the Central Georgia Bank (1871-94), the Macon Savings Bank in 1915, and the Continental Bank, one of those that joined to form First National Bank, in 1927; later, of course, it housed Macon Federal Savings and Loan. The original bank vaults were retained and restored in the building's latest renovation.

finally loosening in response to the new business activity. As soon as banks were allowed to open branches in the late 1950s, many did, significantly expanding facilities and services. The sixties brought even greater investments: Home Federal Savings and Loan built an eight story office building on Cherry and First, C & S planned several ambitious building projects, one of which came to fruition, and First National added an annex to its downtown headquarters. American Federal Savings and Loan Association was organized in April, 1965, with assets of $600,000 which grew to $4 million by its first anniversary, and soon opened new offices in the Lanier Plaza. As the only locally owned and managed public bank in the city, Georgia Bank was well positioned to thrive.

Which it did, despite pre-opening concerns about an "economic decline" in 1960. The first year-end report, issued after the close of business December 30, 1960, noted deposits of $4,745,073.80 in the first six months.[30] When the *Telegraph and News* published its annual "Parade of Progress" business section later that winter, the story on the Georgia Bank cited that total as well as a net profit in excess of $15,000. President Ernest Lee was quoted as saying that "The progress far exceeds the expectations of even the most optimistic of our stockholders." It didn't hurt that the bank had been one of the largest in the nation to open that year: capitalized at $1.3 million it ranked fifth among the 134 new banks in the United States according to The American Banker.[31] In an article on the business climate in the same "Parade of Progress," First National's Tom Greene said the current decline "continues to shape up as the mildest of the post-war recessions," and he looked to acceleration of the interstate highway program and education construction to keep the local economy moving. For his part, Lee claimed that "Most of the recession talk [has been] caused by the fact that predictions for the year were too glowing and the high point of the year's activity was in the [first] winter quarter." The tremendous influence, he added, of Warner Robins' payroll (then being increased by the establishment of CONAC headquarters) "has been a big help in maintaining our business volume at near top level."[32]

Naturally, the path to success was marked by a few bumps in the road. While Ernest Lee was a fine banker, he was not a pliable person and his experience in an older, larger bank appended to an Atlanta headquarters did not equip him to implement the flexible, customer-centered policies the Board set out. Assessing the situation a year after the bank's opening, Logan did not shrink from addressing the conflict and the two came to a mutual agreement that Lee should resign. The Board of Directors then named Logan president. "We just felt like he was the strongest man we could get," says Persons.[33] Not, however,

30 Copy from Hatcher Collection, ibid.
31 "Georgia Bank & Trust Co. Grows Rapidly in 1st Year," *Macon Telegraph and News,* Sunday, February 26, 1961, p. 7 E.
32 "Macon Bankers Optimistic," ibid., p. 14 A.

because of his employment history: "Logan called himself an 'investment banker' but if he ever worked a day in his life I'm not familiar with it," his friend grinned. Logan was, however, extremely devoted to the concept of the Georgia Bank, and determined for it to succeed. So devoted that he personally provided short-term financing for the stock purchases of several holders.[34] So determined that his personality, by several accounts, changed in response to his new responsibilities. Although he had always been pleasant enough, his general demeanor had been retiring, a manner that some people had interpreted as "stuck up." But "after he became president . . . he became a real glad-hander; he greeted everybody who came in the bank as though they were his long lost buddy." He maintained an "open door" policy, and saw anybody who wanted to see him. His first floor office opened right onto the bank lobby, enabling him to "jump up to shake the hand of anyone who walked in the bank." He "just became a tiger—a fireball—in that bank," Pink recounts, and "seemed to love every second of it."[35]

While he had great enthusiasm, Logan lacked Lee's banking experience, which, with the bank's growth, created a need for more hands-on banking skills. Logan asked Herman Sancken of Colonial Dairies, a firm that had outlets in several other Georgia cities, if he knew of any talented young bankers down in Albany who might be interested in coming to Macon; that is how Neal Ham happened to come to work for the Georgia Bank,[36] joining Don Gordon as a vice president. It was a good fit. Logan introduced his new associate to the Macon business community—Ham remembers that he made a point of his meeting Frank Jones "because you'll be working with him on civic affairs"[37]—just as he had earlier introduced Gordon, who took a seat on the Greater Macon Chamber of Commerce board of directors only a few years after moving to town.[38] The two worked hard, regarded Logan Lewis as a mentor,[39] and were philosophically in tune with his vision for the Georgia Bank. The bank, Logan believed, should focus on the customer's needs; the customer must always come first. "Everybody's money is green," Ham remembers; "success in banking depends on service."

And there were customers to serve. The advantage of having so many stockholders was in building an initial base of clientele. In addition, both stockholders and board members devoted themselves to soliciting business

33 Interview #2.
34 According to records in his personal ledgers there were at least four, possibly five of these loans for stock purchases between 1961 and 1963.
35 Persons interviews #1 and #2. It became a fairly common local understanding that, as one wag put it, "You know, Logan didn't speak to anybody until he started a bank." On the other hand, perhaps the change in personality had other origins. A vignette that Jordan Massee attributed to his father in *Accepted Fables: An Autobiography* (compiled by Richard Jay Hutto, Henchard Press Ltd., Macon, Ga, 2005) implies another reason for the transformation: "It's funny how some people change. You know, young Logan Lewis used to be a first class horse's behind. It took a world war to change him. Now he's as good a friend as I've got in Macon. Crosses the street just to speak, whenever he sees me coming. Damn good-looking boy, too." P. 61.
36 Ham, Interview #1.
37 Ibid.
38 "Chamber of Commerce Notes Success Recently in Quest for New Industry," *Macon Telegraph*, Sunday, February 27, 1966, p. 11.
39 Ham noted this in his interview; Don Gordon was deceased by the time this book was researched but his widow, Lucy, confirmed

for the bank, starting with family, friends and their own vendors and business associates, but moving on to involve any other contact they could think of. Letters in Dr. Hatcher's files reflect the perseverance with which both directors and their president sought new depositors, and numerous interviewees reported the same. Also key, in that less regulated era, said Pink Persons, was Logan's insistence on "lending based on what he thought of the guy."[40] Neal Ham confirms this predilection: Logan was "an excellent judge of character," he noted, and the technicalities of making the loan were less important in its approval than what he thought of the applicant. He had, after all, been lending money to various businesses and individuals since 1928 when his mother, as guardian, had lent the funds inherited from his grandmother Mallary on his behalf. He also had an unusual ability to relate to and empathize with people of stations in life other than his own. It was not unusual for President Lewis to bring someone to Ham's desk and tell him to work out a way in which the bank could make the man a loan because, while the collateral might be a problem, "he's going to pay us back."[41]

Another of Logan's instincts had to do with location: "Pink, go buy the corner of Third and Mulberry," he told his business partner/realtor/friend. It was a much more visible site, strategically situated between the federal and county courthouses. Crowell Stewart was operating the Stewart Oil Company there, and the owner of the property, Mrs. Thomas Jefferson Stewart (no relation), was not interested in selling. Nevertheless, Pink finally talked her into leasing the property, pointing out that it was too valuable a part of downtown to be used for a filling station.[42] James Berg, the architect who had designed the Lewises' Country Club Estates home, was commissioned to draw plans for the new building, which opened early in 1963. Once in their new location, according to Ham, the bank had the physical space it needed and it "didn't have time to solicit business."

Not a few of the bank's employees were intimidated by the new President Lewis, which lay behind their occasionally flustered responses when he requested information or assistance from them. He could be fairly short in conversation, not elaborating or making small talk, and he sometimes got "weird" expressions on his face.[43] More problematically, his desire for perfection in the way the bank presented itself to the public, combined with his hair-trigger temper, sometimes led him to be abrupt in correcting situations that concerned him. Still, he usually saw the error of his ways afterward, and seemed to sincerely regret causing distress; he clearly had a deep affection for those who labored on the bank's behalf. And "Mr. Lewis" set no less exacting standards

that her husband also admired and respected Logan Lewis. Oral Interview January 24, 2004.
40 Interview #2.
41 Interview #1.
42 Interview #2.

for himself than those in his employ. Having been known to enjoy a high stakes poker game, he came to realize that being seen gambling was incompatible with being entrusted with the management of other peoples' money, and gave up the indulgence.

The bank made solid progress. In a "Message to Stockholders" accompanying the 1962 annual report the Chairman of the Board noted the "steady growth" in average deposits, which had climbed from 1961's $4.4 million to $6.2 million, "an increase of approximately 40 percent." In 1961 net earnings were $.65 per share, in 1962 they increased 50 percent to $.99. However, the Chairman warned, "we have an even greater challenge for the year 1963 as we prepare to move into our new bank building at the corner of Mulberry and Third. . . . We will be faced with some very sharp increases in overhead and operating expenses. In view of this, we would like to urge each and every stockholder to put forth extra effort to attract new business and deposits to offset this additional expense, so that our progress will be continuous." Apparently they did, and it was.

The next year Logan reported that the decision to construct to new quarters "has been justified by the public's enthusiastic acceptance, by the civic pride it generates and by having adequate space for our expanding services and the efficiency and comfort it offers our customers and staff." The bank had embarked on a business development program, had secured a number of correspondent bank customers, and was petitioning for the activation of a trust department. Drive-in banking hours had also been extended: "The bank with customer's hours . . . not banker's hours," the slogan under the Georgia Bank logo boasted. Not surprisingly, profits per share had increased to $1.22. "Without your efforts in our behalf the Georgia Bank & Trust Company would not enjoy as important a place in the community as it does today," the Chairman concluded, adding that he anticipated more progress in 1964.

And more progress there was. "Progress and solid growth" were the "key words at Georgia Bank & Trust Company during 1964," Logan wrote the next December. In May the directors had transferred $175,000 from undivided profits to surplus, increasing it to $500,000; in October they voted to ask the stockholders to amend the bank's charter by increasing capital to $1 million via a 23 percent new stock dividend, three shares for every thirteen held. The stockholders had voted approval in November. An active trust department had been established that year and the correspondent banking department expanded. In his year-end report Logan was pleased to report net earnings of $1.57, an increase of 45 percent, and total assets of $16,466,045, with deposits of $14,321,830.

But it was in 1965, Logan wrote with obvious pride in the next year's report, that "Georgia Bank had its greatest growth" yet. The bank paid its first cash dividend, enlarged the staff to accommodate growth, decided to automate the bookkeeping department, and made plans for its first branch. "The bank's total resources as of December 31, 1965, were $22.25 million, an increase of 37 1/2 percent. The daily deposit total average . . . was 40 percent higher than in 1964. Net earnings for the year were $170,486.36, or $2.13 per share, an increase of 35 1/2 percent. The Directors and the entire staff of the bank would like to express their appreciation to all of our customers and stockholders for their confidence and urge their continued support."

If the responsibilities of managing the bank infringed on Logan's personal habits, they also gave him a platform from which to exert an influence on the direction of the community he loved. Many other cities around the South were drawing athletic and special events via large multi-purpose arena/ civic centers, and for Macon to effectively compete it needed such a venue. Unfortunately, concerns about usage and cost caused discussions to drag on for several years.[44] Wanting to convince civic leaders that it was an important and feasible project which would benefit the city, the Georgia Bank chartered a plane and took twenty or twenty-five people to Jacksonville, Florida, to see the facility that city had built, one which included offices for a unified city-county government.[45] The effort may have proved a catalyst for getting the project in motion; after overcoming numerous hurdles of location, financing, and administration, the Macon Coliseum finally opened in 1968—led by an administrator recruited from the Jacksonville center.

While Macon's economy was expanding, Houston County's was accelerating rapidly, and over the winter of 1963-64 Georgia Bank helped organize a national bank to be based in Perry, for which it would become correspondent. The new bank was to have $150,000 in stock and another $150,000 in surplus and reserve, with at least 50 percent of the stock subscribed by residents of the Perry trade area. Proposed directors included State Senator Stanley E. Smith Jr., who chaired the steering committee, Emmett Akins, J. M. Tolleson Jr., J. A. Davis Jr., Cooper Etheridge, Hugh Beatty, Dr. H. E. Weems, Eric Staples, and Dan Nelson.[46]

Clearly, as the Georgia Bank's fifth anniversary drew near, a celebration of its progress was appropriate. Fortunately, a copy of the Chairman/President's remarks on that occasion has survived.[47] Recalling the bank's early days, Logan

43 McCook interview.
44 See "Committee is Planned To Study Coliseum," *Macon Telegraph*, November 18, 1960, p. 29A, and "Coliseum Placed on Priority List," ibid., March 6, 1962, p. 1A,
45 Neal Ham remembers this trip as primarily designed to spur the coliseum project; Richard Domingos, at that time a member of the Georgia Bank Board who went with the group, remembers it as directed at illustrating the virtues of city-county consolidation. Oral Interview, February 17, 2004. What is important as far as this narrative is concerned is the Logan Lewis-endorsed civic-mindedness of the bank in supporting a public endeavor. In an interesting sidelight reflective of the times, Eleanor Adams Scott Lane reported that she and Miriam Glover were invited to go along as representatives of the League of Women Voters; when the visiting dignitaries ate lunch at a downtown "men only" club, she and Mrs. Glover were taken to the dining room via the freight elevator. Oral Interview, March 11, 2004. Unfortunately, she was unable to certify the purpose of the trip.
46 "National Bank for Perry Is Approved by Comptroller," *Macon Telegraph*, March 26, 1964, p. 2A.
47 "Untitled Remarks," which internal evidence indicates were prepared for delivery by Logan Lewis at Georgia Bank's fifth anniversary celebration, found in Mrs. Lewis' records after her death; now in Lewis Archives.

said, "We were full of enthusiasm and confident as to the future of the bank, but a little apprehensive as to what we would be able to accomplish in the first few years of operation. We were delighted and amazed that in excess of two million dollars was deposited with us on the day we opened." Subsequent growth and success, he noted, "can be attributed to our fine group of employees [by then numbering forty], as well as our stockholders and friends." Happily, the trajectory had exceeded expectations: "I recall that when we met with the Bank Examiners prior to the granting of our Charter, the incorporators were asked to estimate the deposit total at the end of five years operation, and I am quite sure I am correct in stating that it averaged out at eight million dollars." As it turned out, he continued, "we are very glad to report . . . that our deposits at the close of business today were in excess of sixteen million," approximately twice the pre-opening estimate and 25 percent above the previous year. He then announced that the previously uncompensated members of the hard-working[48] Board of Directors would begin receiving a small fee for their services. Also for the first time, a $.25 dividend would be paid to all stockholders of record— nevertheless the primary return to stockholders had been the "fairly substantial appreciation in the value of their stock."

Indeed, the stockholders should have been happy. Dorothy Lewis, who had bought her first stock before the bank opened in 1960 for $20 per share, had to spend $560 to acquire eight shares in 1965 to round out the 392 shares she received as part of 1964's three-for-thirteen stock dividend.

Typically, the event for which Logan had prepared the above remarks involved more than celebrating success and rewarding directors and stockholders. At a business meeting before the anniversary party at which he welcomed new stockholders (by then totaling three hundred thirty-six) the Chairman ended his speech by describing a related venture, the "Galan Corporation." An inspiration of Logan's that was quickly endorsed by the bank's other officers, Galan had been created by the board in 1961 to purchase property for possible future use;[49] it also held stock for sale to potential future directors. The chairman proposed that, in addition, it finance preferential customers as a way of securing business for the bank so that, over time, it might increase and control substantial accounts. Therefore he recommended amending the charter to recall the original stock and issue of new shares at par value of $5.[50] The bank's stockholders were asked to make an investment of $5 in Galan for every share of stock they owned; those present were urged to indicate their participation in this new corporation on the cards they had been handed as

---

48 A number of interviewees credited an unusually enthusiastic and involved board of directors for the bank's success.
49 Neal Ham, Oral Interview #2, August 2, 2004. Ham remembers that many of those involved with its origin thought Galan might evolve into a holding company for the bank.
50 Galan Corporation Audit Report, December 21, 1965, Hatcher Papers, 11.001.

they had come into the meeting. "Let me impress upon you," the Chairman concluded, "that the more money we have at our disposal in this corporation the more the bank and the corporation will prosper." Officers and directors, he said, were available to provide any additional information desired.[51] Galan, like the bank that organized it, was oversubscribed by investors who clearly took his words to heart. A July 16 letter to prospective stockholders noted "the Officers and Directors have been most gratified by the fine response of Georgia Bank stockholders . . . to Galan's plan to enlarge its activities by the issuance of stock."[52]

The Bank continued to do well. In 1968 Don Gordon told the stockholders' annual meeting that assets for the previous year had reached $32 million and deposits were up 18 percent, more than four and one half million dollars; earnings increased to $3.01 per share and dividends to 75 cents, representing increases of 13 and 50 percent respectively.[53] A letter from Cubbedge Snow to stockholders regarding a meeting to approve an increase in capital by 5000 shares quotes the Superintendent of Banks as having said "our bank has been, without doubt, the fastest growing bank of its size under his supervision."[54] In a 1975 newspaper ad containing the "Consolidated Report of Condition of Georgia Bank and Trust Company" (attested to by P. D. DuBose, Vice President and Cashier), the bank's assets were listed at $79,000,869. A typed sheet[55] attached to that torn clipping reported that the cost of 100 shares of stock in 1965 had been $3,000; its increase in book value through December 1974 was $2440, in addition to dividends paid of $1390, for a return per year of 13 percent and ten year yield of 128 percent.

It should not be surprising that Logan Lewis found his calling with the Georgia Bank. He had, after all, been bred to the vocation. His father had worked in a bank. His grandfather, and great-grandfather Lewis, as well as at least four Lewis great-uncles had been bank presidents around the state, and his maternal great-uncle John Callaway had been President of the Bank of Lee County. His step-grandfather Edgar Mallary founded and later sold two banks. In addition to founding and presiding over a bank, his great-uncle Elijah Banks Lewis had served on the Banking Committee while in Congress.[56] While most

51 "Untitled Remarks," ibid.
52 Letter from Galan President H. T. Anderson to Prospective Stockholders, July 16, 1965, Hatcher Papers 11:005.
53 "Georgia Bank Says Assets Show Gain," *Macon Telegraph*, January 11, 1968, p. 19A.
54 Cubbedge Snow to Stockholders, July 17, 1968, Hatcher Papers, 13.004
55 Both the clipping and typed sheet were found in Mrs. Lewis' files.
56 Though it's unknown if or how much E. B. Lewis' fate impacted Lewis family in Macon, it provides a context that should be noted. The former congressman ran two banks in Monticello, the Lewis Banking Company and the First National Bank, before committing suicide (apparently for reasons unrelated to the otherwise sound banks) in 1920. The former company closed immediately after his death, while the latter hung on for a few months before, at the request of its directors, it too closed its doors. A new bank, the Citizens National Bank of Montezuma, capitalized at $100,000, was organized by a group led by E. B. Lewis' youngest brother, William Minor Lewis, who had presided over banks in Valdosta and Atlanta, and been the first president of the Fourth National Bank in Macon. Logan Lewis was thirteen at the time his great-uncles were involved in these events. "Another Lewis Bank is Closed," *Macon Telegraph*, February 2, 1921, p. 1A; "New Montezuma Bank Organized," *Macon Telegraph*, February 12, 1921, p. 2A; "W. M. Lewis Elected Head of New Montezuma Banking Institution," *Macon Telegraph*, February 24, 1921, p. 9A.

of these men had died by the time Logan was in his late teens, their genetic material shaped his sensibilities; banking was in his blood. He was fifty-two years old when he became the driving force behind the Georgia Bank, an age when he might well have begun to think of reducing his business activity rather than taking on the leadership of an ambitious new enterprise. But he loved Macon and wanted to see it grow; he believed a locally owned and controlled bank was best positioned to foster that growth, and organizing and expanding that vehicle for growth became the most fulfilling activity of his life. Not incidentally, it was an investment that produced an excellent return.

However his involvement with Georgia Bank did not preclude continuing real estate activities, in both his and his wife's name. He and Pink formed a joint venture to build an office building on land leased from an out-of-town property owner at First and Pine streets, and he and Eden bought a piece of property downtown on Riverside Drive; he sold some lots on Pio Nono that he had been holding awhile. Dorothy bought a lot on Pio Nono Avenue adjacent to the Cherokee Shopping Center that same year. It was in 1963 that the Georgia DOT condemnation proceedings on her Riverside-at-Pierce land began. Logan became a trustee of the Riverside Cemetery, where both of his parents were buried, and where he and Dorothy planned to be interred, in 1964. In 1965 he oversaw Dorothy's sale of Cherokee Shopping Center to a group that included Murphey, Taylor, and Ellis and several doctors and lawyers. The purchasers had proposed taking over Dorothy's loan with Macon Federal, providing she could increase it to $250,000 before the transfer, and asked her to take a second mortgage. "The Sales Contract," Logan wrote Pink, "will be satisfactory [should] the following exceptions" be included: that the purchasers also assume Dorothy's lease contract with the primary landowner; that the balloon note on the second mortgage be due three years earlier than specified; and that the purchasers would individually endorse that $150,000 note.[57] His terms were accepted and the sale was finalized in June of 1965, with Dorothy realizing an approximately 25 percent profit on her original investment. They immediately set about planning an expansion of the Town and Country Shopping Center in east Macon: the existing grocery store, pharmacy, cleaners, and dentist's office totaled 24,520 sq. ft., to which they decided to add 14,920 sq. ft. of new space housing seven additional stores at an anticipated cost of $142,000. Clark-Wincey was again the contractor with Fulton National providing the financing, and Fickling and Walker, which was managing that center for the Lewises, soon began signing leases with prospective tenants.[58] In December of 1965 Logan bought one hundred fifty shares of A. G. M. C., by now known as Mirro, and gave seventy-

---

57 Copy of January 26, 1965 letter from Logan Lewis to H. P. Persons, Jr., Cherokee Shopping Center File, Lewis Archives.
58 Town and Country Shopping Center File, Lewis Archives.

five to Dorothy.[59]

But Logan's interest in banking shaped his other activities. He had bought 2000 shares of stock in the Bank of Fort Valley and he owned 100 shares of the Citizens Bank of Washington County, another correspondent bank for Georgia Bank. He encouraged Neal Ham to draw on Georgia Bank's resources to host a series of meetings that led to the organization of the Independent Bankers Association of Georgia, the first two conventions of which were held at Idle Hour Country Club. Furthermore, his interest in banking, especially independent banking, is evident by the enthusiasm with which he embraced another investment opportunity that presented itself in the spring of 1965.

The Farmers National Bank

Pink Person's uncle lived in Monticello, thirty miles northeast of Macon in Jasper County, and he asked whether his nephew knew of "anyone who wanted to buy a bank."[60] It seemed that the folks running the Farmers National Bank were up in years and anxious to retire, but there was no one to take over; no one had been brought along and trained to succeed them. O. H. Banks of Shady Dale, one of the directors of FNB who was also a customer of Georgia Bank, approached Logan about the situation. John Crandall of Kohlmeyer & Co. was also involved in helping find a potential buyer, having worked with at least one Macon businessman whose offer had been withdrawn when federal rules pertaining to the acquisition of national banks placed limitations on his investment.[61]

Once Logan became interested he asked Neal Ham to do a personal audit and advise him on the bank's condition and whether the price was right. After spending a couple of days looking at its loans—which weren't many, given the conservative nature of the men who ran the enterprise—Ham concluded that it was a good buy and that Logan could make money on it. True, the bank was small and old-fashioned, management having "delayed making essential decisions regarding modernization of . . . facilities and operation."[62] But Logan's progressive approach to the business would cause it to grow, and it had the further potential of being a good correspondent for the Georgia Bank; as noted above Georgia Bank's business development activity had already led it to assist both the First National Bank of Perry and the Citizens Bank of Washington County to secure charters as well as to lend funds to potential investors without

59 According to Betty Curtis (Interview #2) the Lewises did not usually exchange gifts on ceremonial occasions: "If you've got everything you want what do you need?" The timing of this presentation, however, suggests a Christmas present, albeit of a unique sort.
60 Interview #2.
61 Envelope inscribed "The Farmers National Bank-Original Purchase Info" in Farmers National Bank file included in Mrs. Lewis's business records found in the Lewis home after her 2002 death; Lewis Archives. Kohlmeyer & Co., a national brokerage firm of which R. A. McCord Jr. was a General Partner, had a branch office in the First National Bank Building.
62 Letter from Board of Directors to Stockholders of Farmers National Bank, June 1, 1965, FNB file, ibid.

ready cash to put into the new enterprises.[63]

Given Ham's positive report Logan wrote to the bank's Board of Directors on May 27, 1965, offering to purchase up to 400 of the 500 shares of outstanding common stock for $550[64] per share net to stockholders, subject to approval of the purchase and his right to exercise control by state and federal regulators. On June 1 the bank's directors wrote to stockholders to apprise them of the offer, noting that he had also told them, in keeping with his philosophy of banking, that while finding a successor to "present management" had been the primary motivation for the sale, "a majority of the present directors" would remain involved.[65] While it might seem inconsistent for a man who believed in local ownership to have become the majority stockholder of a bank in another community, it soon became apparent that Logan Lewis intended to operate the Farmers National Bank as if it were a local bank.

Meanwhile, he set about getting his own affairs in order to consummate the purchase by the July 15 date in his offer letter. Attorney John B. Harris Jr. contacted the Office of the Comptroller of the Currency on his behalf to discuss the impact of various regulations on the acquisitions, after which long forms detailing his business and financial affairs were filled out and filed with that office in early June.[66] Financing was a part of what had to be disclosed; it was arranged with Gordon Jones at Fulton National. Georgia Bank stock and life insurance policies were used as collateral for a short-term loan of up to $300,000 (depending on the number of shares actually purchased). A note was attached pointing out that "applicant will reduce loan by approximately $100,000 within 60-90 days;"[67] that was possible thanks to the fortuitous timing of the City of Atlanta's condemnation and purchase of Logan's Whitehall/Hunter Street property. Thus the sale of those three lots, two of which had been in his family for nearly one hundred years and had capitalized a number of Logan's previous business activities, provided a substantial cash infusion for his most ambitious venture.[68]

63 Interview.
64 As it turned out Logan purchased 366 shares, of which he sold ten each to Pink Persons, John Harris Jr., and Billy Nalls, the only non-Monticellans who owned part of the bank, leaving him with 336 of the original 500. According to a hand-written analysis of the bank's assets found in the folder described above, the book value of the shares was $440. Capital, $50,000, Surplus, $50,000 and Undivided profits of $42,000 totaled $142,000, which with $41,000 worth of building, land and fixtures, and 5 percent of $746,000 in deposits ($37,300), amounted to $229,300 divided by 500 shares. Obviously Logan saw potential in the bank to have paid 20 percent above the book value for its stock.
65 Several copies of both letters found in FNB file, ibid.
66 Copies in the FNB file, ibid.
67 Biographical Report to Comptroller of the Currency under "Proposed National Bank Stock Acquisitions," ibid.
68 The condemnation/sale of this property, the first parcel of which had been purchased in 1869 by Logan's great-great-grandfather, John Jones, clearly facilitated Logan's bank acquisition. Its $350,000 sale price was divided amongst numerous Jones heirs, but Logan got the largest portion, owning a half interest in #92 Whitehall (later Peachtree Street S.W.), and one-third interests in the other two parcels, #94 Whitehall and #121 Hunter Street. As his financial report to the Comptroller of the Currency filed in June revealed, Logan had also netted close to $100,000 in 1964 as a result of the sale of the Vineville Avenue stores. An aside: widening Hunter Street (later Martin Luther King, Jr. Boulevard), which ran next to the Keely building, was the reason for the condemnation, but while that took about ten feet off the side of the building, it did not cause the whole structure to be destroyed. The sale closed in September and the building was vacant while the road construction was underway; according to *City Directory* listings it re-opened in 1967, albeit with other businesses replacing the Kessler Company as tenant. The building has recently been re-habbed by an Atlanta developer (The Vision Group) and remained ready for a new tenant in the winter of 2003-4.

The next step was to find someone to run the new bank, and Ham helped Logan recruit a young banker he had known in Albany, Billy Nalls, a thirty-one year old father of two who was then cashier in charge of personnel and operations at the First National Bank of Newton County in Covington. Ham remembers that it was not easy to convince Nalls that Monticello could generate enough business to warrant his making the move. "I told him that it wasn't that there wasn't enough business, but that these old gentlemen had not been willing to do business: 'When word gets out that you are . . . you'll be calling me in Macon asking me to buy your loans.'"[69] Nalls was persuaded and began arranging to relocate his family. On June 30 Logan wrote him "I am looking forward to a very pleasant association with you and assure you of my full cooperation without interference. During the brief visits I had with the directors yesterday after our meeting they informed me they were very much impressed with you and I am sure you will get off to a good start."[70]

During the summer of 1965 Logan was immersed in planning for his new venture. The extent of his enthusiasm and the attention he gave to every aspect of the project is documented by the thick file on the acquisition found with Mrs. Lewis' business records. Realizing the necessity of a new building, given both the size of the bank's current structure and the fact that the competing Bank of Monticello was about to construct new facilities, he took an option on two pieces of property that would accommodate the larger, more modern financial institution that FNB was about to become. The extent of his collaboration with the extant staff is evident by the names of those witnessing the option documents: Board Chair O. H. Banks and Cashier C. T. Pope.[71] He recruited two new board members (Lucien Ballard and Ernest Key Jr.), both important players in the Monticello business community, and made sure that they were given an opportunity to acquire stock.[72] He drafted letters for President D. N. Harvey to send to the Comptroller of the Currency reporting the sale/ acquisition, as well as a notice to shareholders of a called meeting, along with proxies for their votes on the issues to be presented for approval.[73] He wrote Harvey again shortly before the July 19 stockholders meeting to suggest that "it would be appropriate" for the three ladies employed by the bank, while not stockholders, to be invited to attend the meeting "if it meets with your and Mr.

69 Interview, ibid.
70 Logan Lewis to B. E. Nalls, June 30, 1965, FNB file, ibid.
71 Options from W. Travis Lynch and Myrene P. Jordan, both dated June 4, 1965, ibid.
72 Logan Lewis to Ernest D. Key, Jr., June 30, 1965; Logan Lewis to D. N. Harvey and Herschel Allen, June 30, 1965, ibid. Mr. Ballard, who was Pink Person's brother-in-law, wrote Logan on July 24, 1965: "Once again I would like to take this opportunity to thank you for all you have done for me in my election to the Board of Directors of the Farmers National Bank. It is an honor and I sincerely appreciate it. Your interest in the Bank has solved a problem the Bank has been faced with for years and I think it a real blessing, particularly for Mr. Harvey and Mr. Allen. I also know that no matter what they had done they could not have found a better man than you to guide it in the years to come." ibid. In fact, Logan's enthusiasm was such that he had to correct the misimpression that he himself was moving to Monticello; writing to O. F. Holland on June 30, 1965 to disabuse him of that idea he nevertheless ended his letter by saying "The first opportunity I have when I am in Monticello I plan to come by and see you." ibid.
73 Logan Lewis to C. T. Pope, July 6, 1965, ibid.

Allen's approval." Noting that John Harris Jr. and Pink Persons would accompany him that day, he also asked the president to ascertain how many Monticello stockholders planned to be present, suggesting that "it might be best, even at this late hour, to change the place of the meeting to the American Legion."[74]

On July 12, three days before the stated end of the purchase period, he met with the existing board to outline the sweeping changes that, in consultation with Messers Harvey and Allen, he planned to recommend to stockholders the following week. President Harvey and Vice President Herschel Allen would step down after a thirty-day transition but remain honorary members of the Board of Directors, with the former also serving as Honorary Board Chair, and the latter as Chair of the Executive Committee. That committee was to be established by amending the by-laws (which amendment would also be submitted to the stockholders for approval) and would be authorized to act as a Loan Committee between regular meetings of the Board. Another by-law change would enable the board to add directors between annual meetings of stockholders. He recommended that Mr. Nalls be elected President and Chief Executive Officer, and that Cashier Pope remain in place with a raise in salary. Four new directors, Mr. Nalls and himself, as well as the two Monticello businessmen, should be added to the board. The capital of the bank should be increased to $100,000 by transferring $50,000 from the surplus account, and increasing the number of shares to 1000. He further recommended a reduction in the par value of the stock from $100 to $10 per share with a consequent increase of the number of shares from 1,000 to 10,000.[75] An architect (W. Thomas Little of Macon) had been selected for the design of the new building, on which he hoped construction would start within thirty days. At the subsequent meeting he concluded his outline of these initiatives by saying,

> I want to take this opportunity to thank the Board collectively, and the members individually, for the wonderful acceptance I have had and to assure you that I am very grateful and appreciative of your cooperation. I know this situation will continue and it is my sincere hope that at all times you will express your opinions. It has been my experience that a bank is no stronger than its Board of Directors and management. I am most optimistic about the future of this Bank and I am positive that, if this Board will cooperate with Mr. Nalls, it will be a marvelous success. Although it has not been my pleasure to know Mr. Harvey and Mr. Allen prior to this, it is certainly appropriate that I say it has been a real privilege for me to be associated with them during the past few weeks and I hold them in high esteem, and this certainly applies to Mr. Pope and the Directors of the Bank.

---

74 Logan Lewis to D. N. Harvey, Sr., President, July 16, 1965, ibid.
75 This had the effect of making the shares more liquid. While Logan ended up with majority ownership he wanted to be certain that Monticellans held significant portions of the stock, and that there was always some available for future board members to purchase.

Two days after that meeting Logan wrote Joe Andrews of Southeastern Services, a public relations firm in Macon, enclosing a copy of his remarks to the Directors and requesting that he prepare an article for the Monticello newspaper to be published after the July 19 stockholders' meeting; Andrews' draft was submitted to both Harvey and Allen before being sent to *The Monticello News* for its July 22 edition. Commenting on the appointment of Mr. Nalls as President and C.E.O., Mr. Harvey and Mr. Allen were quoted as saying that they "welcome the opportunity to bring an aggressive, community minded executive into Monticello to join in the progress that will be ours in the years to come." And Mr. Nalls, in accepting the position, told the Directors "I am delighted to have the opportunity to work closely with these two men who are held in such high professional and personal esteem in Georgia banking circles."[76] Logan Lewis is not quoted by name in the article, or even mentioned, save when listed as a new member of the board. But a typed sheet of his remarks inscribed with the date of the meeting shows that he thanked Harvey and Allen for their past service to the bank, and asked John Harris to prepare an appropriate resolution of gratitude for insertion into the minutes. He expressed his confidence in Mr. Nalls and optimism about the bank's prospects for growth and concluded by saying "Due to my own job I will not have an opportunity to visit Monticello as often as I would like but I am positive that if this Board gives its full cooperation to Mr. Nalls there will be little or no reason for me to come . . . except for the pleasure of seeing and meeting with you. . . . I will see you at the next Directors' Meeting."

Leaving no stone unturned in his cultivation of the Monticello business community, Logan wrote the newspaper's editor as soon as the story came out to thank him and let him know that he intended to place a large ad, possibly with photographs in it, in the near future. To Billy Nalls he wrote, "I enjoyed seeing you at the meeting yesterday. I thought your remarks were very appropriate and well said." Then reiterating his management philosophy he added, "again, I want to assure you that as long as everything goes well, and I know it will, you will have no interference from me. Naturally, I think after you get settled in Monticello we should have a discussion as to what your policies should be with reference to the bank, and after that it will be entirely up to you."

Which was not to say that the new owner didn't concern himself with details: he enclosed some form letters used in his own bank, suggested that Nalls order "personal cards" now so as to have them ready for immediate use once he arrived in Monticello, and finally, "I am also enclosing a check I picked up in Milledgeville the other day which I think is unusual and attractive. I don't

---

76 "Farmers Natl. Bank Holds Directors and Stockholders Meeting," *The Monticello News*, Thursday, July 22, 1965, p. 1A. Copy, ibid.

particularly care for having the building on the check, but this did attract my attention."[77]

Two days later he wrote again. "I was in Monticello for a very few minutes this morning and I think quite a few people are anxiously awaiting your arrival and the beginning of the new regime. Every time I am up there I think we have an even better opportunity. The paper I am sending carried an ad of the McIntosh State Bank of Jackson advertising 4 1/2% on Savings Certificates. Just this morning a customer of the bank advised me that they were sending a $15,000 check to some Atlanta Federal Saving and Loan Association due to the better interest rate, as the two banks in Monticello are paying a maximum of 4%. I realize that we have to put the money to work, but at the same time I certainly dislike seeing the money going to the competition. Give this some thought." He was not yet finished, though:

> As I may have told you, I am adamant about only one thing, and that is customer relationship. This morning on the way to Monticello I stopped by the Peoples Bank in Eatonton and the minute I walked in I felt as though everybody in the bank was glad to see me. Maybe that's because they didn't know who I was. Seriously, it was the nicest reception I think I have ever had in any place of business. Everyone in the bank spoke to Neal and me very cordially and I came out with a real warm feeling for the bank and the people in it. I was so impressed that I advised Mr. Adams, the President of the bank, and complimented him and asked him to convey my thanks to his employees. I am sure you will do your utmost to inaugurate [*sic*] this policy in Monticello. Certainly you know it pays off in the long run.[78]

Nalls replied on July 26: "I was pleased to get your letter and find you also have been thinking about an increase in the time certificate rate of interest. . . I plan to have that as the first order of business at the Board of Directors meeting August 10."[79]

The Lewises' FNB file contains a "Statement of Conditions" for the months of August, September, October, and November of 1965 (if such a comprehensive document had been prepared before Billy Nalls took over as President August 2 it is not with the other papers.) An examination of the statements shows the volume of loans steadily rising, to Logan's evident pleasure. "Sorry I was unable to attend the meeting yesterday," he wrote October 13; "Neal brought me the report which I have in hand. I think you are making excellent progress."[80] The next week he wrote again: "I read in the Monticello paper on Thursday that you had been elected president of the Kiwanis Club and

77 Logan Lewis to B. E. Nalls, July 20, 1965, ibid.
78 Logan Lewis to B. E. Nalls, July 22, 1965, ibid.
79 Billy E. Nalls to Logan Lewis, July 26, 1965, ibid.
80 Logan Lewis to B. E. Nalls, October 13, 1965, ibid.

certainly, I want to congratulate you. Also, I think it is fine for the bank."[81] He went on to discuss the "very good demand" in Monticello for the bank's stock, and his plan to sell down his holdings to just over 50 percent.

That plan was consistent with Logan's belief that banks should be locally owned: he wanted as many shares as possible owned by residents of Monticello. Another principle was at work: individual stock purchases in the Georgia Bank had been limited initially, in order to spread ownership, thus vesting numerous people in the bank's success. So it is not surprising that Logan, while wanting to protect his investment by maintaining a majority ownership,[82] decided to sell off more than ten per cent of his stock, up to 1600 shares. From November 20, 1965, to April 30, 1966, he sold 1225 shares to sixty-three people at $30 or $31 per share, leaving Nalls with 375 that he had been willing to sell but which had not yet been issued to other owners by the following May.[83]

Things continued to go well, as he wrote Nalls in January: "I thought you had a real fine meeting yesterday and also I think it was nice of you to let C. T. Pope participate in the program and he did a commendable job, as did you."[84] The next day the majority stockholder sent another letter to the editor of *The Monticello News*, enclosing an article for publication reporting on the annual stockholders meeting of the Farmers National Bank. It read "Billy E. Nalls, President . . . stated that the bank had enjoyed a 20% growth during 1965 and that as of December 31, 1965 had deposits in the amount of $2,430,500 and total resources of $2,673,000. Mr. Nalls also stated that the bank would move into its new quarters in the early spring."[85]

The Mission Comes to an End

The seeds of success had been planted but, as an incident some months before Logan's fifty-eighth birthday revealed, the sower would not reap the harvest. In the midst of a doubles match he and Pink were playing at the club that fall, Logan excused himself "to use the facilities." When he came back, as Pink tells it, he was "white as a sheet" and said he had to quit, that he had "passed blood." Dr. Ben Bashinski confirmed cancer as the cause of his symptoms; Dr. Milford Hatcher later found a mole on his back, a melanoma that had metastasized.   Six months later he was dead.

The spring of 1966 was doubtless a painful one for Dorothy and Logan Lewis, with new life coloring the landscape around them while Logan's strength

81 Logan Lewis to B. E. Nalls, October 22, 1965, ibid.
82 As Neal Ham points out, the C & S Bank was known to be interested in acquiring small banks from time to time, and should it have moved in and bought a majority share from various stockholders, the bank's future would have been in doubt. Oral Interview #2, August 2, 2004.
83 Billy Nalls to Anne Bryant, December 27, 1966, and January 6, 1967, ibid.
84 Logan Lewis to B. E. Nalls, January 26, 1966, ibid.
85 Logan Lewis to James W. Haney, January 27, 1966, ibid.

ebbed away. But like much of the rest of their affairs, they kept their grief to themselves. Logan's last weeks were spent in near isolation in a private room at the Middle Georgia Hospital. Although in those days the *Macon Telegraph* printed all admissions and dismissals to and from area hospitals every day, Logan's could not be documented in the newspaper—in all likelihood omitted at the Lewises' specific request. His illness can be inferred, however, from a *Telegraph* story reporting the paper's interviews with leaders of all the local banks that appeared in its annual "Profile of Progress Business Review" published in February: it was Vice president Don Gordon who was quoted regarding the Georgia Bank, even as President Tom Greene spoke for First National and President Ralph Eubanks for C & S.[86] In late February it was Anne Bryant who wrote to the trust officer managing Anne Vits's finances on Dorothy's behalf "due to the critical illness of Mr. Lewis."[87] Bib Anderson recalls that during a trip to Palm Beach that winter Logan became so ill that he had to go to bed when they got home, and apparently was never able to go back to work afterwards. The next month two announcements from Georgia Bank, the hiring of assistant cashier Roland May (from Atlanta) and the construction of its first branch in the Pio Nono Plaza Shopping Center, were also made over Don Gordon's name, rather than that of the bank's president.[88] In late March Billy Nalls wrote Anne Bryant in response to her query as to the number of shares in the Farmers National Bank that had been sold, and ended his letter by asking her to "Tell Mrs. Lewis . . . that we are thinking of her and Mr. Lewis every day."[89] On May 2 Frank Jones addressed an update on the Riverside Drive condemnation case directly to Dorothy, rather than to Logan.[90]

It grieved Pink Persons, who loved Logan "like a brother," that Dorothy wouldn't let her husband have visitors: "I went every day and signed the sheet on the door, hoping he'd know I was thinking about him," he recalled. During an earlier visit Logan had suffered a seizure in his presence and it was clear to Pink that Dorothy Lewis did not want anyone to witness such an episode again. Jimmy McCook too, remembers the "no visitors" regimen as Logan became sicker.

Curiously, and perhaps revealingly, however, Dorothy did venture out in early May to meet with the board of directors of the Farmers National Bank. On May 12 she wrote Billy Nalls that the meeting had been "a distinct

86 "Macon in 1965: All Indicators Point to More Progress," *Macon Telegraph*, February 28, 1965, p. 6 C. Early in the month Logan had written, in an undated notice of the February 8 Board Meeting, that January's net after taxes, shown on an enclosed operating statement, "was disappointing to me." Mentioning adjustments made in response however, he added, "At this moment I do not plan to be at the meeting next week, so if there are any questions may I suggest that you call me Thursday or Friday of this week." Hatcher Collection, ibid. The letter does not give illness as the reason for his missing the meeting; it may have been his trip to Palm Beach.
87 Anne Bryant, Secretary to Mr. Logan Lewis to David G. Owens, February 28, 1966, on Mrs. Lewis's stationery, Anne Vits Estate File, Lewis Archives.
88 "Georgia Bank Appoints May," *Macon Telegraph*, March 15, 1966, p. 16, and "Georgia Bank to Open Branch on Pio Nono Ave," *Macon Telegraph*, March 18, 1966, p. 3.
89 Billy Nalls to Anne Bryant, March 22, 1966, FNB File, ibid.
90 Frank Jones to Dorothy Lewis, May 2, 1966, State Highway Department Condemnation File, Lewis Archives.

pleasure for me. It soon became evident why Mr. Lewis has always had the greatest confidence in your ability and that of the Directors. Mr. Lewis feels their diversity and positive interest contributes substantially to the sound progress the bank has been enjoying. I thank you for affording me the opportunity of meeting the 'Bank Family.' Mr. Lewis joins me in sending to each of you our warm personal greetings."[91] It is impossible to escape the conclusion that Logan Lewis was preparing his wife to manage their business activities on her own.

Preparations had to be made to fill another gap Logan was leaving. Even before Jelksie Lewis's 1946 commitment to the State Hospital, her nephew had been, despite her paranoid suspicions of his intentions, the primary guardian of her interests.[92] After she went to Milledgeville he kept her few pieces of jewelry in his safe deposit box, and when the Georgia Bank opened he placed her meager funds in a savings account there. He sent the hospital periodic checks for deposit to her account and was the hospital's contact for information or permission for various medical procedures, about which he sometimes solicited Milford Hatcher's advice.[93] Now Jelksie's older sister, Martha Lewis Kaderly, would have to take over that responsibility, and Anne Bryant sent her signature cards to effect the change.[94]

In what was surely a consolation for Dorothy at this difficult time, her husband's death was preceded by his conversion to her faith. As a firm believer that "the Roman Catholic Church was the one true religion, the Mystical Body of Jesus Christ, appointed by Him to be the perennial and infallible voice of Christian truth," as well as "the only way to be joined with Christ the Savior," she would have feared for Logan's eternal salvation, had he not taken this step.[95] Jane Protz remembers once confiding to Dorothy that her own husband, Bill, had not yet converted. "Pray," her cousin replied, "and give him time."[96] For Dorothy, Logan's acceptance of "the Real Presence of the Living Jesus" not only made him "one with the Lord," but also enabled him to receive the sacraments of the Church, both of which must have given comfort to his devout wife. Vatican II would bring changes in the way Catholicism is practiced, as well as in the way other religions are perceived by the Church, dramatic changes that, according to

91 Dorothy Lewis to Billy Nalls, May 12, 1966, ibid.
92 A strained letter and several receipts attest to Logan's stewardship: Logan Lewis to Miss Jelksie Lewis, February 7, 1942, receipts dated July 6, 1942, and January 18, 1946, Miss Mary Jelks Lewis File, Lewis Archives.
93 Logan Lewis to Dr. Milford Hatcher, August 22, 1963, ibid.
94 Anne Bryant to Mrs. William F. Kaderly, May 11, 1966, ibid.
95 This pre-Vatican II expression of the Catholic faith is taken from Paul Whitcomb's *Confession of a Roman Catholic*, Loyola Book Co., Los Angeles, 1958, found with other religious materials in the Lewis kitchen. The booklet chronicles Whitcomb's conversion from Methodist minister to "a lay apostle of Christ's holy Church" through study of scripture and the primitive Christian fathers. While it's impossible to know whether Whitcomb's spiritual journey from Protestant to Catholic was ever read by Logan Lewis, given its date and the dates of the materials with which it was found, he may well have seen it. Not surprisingly, Logan's friends were less enthusiastic about his conversion, as illustrated by the following story shared by Laura Nelle O'Callaghan: unable to find a place for his car at St. Joseph's when he, his wife, and the O'Callaghans arrived for his old friend's funeral, Herbert Birdsey ended up across the street at the First Baptist Church, which shares the top of the Poplar Street hill with its Catholic counterpart. With a wry smile he said "I'm glad we're going to park in the Baptist parking lot while we say good-bye to Logan." Oral Interview #4.
96 Oral Interview, March 20, 2004.

her pastor, Dorothy accepted.[97] That far-reaching convocation had ended less than half a year earlier, however, and the full impact of its engaging, ecumenical spirit had yet to filter down to individual parishes and communicants.

Logan died on Wednesday, May 25, 1966. A front-page story in the *Telegraph*[98] announced both his death and the consequent arrangements. The Rosary would be said in the Lewises' commodious Old Club Road living room on Friday evening; afterwards a group[99] that included a devastated Pink Persons sat with Logan's remains through the night before Saturday's funeral.

On May 28th Monsignor Thomas Sheehan officiated at an 11 a.m. Mass at St. Joseph's, the soaring, dome-topped Catholic church where Dorothy had worshipped without Logan for nearly thirty years. Now he too was surrounded by the exquisite carvings and mosaics, statuary and stained glass representing the angels and saints, the Blessed Lord Jesus, and his Holy Mother Mary—"the consolations of the faith." Neither her mother, in failing health in Wisconsin, nor her brother, then living in California, nor any other member of her family, was present. Seated next to her, Pink Persons was startled when she began fumbling near his suit coat: at first thinking that she wanted to clasp his hand, he finally realized that she was simply trying to put her rosary beads in his pocket.[100]

That afternoon Logan Lewis was buried under a simple granite slab in the Riverside Cemetery plot where his parents and grandmother Mallary had previously been laid to rest. An adjacent gravesite was held in reserve for his wife.

The new Georgia Bank & Trust Company readies for its first day of business, July 1, 1960, with numerous flowers and the presentation (by an unknown representative of the American Legion) of an American Flag to Chairman of the Board Logan Lewis. Courtesy Middle Georgia Archives, Washington Memorial Library, Macon, Ga.

97 Monsignor John Cuddy, Interview #2, March 12, 2004.
98 "Death Claims Logan Lewis," *Macon Telegraph*, Thursday, May 26, 1966, p. 1A.
99 Jimmy Cassidy, Art Barry, and Chris Sheridan, all of whom were communicants at St. Joseph's, are the only others who are known with certainty.
100 Interview #3, February 12, 2004.

On opening day President Ernest Lee watches Mayor Ed Wilson make a hefty deposit to a smiling Georgia Bank teller. Courtesy Middle Georgia Archives, Washington Memorial Library, Macon, Ga.

The new bank building, going up at the corner of Mulberry and Third, February 1963. Courtesy Middle Georgia Archives, Washington Memorial Library, Macon, Ga.

The completed Georgia Bank after its summer 1963 opening. Courtesy Middle Georgia Archives, Washington Memorial Library, Macon, Ga.

Don Gordon, Logan Lewis, and Margery Pate watch as a customer makes a deposit at the grand opening of the new building at the corner of Mulberry and Third in 1963. Courtesy Middle Georgia Archives, Washington Memorial Library, Macon, Ga.

The spacious lobby in the new building, of which Logan had a clear view from his office. Courtesy Middle Georgia Archives, Washington Memorial Library, Macon, Ga.

Posing for Drinnon just before the opening of their new building, after which they "didn't have time to solicit business," are from left, Vice Presidents Don Gordon (seated) and E.B. Barker (standing), President Logan Lewis (seated), Vice President Neal Ham (standing), and Assistant Vice President Margery Pate and Assistant Cashier Jack Haugabook III (seated). Courtesy Middle Georgia Archives, Washington Memorial Library, Macon, Ga.

An aerial view of the new bank building in the heart of downtown Macon, fall 1963. Courtesy Middle Georgia Archives, Washington Memorial Library, Macon, Ga.

The eighteen members of the Georgia Bank Board of Directors, with Secretary Cubbedge Snow, at the beginning of the bank's fourth year in business. Courtesy Middle Georgia Archives, Washington Memorial Library, Macon, Ga.

This Constantine Chakov portrait of Logan Lewis, along with his World War II medals, hung in the Georgia Bank Board Room decorated by Dorothy Lewis following his death. Courtesy Middle Georgia Archives, Washington Memorial Library, Macon, Ga.

Chapter 5

Stewardship
and Legacy

The Widow Takes Charge

Following the pattern set in previous years, Georgia Bank's June 30, 1966, Report to Stockholders brought still more good news of the bank's continued progress: deposits were up to $22,366,901, an increase of 36 percent over the previous year, while earnings had increased 16 percent, from $.90 to $1.05 per share. A second cash dividend of $.25 per share had been paid June 15 and further periodic disbursements were anticipated. In addition, plans for the bank's first branch in the Pio Nono Shopping Center were well underway.

Unlike its earlier counterparts, however, this Report was not entirely upbeat: "Gratifying though they are," it said, "the figures cannot reflect all of the vital happenings of the first six months of 1966 . . . . Foremost was the untimely death of our friend and colleague, N. Logan Lewis, on May 25th. Mr. Lewis was in his sixth year as Chairman and President, and made many outstanding and unselfish contributions to our bank."[1]

When the stockholders met a few months later, the man who succeeded Logan as Chairman went to the trouble of writing out his remarks, so there is a record of what he said: "At this first annual meeting without the presence of our Founder and First Chairman of the Board of Directors we cannot fail to pause and pay tribute to Logan Lewis, his inspiring leadership, and his invaluable and continuing contributions to this institution." After acknowledging the service of vice president E. B. Barker, who had also died that year, the new chair went on to spell out the bank's next challenges: "This was a year of great personal loss; however, due in large part to these men's efforts, along with the other officers and employees, Board of Directors, stockholders, and many friends, you will see from the following reports that your bank has continued in its upward course and has completed [the] most successful financial year in its history. We are suffering from the growing pains of success and there will be many more adjustments

---

1 Report to Stockholders, June 30, 1966, 13.023, Dr. Milford Hatcher Papers, Middle Georgia Archives, Washington Memorial Library, Macon.

to be made such as we have in the past year. . . . Our problems have become those of a large bank, and our glamour and enthusiasm as a new and untried organization are not enough to sustain us. We are now expected to fulfill [*sic*] all the functions of a first-class, full-service banking institution and must plan and act accordingly."[2]

While the directors were determined to carry on, the loss of their founder had clearly left a void. How large can be inferred by the way in which the board went about filling his shoes: three men took over his duties. Milford B. Hatcher, M.D., became Chairman of the Board, Halstead T. Anderson was named to a newly created position as Vice Chair, and Don W. Gordon, who had joined the board in 1965, was chosen President. The next year popular Macon businessman J. Vernon (Buncie) Skinner was appointed yet another co-chair of the board, a move designed to generate additional good will. Even though she was its largest stockholder,[3] Dorothy Lewis was not asked to play a role in setting the course of the bank her husband had organized and led.

Not so with the Farmers National Bank of Monticello. At its first meeting after Logan's death (June 14, 1966) the board of directors elected his heir, who owned 5,295 of the 10,000 shares outstanding—admittedly much greater proportion than she held in Georgia Bank and Trust Company—to its ranks. Later she also took Logan's place as a principal of Idle Hour Development Co., and its spin off, Country Club Development Co. In the meantime, of course, her own business activities went forward, including the expansion of the Town and Country Shopping Center to which she and Logan had committed some months before his death. In June, having paid off her original $150,000 loan from Macon Federal, she began borrowing from Fulton National to finance that construction.

Her mother's deteriorating health, however, meant the new widow spent long months tending to Anne Vits's needs in Manitowoc. She asked Neal Ham, who had helped Logan to analyze the Monticello bank's potential, to take her seat on the Farmers National board, to attend its meetings, and to cast votes "as if I owned the stock,"[4] Ham remembers. He agreed, filling in for her for well

2 Seventh Annual Stockholders meeting, Typed 3"x5" cards, 1307, ibid.
3 According to Logan's Estate Tax Return he owned 4,312 shares (of the then 80,000 shares outstanding) of Georgia Bank and Trust Co. at his death. Initially, in order to increase the number of owners each investor had been limited to purchasing no more than 1250 shares @ $20, or $25,000 worth of stock, but the Chairman's great enthusiasm for the bank had led him to acquire additional shares from holders needing or wanting to sell after the bank was up and running. He got more when the capital was increased and a stock dividend declared in 1964 (each stockholder received three additional shares for every thirteen owned; fractional shares thus created were sold by lot to those interested, which certainly included Logan Lewis.) In addition to what she inherited from her husband, Dorothy owned 2100 shares in her own name, having purchased her first fifty in June, 1960, before the bank opened. She purchased fifty more in November of that year, 500 in May of 1961, 1000 in 1962, and eight more in 1965, to even out the 392 she received in 1964's 23 percent stock dividend. The Lewises' combined holdings gave Dorothy 6412 shares, which, with a 1968 split, totaled 7213 when the estate was settled. (She had purchased and given Anne Bryant 20 shares in 1967.) With more stock dividends, a split in 1969, and the purchase of another 2005 shares in 1969, she owned 18,033 by 1972, the first year for which Dr. Hatcher's files include a list of board members that enumerated the shares each "owned directly and beneficially." None came close to her total, although four directors (Halstead Anderson, Nat Hardin, Lee Newton, and Tom Standard) had fairly substantial holdings. As an interesting aside, s⌴
1965. (Information drawn from handwritten ledgers in the Lewis business records now in the Lewis Archives, and the Hatcher Papers, 13.003.)
4 Oral Interview, November 19, 2003.

over a year, all the while making sure that Billy Nalls sent her meeting minutes and financial reports. She called occasionally to ask questions or to comment on what she had read, but not with any regularity. "She learned a great deal," he remembers; being "very bright, she picked up on things very fast." Even after Anne Vits died on October 8, 1967, the numerous issues involved in settling her estate kept Dorothy physically in Manitowoc for weeks afterward.

As for managing the details of Logan's estate, she accepted the advice of her husband who had written, in the item of his will naming her executrix, that "She shall be authorized to employ [a] . . . corporate fiduciary to assist her in the performance of her duties . . . and I strongly recommend to her that she do so in order to relieve her from the burdens of that office."[5] Enlisting the help of the people upon whom he had relied, she asked Frank Jones to draw a contract between her and Fulton National Bank, which was to serve as the primary administrator, and Georgia Bank & Trust, which agreed to make its banking facilities available as a clearing house and contact point.[6]

Anne Bryant,[7] who had been Logan's trusted bookkeeper and secretary for over a decade, was the point person for both Jones, as the lawyer representing the estate, and the trust officers in Atlanta who were trying to tie up the loose ends of—or simply identify—the various ventures in which her employer had been involved. Naturally there were numerous hospital bills and insurance claims to take care of, some of which she and Dorothy had begun to address even before Logan's death. Mrs. Bryant also continued to maintain Mrs. Lewis's own ledgers, responded to day-to-day matters regarding the properties she owned, and handled her mail during her long absences from the city, working from a space provided by the Georgia Bank. Keeping tabs on the ongoing projects in combination with settling the estate must have been a juggling act, and it was doubtless in gratitude for her assistance during a difficult time that Dorothy gave her twenty shares of Georgia Bank stock.[8]

As the second year of Dorothy's bedside vigil in Wisconsin began, Logan's aunt, Martha Lewis Kaderly, also suffered a critical illness, one that necessitated Dorothy's taking over the management of Jelksie Lewis's affairs. All of the Kaderly children had by then moved away from Macon save the remaining son, Nathaniel, who was nearly incapacitated from multiple sclerosis and eventually confined to a nursing home. Anne Bryant typed a letter to Central State Hospital in Milledgeville to change the contact name on its records,

5 Item VII of Last Will and Testament of Nathaniel Logan Lewis as quoted in Agreement Between Dorothy Vits Lewis, Fulton National Bank and Georgia Bank and Trust Company, June 1966. Logan Lewis Estate File, Lewis Archives.
6 Frank Jones to Virlyn Moore, June 16, 1966, with copies to Don Gordon and Dorothy Lewis; ibid. The contract was enclosed with this letter.
7 Neal Ham described Mrs. Bryant as "the finest of people . . . so efficient," and said he'd tried to hire her for the bank after Logan's death, but that she had preferred to continue working part time for Dorothy Lewis. Oral Interview #2.
8 The gift is documented in the ledgers on the sheets summarizing the Georgia Bank stock transactions, as well as the page on which each year's stock acquisitions and disposals are recorded. Lewis Archives.

and arranged for Dorothy to become representative payee for the small Social Security award that Jelksie began receiving after Congress passed the Medicare Act; the checks went to 515 Mulberry Street for Mrs. Bryant to retrieve when she came in to work on Lewis business matters. Concerned that she did not have enough information to make final arrangements in the event that the by-now seventy-six-year-old Jelksie should die, Dorothy got in touch with Mrs. Kaderly's daughter, Martha Zebrowski, to find out how to locate the Lewis lot in the Hawkinsville Cemetery, and which relatives she should notify.[9] Dorothy was also concerned with Anne Vits's younger sister, Emma Auton, in poor health and living in a nursing home, similarly short of funds. Her mother's will established a small trust for Mrs. Auton's benefit, and Dorothy asked her cousin, Jane Protz, then still living in Manitowoc, to attend to their aunt's personal needs, an arrangement that was carefully spelled out in a letter to David Owen at First Wisconsin Trust in Milwaukee before she returned to Macon.[10]

It cannot have been a pleasant period, with multiple people and business matters to look after and worry about. Correspondence from the lawyer who handled the estates of her parents gives an inkling of the pressures she was under in those months: "On the afternoon of Wednesday, October 11, when I was at the home conferring with you, Abby and Florence relative to these matters," Pat Clark wrote Dorothy in a letter addressed to 1304 Michigan Avenue shortly after her mother's death, "you seemed to be quite anxious to have . . . distribution made at an early date because you stated you were heavily indebted and needed these funds." She had also, apparently, expressed concern as to whether she would owe taxes in Georgia, saying she needed to consult with her tax advisor.[11] The previous May she had asked First Wisconsin's David Owen whether the remainder interest she held in her mother's trusts could be used as collateral for loans, but he had replied that, given the structure of the three trusts the bank was administering, it could not.[12]

While it's impossible to know Dorothy's frame of mind, she had every reason to be "anxious." With the development of the shopping centers and other investments she had already built up an impressive net worth and Logan had left her more assets, to which her mother's death added substantially, since the trust her father had established for his wife was now to be divided between Dorothy and Abby. Yet the taxes she expected to owe were also considerable,[13] and both hers and Logan's properties were heavily mortgaged on behalf of their

9 Mrs. Edward Zebrowski to Dorothy Lewis, May 25, 1967, Mary Jelks Lewis File, Lewis Archives.
10 Two drafts of this letter dated November 2, 1967, one in pencil, the other in ink, survive. Anne M. Vits Estate File, Lewis Archives.
11 Walter J. Clark to Dorothy Lewis, October 20, 1967, ibid. As Mr. Clark points out, he was not, obviously, able to answer questions concerning Georgia tax law.
12 David G. Owen to Dorothy Lewis (in Manitowoc), May 3, 1967, ibid.
13 In a 1977 letter to her brother responding to queries about the cost-basis and value of some of the stocks they had inherited she wrote "Because I needed great sums of money to pay estate taxes, personal taxes, and debts, I sold about everything including all 3800 shares of Georgia Pacific in 1969-at the time the list of stocks and bonds sold numbered 25 so you see I was pretty well cleaned out." Dorothy Lewis to A. J. Vits, Jr., "Ab," pencil draft on yellow legal sheet dated July 13, 1977, Personal Notes File, Lewis Archives.

most recent business ventures: in addition to Logan's $230,000 loan with Fulton National for the purchase of the Farmers National Bank (secured in large part by life insurance policies which consequently generated a diminished cash benefit), Dorothy had borrowed nearly $150,000 to expand Town and Country Shopping Center. She anticipated needing cash to pay upwards of $30,000 to settle Logan's estate before the end of the year, as well as a large income tax estimate. The State Highway Department's continued recalcitrance regarding the Riverside Drive condemnation case meant that dispute might still go to trial, an expense in and of itself, but which might, more problematically, result in Dorothy's having to repay thousands of dollars from the Special Master's Award she had received in 1963. She had come of age in a financially sophisticated family with complex business interests; she herself had been involved in real estate, and buying and selling securities for nearly twenty years. But her husband had handled most of the details of her investments and helped with decision-making; the loss of his assistance, expertise, and business contacts left her to shoulder everything alone. It must have been more than a little daunting.

She did not shrink from her new responsibilities, however. Indeed, she seems to have set about preparing herself to manage them effectively. She did not hesitate to obtain issue-specific advice from professionals as needed, and one of those to whom she turned was Sidney McNair, the CPA who had handled the Georgia Bank's accounting since its inception. McNair and his wife, Katherine, had been Dorothy and Logan's contemporaries in Macon's young married set, part of the group that recreated on the Georgia coast in the thirties. Logan had used another accountant (one to whom he had made unsecured loans) before his death, and while her records do not reveal why his widow made the change, she took her business to McNair in 1967 and they developed a great rapport and mutual respect, although McNair's associates often did a good bit of her work. One who joined the firm some years later was astonished to find that she kept double entry books, an arrangement usually reserved for businesses. Yet, "Once I saw what all she was involved in," Bill Epps explained, "I understood. She was a business all by herself."[14] It became her habit to bring the ledgers in at year-end so the accountants could go over them and run a trial balance: it was important to keep on top of how all her ventures were doing. In a revealing anecdote Epps said the first time he tried to achieve that balance he found he was off by a large number. Seeking guidance from another of McNair's associates, he discovered that in what was no doubt an effort to maintain her privacy, their client had removed the page listing all her equities, making an accurate balance of assets and liabilities impossible.

---

14 William H. Epps, Jr., Oral Interview, May 31, 2005. Epps joined McNair, McLemore, and Middlebrooks in 1976, some eight years after Dorothy Lewis became a client of the firm.

Frank Jones drew a will for her in the summer of 1968. Billy Nalls had expressed concern about his future and that of the Farmers National Bank, given her majority holding, suggesting that she consider giving him an option on her stock at her death, or if she decided to sell. A note in her hand at the bottom of his letter to that effect read: "This was answered to Mr. Nalls satisfaction [by] my will made 8/68."[15]

She had used several brokers in managing her portfolio, and continued to do so, getting advice from Righton Lyndon at Robinson-Humphrey on occasion. Depending on who had what securities for sale, she also did business at Merrill-Lynch, and bought bonds at Clisby & Co. She maintained the paper herself, however, with Anne Bryant's help, rather than letting the brokerages keep track of it.

Finally, she also educated herself with written materials. A young banker to whom she became close in later years believes that in addition to consulting her husband's colleagues she did a lot of reading, and dates on books with business titles in her library bear this out:[16] a well-read 1965 copy of Paul Sarnoff's *Wall Street Wisdom, A Key to Investment Theory Through An Understanding of the Language of the Stock Market,* for example; a 1969 pamphlet published by the New York Stock Exchange, apparently sent by Righton Lyndon, entitled "Understanding Financial Statements, Seven Keys to Value;" "A. Vere Shaw's Ten Rules for Investors," which was published by Dow Jones in 1967. Not surprisingly, some of the resources she turned to reflected her conservative political views: Gary Allen's 1968 *It's Our Money, The Economics of the Coming Crisis,* published by the John Birch Society's American Opinion; Harry D. Schultz's 1969 *The International Monetary Muddle* from La Jolla Rancho Press; and Harvey Peters's *America's Coming Bankruptcy: How the Government Is Wrecking Your Dollar,* from the equally conservative Arlington House in 1973, in addition to numerous pamphlets from the conservative Constitutional Alliance in Lansing, MI. The Lewises had subscribed to the *Wall Street Journal* for many years, but the meticulously kept ledgers show that in the late sixties she also subscribed to *Forbes* and *Barron's,* as well as, for a time, the "Kiplinger" Letter.

During the first summer after Logan's death, Dorothy had taken advantage of the expertise of the Georgia Forestry Commission, asking it to develop a management plan for the old Callaway property in Monroe County. Herbert Darley sent it to her in care of Mrs. Bryant at the bank in August, along with a booklet describing the Commission's services.[17] The one hundred eleven acres had been divided into four categories and the plan stipulated what should

---

15 Billy Nalls to Dorothy Lewis, May 14, 1968, with note from Mrs. Lewis dated 8/17/68. Farmers National Bank File, Lewis Archives. A copy of the 1968 will was not available for this project.
16 Among those she consulted were Don Gordon and Pink Persons, in addition to the lawyers, accountants and bankers working on Logan's and Anne Vits' estates. Thurman Willis, Jr., Oral Interview, June 2, 2000.
17 H. W. Darley to Mrs. Logan Lewis in care of Anne Bryant, August 16, 1966, Monroe County Land File, Lewis Archives.

be done, and when, on each, along with the Commission's prices for marking timber and mist blowing for the control of undesirable hardwoods.

At the same time Bill Barnett, the young Fickling and Walker realtor charged with managing the Town and Country Shopping Center, kept her apprised of the progress of construction and leasing there during the early summer, and wrote again in August to report that the new stores were open and that things were running "smoothly." Reminding her that his firm would deduct their procurement fees from the first month's rents, he enclosed a list itemizing them. He failed, however, to add up the neat columns of numbers attached, an omission the owner corrected: the totals are written in her hand at the bottom of each column, with marks demonstrating that she had calculated the sums without the assistance of a machine.[18] Clearly, despite being out of the city and new to handling details, Dorothy Lewis intended to be on top of things. When tax assessors increased the value of her center from $91,220 to $146,510 the next year, she considered filing an appeal,[19] instructing Mrs. Bryant to consult Sanders Walker, a principal in the firm managing the center, and an old friend of Logan's who had been at their Manitowoc wedding. Walker's somewhat patronizing effort at tutelage can be read between the lines of his reply:

> I have discussed this matter thoroughly with Mr. Barnett and Mr. Marvin Newberry, who is our tax negotiator. . . . You will recall that extensive additions have been made to the shopping center since the last return. [It] now produces an income of approximately $60,000 a year. Applying a rule of thumb of 12% gross, this will result in a valuation in the neighborhood of $500,000. There are approximately 40,000 sq. ft. in the center. At a reasonable cost of $10 a sq. ft. this would amount to $400,000, and certainly, the land is worth $100,000. We, therefore, come up with a valuation of approximately $500,000 for the center. The County is supposed to return property at 40% of value, and on this basis the return could be as high as $200,000. We, therefore, feel that the assessed valuation of $146,510 is reasonable . . . and do not think anything is to be gained by appeal. By a copy of [this] letter I am inviting Mrs. Lewis to consult with me if she has any difference in opinion.[20]

Earlier Dorothy had written to Barnett about the sign at Town & Country. While her letter does not survive, his response to it is revealing:

> Thank you for your thoughtful letter . . . . It is true that I am leaving

18 Bill Barnett to Dorothy Lewis, August 12, 1966, Town and Country File, ibid.
19 Logan had filed a number of appeals over the years. Note has already been made of his 1963 objection to the rise in valuation on Callaway Drive; he had also protested in 1962. In 1964 he objected to the doubling of value on the Abel part of the Cherokee property (from $3000 to $6000), noting, "In the opinion of Mrs. Lewis, who is responsible for the taxes, this amount is excessive." (Logan Lewis to Board of Tax Assessors, March 3, 1964, City-County Tax File, Lewis Archives.) "Mr. Tom" (as Logan addressed him in some letters) replied pleasantly "We still think the value on this land should be $6,000. So we are leaving it at that value. If you care to come up and discuss it further with us, we will be glad to see you." (T. J. Cater to Logan Lewis, March 9, 1964, ibid.) Dorothy was more successful when she appealed an increase (from $190,572 to $209,760) on her home in 1980, with the board writing back that "As a result of our review, we feel that a change is in order," which lowered the valuation to $200,105. (J. A. Leggett, Dan Bullard Jr., and John S. Miller to Property Owner, June, 1980, ibid.)
20 Sanders Walker to Anne Bryant, March 14, 1967, Town and Country File, ibid.

Fickling & Walker . . . to become Director of Real Estate for Rose's
Stores, Inc. . . in North Carolina. In anticipation of my departure . . .
I had asked Clark Ballard, who is one of my very capable assistants, to
correspond with you concerning the sign for your shopping center. I
am fully familiar with this situation, but wanted him to take over the
correspondence with you. In addition to Mr. Ballard, I'm sure you
remember Donald Barkley, who is also in my department. These are
two capable young men who, I'm sure, will continue to give you good
service in the management of Town & Country. In addition to them I'm
sure you know that all of the personnel at Fickling & Walker, including
the principals, are available to you at any time. [21]

Dorothy's notation on the back of Barnett's letter is also revealing: "To
this I replied that I would delay any action until I found out who was going to
handle my account—I have not had a reply—He sent a copy of the proposed
sign for $1400.00—I thought it best to wait until I get there in May—Perhaps the
old one could be repaired." And in an aside to Mrs. Bryant: "Put this in the files
please. DVL" Her angst had been noted by the "principals" in Macon, however;
Walker wrote back shortly thereafter:

The correspondence concerning Town & Country has been referred to
me, and I can naturally understand your concern. Please let me assure
you that your center will be given the very best service and attention.
Since all of the center is rented with the exception of the small
corner store . . . the matter now becomes one more of maintenance,
supervision and upgrading rather than new leases. I have instructed
Clark Ballard to give this center his personal attention and to report
every matter of any concern directly to me . . . I am told that we have
several prospects for the vacant space. The center looks good and
healthy and the tenants are apparently happy. . . Referring to the sign, I
rode over myself yesterday to make a personal inspection of the sign on
the premises; and I frankly, believe that a new sign is in order. We will,
of course, await your instructions . . . . Our entire organization is, of
course, at your disposal, but I would consider it a pleasure to personally
serve you in any way that I can. I assure you that this account will not
be neglected.[22]

While the conclusion of the sign saga is not in the file, it is no wonder
that Dorothy gave up the hassle of owning a shopping center the next year when
she sold Town and Country to A. Emmett Barnes III for, in keeping with Sanders
Walker's analysis of its value, $525,000. Brokered by Pink Persons for Murphey,
Taylor and Ellis, the deal called for her to take a fifteen-year note with a seven-
year balloon, on eighty-five per cent of the price, from the buyer.[23] Dorothy was

21 Bill Barnett to Dorothy Lewis, February 22, 1967, ibid.
22 Sanders Walker to Dorothy Lewis (at 1304 Michigan Avenue), March 7, 1967, ibid.
23 Sales Contract, dated September 30, 1968, ibid. Baxter Evans of Batchelor Realty Company had inquired as to whether Mrs. Lewis
was interested in selling either Town & Country or the Pio Nono lot adjacent to Cherokee Shopping Center a year earlier, and been
declined. Baxter Evans to Dorothy Lewis, February 3, 1967 and Anne Bryant to Baxter Evans, February 13, 1967, ibid.

well acquainted with Barnes, having begun acquiring stock in his Security Life Insurance Co. in the late fifties, and was doubtless comfortable doing business with him. By the time that note would come due she would be hitting her stride as a businesswoman; in late 1960s she was still feeling her way. Yet her attention to details is revealed in some work papers found in the file: attached to Pink's handwritten analysis of the sale price, down payment, mortgage payments and interest, etc., was another sheet on which the same information had been typed on notebook paper in a font that appears to match that of a machine on which Dorothy often drafted notes. But whereas the handwritten sheet, while noting that the $24,000 commission was to be paid over three years with the first installment not due until October 1, 1969, did not calculate the 7 1/2 percent interest, it was calculated on the typed sheet, written out in Dorothy's hand and then totaled, with the observation that it "really amounts to $29,284" rather than $24,000.[24]

A letter from Frank Jones dated January 31, 1967, indicates that she had written him to express concern about the still unsettled Riverside Drive condemnation case. She had apparently enclosed a clipping regarding what must have seemed a similar suit, Calhoun v. State Highway Department of Georgia. "That decision has no effect on your case," the attorney wrote back. He also summarized his unsuccessful efforts at working out a settlement over the previous year, after having obtained, in preparation for going to trial again, yet another valuation (this time for $85,000) from an Atlanta appraiser completely unacquainted with either of the Lewises. Jones then went on to reassure his client that the "case is in no way related to the administration of Logan's estate since the property was owned by you individually. Consequently, the continuance of this litigation will not delay the closing of the estate or have any other adverse effect." In addition, because payment of the Special Master's $68,750 award had been made when the issue was initially decided in the fall of 1963—and the subsequent jury award was only $52,500—"You have everything to gain and nothing to lose . . . by allowing [it] to continue in a dormant condition."[25]

When Dorothy returned to Macon briefly later in the spring she apparently gathered and analyzed some data herself to assess her prospects in that case: a pencil-written list in her hand records not only the multiple valuations on her Riverside Drive property (Julian Reynolds's, Pink Persons's, the first Highway Department offer, the Masters' Award, and finally, what the jury brought back), but the appraisals and subsequent jury awards for two other,

24 Dated 9/5/68 in Dorothy's hand, the two sheets were in a file titled "1968" now in the Lewis Archives. Persons' handwritten sheet contains a note from Anne Bryant that "Mr. Barnes will pay 1/2 Intangible Tax."
25 The Atlanta appraiser was Stewart Wight. Frank Jones to Dorothy Lewis in Manitowoc, January 31, 1967, State Highway Department File, ibid.

similarly situated, properties; in both of the other instances jury awards came in substantially lower than the appraisals. "Info obtained from MTE May 21 67" she wrote at the bottom of the page.[26] With Jones' conclusions thus verified, it was over a year later that the case (which had been on the calendar for the week Anne Vits died, and hence continued), was finally settled for $61,000. Dorothy had to repay $7,750, but, as the lawyer reminded her, she had had the use of the money for nearly five years.

The most frustrating experience, business wise, in the months following her mother's death, was no doubt the action of the IRS, which, after reporting in a December 13 letter that it had accepted Logan's estate return as filed, wrote back January 31 to say that the "closing letter" had been issued in error; an audit was scheduled. Fulton National Vice President Virlyn Moore's reply noted that he was "of course amazed at the proposed action . . . in revoking an Estate Tax Closing Letter," although the tone of his missive is one of righteous indignation rather than amazement. He asked Frank Jones to look into grounds for protesting the revocation; unfortunately, came the response, while Jones fully agreed with the "spirit" of Moore's reply and "it is certainly possible that your request for a reconsideration . . . will be granted," he had "reluctantly concluded" that because there had been no mutual closing agreement within the meaning of the IRS Code, there was no legal basis for forcing the agency to adhere to what it termed an "inadvertent" notification. The spiral bound copy of the original estate return contains numerous notations in Dorothy's hand, specifying which valuations had been challenged, as well as her calculations as to their potential effect. A conference with the agent conducting the audit was set for May 6, 1968, and in all likelihood Dorothy was present, since the file also contains a highly detailed list of each item for which the value was disallowed (primarily the stocks in the closely held corporations), and the rationale for the IRS's action.[27] As a result of the audit the estate tax increased from $24,500 to $50,550. The estate was finally settled in late 1968—just a few months after the 1963 condemnation case also came to a close.

If that winter had its difficulties, there were also bright spots. Distribution of Mirro stock from her parents' estates had begun in November and she received another large parcel in February, which meant her dividend income was now substantial. She and Logan had been in the habit of visiting Palm Beach in February, often with Bib and Halstead Anderson, and in 1968 she spent a few days at the Brazilian Court Hotel. Once back in Macon she picked up her social connections, eating frequent Idle Hour suppers with Pink and Eden Persons. She began attending Idle Hour Development Company directors

26 Ibid.
27 These two pages of hand-printed notes are dated 5/7/68. Logan Lewis Estate File, ibid.

meetings and took an interest in that company's affairs. While no longer actively engaged in politics, she continued to make contributions to the Republican Party and to various candidates, as well as to subscribe to and purchase conservative publications. She commissioned Constantin Chatov, the renowned Russian émigré artist who, with his brother Roman, was then working in Atlanta, to do a portrait of Logan. When it was finished she asked local photographer, Walter Pharr, to make a copy of it.

When it came time for the Farmers National Bank's 1968 stockholders meeting, Neal Ham encouraged his mentor's widow to go with him, only half expecting her to agree, or to enjoy it if she did. On the way home, however, he was surprised to be informed that it would no longer be necessary for him to fill in for her on the FNB board; she had asked Billy Nalls or the board chair to substitute her name for his, and the bank quickly became an significant part of her life.

Dorothy Lewis was warmly welcomed and granted a measure of respect in the smaller community that she might not have felt in Macon, a respect that recognized not only her majority ownership but also her increasing business sophistication. "They treated her like a lady," Thurman Willis has said, but a lady whose opinion mattered.[28] She became the board's most active member, attending everything to which she was invited and, in the process, forming close friendships with the other board members, relationships she recognized by sending each of them a box of pecans at Christmas.[29]

Some of her efforts on the bank's behalf can be traced through correspondence. She asked Jack Haugabook, who had once worked at Georgia Bank but was now selling life insurance, to prepare a proposal for Billy Nalls, directing him to submit his plan to D. N. Harvey who was chairing the committee to study how to insure the bank's president.[30] She also, in that most important function of a director, solicited business for the bank: in August of her first year, after having met earlier that month with representatives of Georgia-Pacific Corporation and Jasper County and Monticello officials, she wrote to the President of the company:

> Now that your operation there seems definite with expected expansion, I write to offer . . . the facilities of the Farmers National Bank as well as the time and ability of the President, Mr. Billy Nalls, and his staff. The liberty I take in asking this consideration is due to my fruitful association with Georgia-Pacific which came about through the efforts of an old family friend, Mr. Rawson G. Lizars of Bestwall Gypsum. As a

28 Oral Interview, June 7, 2000.
29 Noted in ledgers, Financial Records, Lewis Archives.
30 John R. Haugabook III to Mrs. N. Logan Lewis, May 23, 1968, with note as to her response in Dorothy's hand dated June 11, 1968, Farmers National Bank File, ibid.

stockholder I send my appreciation to you for the pleasure afforded me from your handsome profits and remarkable progress. May I urge you to allow the Farmers National Bank . . . which I inherited from my late husband, to be of service . . . in this new venture. I join with the entire community not only to "welcome you back home" but to Monticello in particular.

She also added a post script to her letter: "Mr. K. A. McCaskill of Georgia -Pacific had a personal connection with the Georgia Bank & Trust Company, Macon, of which my late husband was Chairman and President. Perhaps you might want to ask him about us."[31] What the gentleman learned of Farmers National Bank must have suited him. Happily, the company chose to bank with FNB, and became its biggest customer over the next decade.[32]

Dorothy Lewis took an intense interest in not only FNB, but in accord with her husband's philosophy regarding the role of banks in their community, the city of Monticello and Jasper County. Logan had believed that its principals should play leadership roles to reinforce a bank's place in the community, and she did. She supported the new Jasper County Library, donated equipment to the Jasper County Fire Department, and made the lead gift to a new recreation complex, helping to provide additional fields on which Thurman Willis's two sons would play ball. Perhaps remembering Logan's passion for golf and Idle Hour Club, she also contributed to improvements at the Hunter Pope Country Club's golf course. Willis, who joined the bank right after his 1971 graduation from college and soon became a protégé of Mrs. Lewis, notes that "she cared about the bank serving the community more than its profits." Yet the two went hand-in-hand. When she learned that the Miller Brewing Company was looking for a site in Georgia, she wrote Willis to suggest he see whether there might be one in Jasper County.[33]

Willis found the majority stockholder supportive without being overbearing. "She understood banking," and was always available if needed, but, "she never overly interfered," Willis recalled, allowing the board and officers "to run and control the bank locally." On the other hand "She made motions that the local board might be fearful of making." Pressed for an example Willis described an instance in the early seventies when the board was about to forego issuing a bonus to employees after an exceptional year, out of a conservative concern as to where the bank might find itself the year after that. "But Mrs. Lewis believed in rewarding good performance," Willis said, so she convinced the directors to respond to this year and let next year be influenced by that

31 Dorothy V. Lewis to Robert B. Pamplin, President, Georgia-Pacific Corporation, August 28, 1968, carbon copy, ibid. The typeface of this letter matches that on the typewriter used by Anne Bryant. It is not surprising that Mrs. Lewis should express "pleasure" over the company's "handsome profits;" the $6232 in annual dividends she received on that stock constituted a substantial percentage of her personal income in the mid 1960s.
32 Thurman L. Willis, Jr., Oral Interview, April 25, 2005.
33 Thurman L. Willis, Jr., to Dorothy Lewis, October 11, 1977, Farmers National Bank File, Lewis Archives.

action. In spite of her inclination to stay in the background, since "everybody knew she owned 51 percent," it did not take much discussion for her perspective to prevail. Unlike her husband, she was not directly involved in credit decisions, but like him she encouraged the bank to be less restrained—albeit prudent—in making loans. Having shared a "warm, mutual respect" with Willis's father, as well as his future father-in-law and grandfather-in-law, all of whom were members of the FNB board, she was extremely supportive of young Willis, and was instrumental in his being named to the board in 1973, two years after he had joined the bank's staff. His respect for the fact that she was "a very private person," and the natural distance created by the difference in their ages made Dorothy Lewis less wary of Willis than she sometimes seemed of other associates. She was also fond of his wife, Angie Lee, and enjoyed keeping up with his sons. Over the years the relationship grew closer: Mrs. Lewis invited the Willises to dinner at Idle Hour followed by dessert and a tour of the classic cars at 455 Old Club Road; she also accepted their invitation to dinner in their home in Monticello. They sent her pecan clusters at Christmas, exchanged cards with her, and took their boys by to visit.

Not long after she had come on the FNB board, the bank's former Vice President, Herschel Allen, approached Dorothy about buying his stock; he still had two hundred shares which he wanted to liquidate in order to assist his son, a Presbyterian minister who was going back to school so as to better support his family.[34] Allen offered to take $30 per share, but whether because of the improved situation of the bank or the poignancy of his request, Dorothy instead bought half of his holdings for $40, encouraging him to hang on to the remainder and stay on the board.

The circumstances were different when she bought additional shares a few years later.[35] Pink Persons recalls her asking if he would be interested in selling the stock he had bought from Logan in 1965; thinking that there was no reason for him to own a piece of a Monticello bank, Pink said yes. The next thing he knew FNB President Billy Nalls called to ask where he wanted the check sent. "What check?" Pink remembers replying. "Well, Mrs. Lewis said she was buying you out for 'X' dollars," Nalls answered. Pink was taken aback at the price. "I said, 'She ain't mentioned 'X' dollars to me and I'm not at all interested in selling it for what she's interested in paying.'" The bank president

34 Herschel Allen to Dorothy Lewis, August 21, 1968, ibid. "Please let me know fairly soon," he wrote; "I will be 71 years old August 25, 1968, and my previous health history tells me that I cannot expect many more years here.... There will be no need for resignation [from the bank's board of directors] as the lack of ownership will immediately disqualify me . . . which I feel physically and mentally unable to carry out. I would not accept honorary directorship. I would not feel right to accept pay during incapacity." Calculations in pencil on the bottom of the letter indicate that Dorothy may have called him to relay her decision-"4000.00" is followed by "Happy Birthday." Apparently he was then able to remain on the board. He sent the stock certificate in an August 24 letter thanking her for the purchase and birthday wishes, adding "The fact that I will own some less stock in the bank here will not cause me to lessen my efforts in the bank's interest and welfare." Stock Information File, ibid.
35 According to her ledgers Dorothy bought Pink's shares in January of 1972—for more than she had paid Herschel Allen.

asked what Pink would accept, and a check for that amount was soon in his hands. "For somebody that never had any business experience, she was tough as nails," Persons exclaims. "Man, she was tough." Furthermore, "she was very close with a dollar."[36]

He had reason to know. In 1972 Dorothy had consulted him as to what she should do with the lots she still owned in the first block of Callaway Drive. Pink suggested that she build some apartments, and proceeded to help her do so by obtaining drawings, overseeing the construction, arranging the financing through Georgia Bank, and finally, renting the units, with Murphey, Taylor and Ellis set to manage the rentals. "Now Dorothy, you don't owe me anything," he told her in reporting the results of his efforts, "I'm not charging you a nickel." "Well," she replied, "I wouldn't have thought you would." Clearly, his widow was not averse to capitalizing on Logan Lewis' relationships as she developed her resources. In the process, as Persons somewhat grudgingly acknowledges, "She became an astute businesswoman."[37]

A businesswoman who understood that maximizing profits was a matter of keeping expenses down. Anne Bryant's ledgers show how very little Dorothy Lewis spent on her properties, as illustrated by her resistance to replacing the Town and Country Shopping Center sign. Bill McCowen, a loyal neighbor who managed multiple rentals for the Lewises for over forty years and found her careful in that regard, was also impressed that while he saw examples of her kindness, she could not be manipulated. In one instance a tenant in financial straits was allowed to substitute upkeep and maintenance for rent; in another a renter who complained about an unkempt parking lot was left agape. Dorothy had agreed to stop by to the latter's apartment to see for herself the source of the complaint, but insisted on bringing her property manager (McCowen) along. Gesturing toward the asphalt outside her unit the woman demanded peremptorily: "What would you do if you had a pile of leaves like that at your front door?" With only a hint of a smile the landlady replied forthrightly: "Well, I'd sweep them up!"

Sidney McNair also had reason to appreciate Dorothy's penchant for controlling expenditures. Her 1969 tax return had been selected for a detailed audit under the Taxpayer Compliance Measurement Program. The tedious process went well; amazingly, the sole resulting change was a $150 deduction from income for unclaimed depreciation on the 441 Old Club Road rental property, a change in the taxpayer's favor. Referencing that audit is an unusually friendly personal letter from the Macon revenue agent found in Mrs. Lewis' files:

I should like to commend you for maintaining good records and extend

---

36 Oral Interviews #2 and #4; Mr. Persons shared this story twice and while the wording varied slightly in each rendering the spirit and the gist of it were the same.
37 Interview #2.

my appreciation for the cooperation you and your accountant afforded me during the recent examination of your 1969 return. . . Various transactions on your records and return involved several technical sections of the Federal Income Tax Laws, and again, your accountant, books and records were of utmost assistance.

The most interesting parts of the letter, though, are the comments on the envelope in which it was enclosed: "Mrs. Bryant-Read this!" is written in red pencil in Dorothy's hand on one side. On the other is an inked scribble. "Sidney probably asked him to write this after I refused to pay him-"[38]

McNair must not have felt unduly short-changed, for he continued to help Dorothy manage her affairs. In 1974 she enlisted the assistance of his office in selling a lot in Ft. Lauderdale that Tero and Annie had purchased from H. C. Jelks[39] in 1926 during the Florida land boom. Having seen the property taxes go up twice since Logan's death she used her banking connections[40] to get a recommendation on the real estate firm she planned to use, and finding it positive, shortly obtained a good price on the lot. McNair's office handled the correspondence with both the realtor and the attorney in Ft. Lauderdale, as well as the duplication and notarizing of documents-but no detail went unnoticed by his client. In a letter to the attorney McNair wrote:

> You . . . referred to the possibility of inheritance taxes that might be due the State of Florida. While it is doubtful that this tax would be of a material amount, Mrs. Lewis is a good businesswoman and feels that this amount should be determined before the sale is closed. I would appreciate your giving me the amount of tax involved . . . ."[41]

The attorney's reply is not in the file but judging from a list of selling expenses on the closing statement, the tax was indeed negligible—$5.00. The property sold, incidentally, for more than four times the appraisal Frank Jones had obtained in 1966, which explains why the taxes had been going up.

By 1973 Dorothy Lewis's interest in banking had become so strong that in June she paid her own way to the Cloister at Sea Island to attend the annual conference of the group Logan had encouraged Neal Ham to help organize, the Georgia Independent Bankers Association. Involvement with the bank had actually become her primary social outlet. She had spent many holidays with the Persons family and, as Pink Persons recalls, seemed to have had a wonderful time accompanying them to young Pink's 1971 graduation from the Citadel in

38 Alton J. Huser, Internal Revenue Agent, to Mrs. Dorothy W. *[sic]* Lewis, February 11, 1972, Lewis Archives.
39 A number of the Jelkses had participated in Florida land purchases during the twenties, some in Jacksonville, some in Pompano, others in the midstate. Howard. C., who was a cousin of Johnnie Logan's first husband (Logan's father) Nat Lewis, and his wife, Beulah, developed the Placido Place subdivision in Ft. Lauderdale.
40 Lucius H. Weeks, President, First National Bank, to Mrs. Logan Lewis, May 24, 1974, Placido Place File, Lewis Foundation Archives. In all likelihood she was following Logan's lead: a 1965 memorandum in the same file which encloses a photograph of the lot and subdivision plat, plus a First National Bank map of the city so that "Mr. Gordon can get an idea of where it is in relation to downtown Ft. Lauderdale," indicates that Logan had used the First National Bank to obtain information earlier.
41 Sidney McNair to John Bielejeski, Jr., October 3, 1974, ibid.

Charleston, a city she and Logan had visited on their honeymoon and enjoyed during his World War II service. But not long after that she told Pink not to invite her to anything again. "I've become too dependent on you and Eden," he remembers her saying. "I'm not going to come anymore." And she didn't. The decrease in the size of her bills from Idle Hour around this time indicates that she was no longer eating there with any regularity. Laura Nelle O'Callaghan confirms the retreat: having frequently joined a group for dinner when Polly McGurk, a dear friend of Logan's to whom the Lewises had remained close, came back to Macon, she suddenly declined to participate. Thinking that going out at night might be the problem, Laura Nelle suggested lunch instead. Dorothy was not persuaded; if she did this, she told Laura Nelle, she'd have to do others, which she did not want to do. Betty Curtis believes, on the other hand, that if she cut herself off, it was not much more than before, and she did not stop making occasional impromptu suggestions: "I've never had a pizza. Would you go with me to have a pizza?" She never failed to acknowledge an invitation, and to remember the children of friends with gifts as they married, but her response was to politely decline.

It was still Dorothy's habit to attend the 6:00 a.m. mass at St. Joseph's; on Sundays she always came in the side door and sat alone in the second row from the back.[42] According to the short history of St. Joseph's written by Sr. Mary Sheridan, those were years of some moment as the changes in church discipline generated by Vatican II, changes which affected all Catholics, both clerical and lay, were felt on the local level. "Fish on Fridays," for example, long recognized as a sign of Catholic identity, began to disappear after the first Sunday of Advent 1966, services were scheduled so that Sunday and Holy Day Of Obligation Masses could be celebrated on the previous evening, and lay ministers of Communion were gradually introduced. There were personnel changes too. When Sr. Fidelis Barragan came to Macon as principal of Mt. De Sales in 1970, Chris and Eleanor Sheridan made sure that she was introduced to Dorothy Lewis one Sunday after church. The two women felt a rapport and they gradually became friends, which furthered Dorothy's interest in the school and its students. Fr. John Cuddy became pastor in 1974.

Sports car racing was no longer part of her life, but she kept most of the cars Logan had collected, and her continuing interest in automobiles is evidenced by the numerous magazines and catalogs on the subject that remained in her living room, as well as the thick file she kept on Road America, the company that ran the track at Elkhart Lake. The reply to a 1972 inquiry about a particular "sedanca de ville" she had apparently sent to Jack Barclay, a Rolls Royce retailer in Berkeley Square, London, was also in her desk after her

42 Sr. Fidelis Barragan, Oral Interview, April 14, 2004.

death.[43] With the condemnation case closed, the shopping center sold, and her apartments up and running, her financial stressors had eased; that year she spent $23,000 to buy 595 shares of Mirro. In 1973 Mirro stock split, giving her a total of 44,000 shares. A 3226-acre piece of Texas land in which her father and uncles had invested before George Vits's death was also sold in 1973, returning $45,900 on a cost basis of $1868.

In 1968, Georgia Bank had decided to increase its capital. It was an opportunity not to be passed up: Dorothy spent $20,062.50 to buy 401 5/16 more shares. She purchased another 1000 in November of 1969, at $32.5 per share, and 1005 more in December (a year in which she had sold a great deal of other stock in order to pay her taxes.) With a stock dividend and another split, she owned a total of 18,033 shares by 1971,[44] considerably more than anyone then serving on the board of directors.[45] The increasing value of this investment was certified in a 3/7/1973 memo from vice president George Hall to Board Chairman Hatcher:

> Assume that a person purchased 100 shares of Georgia Bank stock when it was issued in July 1960, at $20 per share. This 100 shares today would have a market value of $11,520. For each share purchased, the stockholder would now own 2.88 shares of Georgia Bank stock, or each share purchased would now have a market value of $115.20 (2.88 shares times $40). In addition, the stockholder has received cash (cash dividends plus sale of fractional shares) of $9.51 per share during the twelve years covered.[46]

Certainly her holdings in the Georgia Bank had both financial and emotional significance for Dorothy Lewis, and she followed the bank's situation with great interest. It is not known how she came at last to sit on its board, though in hindsight it seems inevitable. Neal Ham speculates that she may have approached Don Gordon or Dr. Hatcher and expressed an interest in serving; she certainly had acquired valuable experience in Monticello and taking such an initiative does not seem out of character given the way in which she reinserted herself into the FNB seat after nearly two years of relying on Ham to fill it. George Hall suggests, on the other hand, that the bank had decided it needed a female member and that she was an obvious choice;[47] indeed there were no women on any Macon bank board at that time, though it was well over a decade before the men that were became conscious of the need for such. Or perhaps, as Thurman Willis postulates, in one of her many consultations with Don Gordon he said "Dorothy, you own more stock than anybody, why don't you come

43 Lewis Archives.
44 Figure taken from draft of Personal Financial Statement prepared by Anne Bryant for Farmers National Bank, dated January 1, 1972.
45 The largest stockholder on the board at that time owned 9,162 shares; three others owned 8,000 or slightly more. From the Proxy Statement, Annual Meeting of Shareholders to be held January 25, 1972. Hatcher Papers, 13.003.
46 Ibid.
47 Oral Interview, May 31, 2000.

on the board?" and she acceded to his invitation. In any event, Dr. Hatcher's handwritten note adding her name to the Advertising Committee on his 1975 committee list,[48] as well as the December board minutes that year, indicate that she joined the board in June of 1975. Anne Bryant recorded the first Directors' Fees for the Georgia Bank on the Lewis ledgers in August of that year.[49]

Interestingly, Milton Heard III had been the only new director named at the March 20 stockholders meeting.[50] A few days afterwards, J. Freeman Hart submitted his resignation "Due to a varied and complex work schedule."[51] The first choice for replacing him, however, appears to have been Cubbedge Snow, who had declined to serve on the board while acting as Georgia Bank's attorney, citing a conflict of interest; the conflict disappeared when he relinquished his legal responsibilities that year, so it was a natural selection. It was after he decided that his age made him ineligible,[52] apparently, that the seat went to the Bank's largest, if female, stockholder. The 1976 committee list shows her as chair of Advertising and a member of the Trust Committee. The 1977 stockholders meeting brochure includes "Mrs. Dorothy V. Lewis"[53] on the list of board members; "Personal Investments" is the explanatory note after her name, in the place where other members' business affiliations are described.

Pink Persons's primary memory of Dorothy Lewis's role on the Georgia Bank board was of her chairmanship of the Advertising Committee: "She did a good job with it," he said.[54] The minutes in Dr. Hatcher's file show that she made frequent reports, keeping the board apprised of both internal and external promotions, and encouraging their participation as appropriate. One detailed announcement in 1979 involved a program that may well have had particular resonance. She brought its coordinator, Mrs. Charles Hollis, to the meeting with her to describe "SOS"—Special Organizational Services—a personal advisory service offered free of charge through the business department to customers and non-customers alike "who have gone through some sort of lifestyle change."[55] Designed to assist clients in record keeping, document gathering, and financial planning, it "affords our Company a competitive edge that no other financial institution has in the Macon community," according to that year's Annual Report, since Georgia Bank held the first SOS franchise in the state of Georgia.[56] Initial plans called for letters to be sent to widows and widowers offering the service, and for staff to make talks at various organizations and civic groups rather than using media to get the message out. A few months later the committee chairman was pleased to report how well the program had been received. Outside her

48 Hatcher Papers, 13.019
49 Lewis Archives.
50 Notice of 1975 Annual Meeting, Hatcher Papers, 13.005.
51 J. Freeman Hart to Milford B. Hatcher, March 25, 1975, ibid.
52 Cubbedge Snow to Milford B. Hatcher, May 20, 1075, ibid.
53 Ibid., 13.025.
54 Interview # 1.
55 Minutes, Board of Directors, October 9, 1979, ibid, 13.011.
56 1979 Annual Report, ibid., 12.001.

chairmanship, Dorothy was often the board member who opened meetings with a prayer; Thurman Willis found hers unusually meaningful. In another role "Director Lewis moved that director fees for monthly meetings be increased to $100."[57] In addition to giving her a leadership position on the board, Dorothy's work on Advertising brought her into close contact with a number of the bank's employees, with whom she developed cordial relationships. The women, in particular, enjoyed exchanging pleasantries, admiring her "well put together" outfits, and sharing limited details of their own lives. Notes accompanying paperwork on her accounts reflect the warmth and friendliness of these contacts.

In remarks prepared for the annual stockholders' meeting in 1976, the year after Dorothy joined the board, Dr. Hatcher expressed hope that the bank's physical expansion was over for awhile.[58] Noting that only five of the board's original directors remained in service, he heaped praise on retiring secretary Cubbedge Snow Sr., who, while never having been an official member of the board, was henceforth listed with it as "Secretary Emeritus." Then, prophetically, he reminded his audience that the "holding company law" had been passed by the Georgia legislature and would take effect on July 1.[59] He would, he said, "be glad to get anyone's reaction who sees fit to send it to me. We have not had any offers, nor have we made any offers, but your board is studying it."

As to the bank's positioning for such offers, its continued growth had been documented in a March 1976 study assembled by Elaine Henderson:[60] assets were nearly $90 million, with deposits at 83.4 percent of that figure. The loan to deposit ratio was 63.1 percent and profits had been well over half a million dollars throughout the seventies. When Dr. Hatcher addressed his annual year-end letter to employees in 1978 he was pleased to congratulate them for "our most profitable year," as he reported that the profit-sharing contribution approved by the Directors that month was "more than twice last year's $71,281." Characteristically, he added, "May I count on each of you to make 1979 even more outstanding?"[61] A study reported earlier that year had pegged Georgia Bank's share of the Macon banking market at twenty-one per cent.[62]

Farmers National Bank was also doing well; from assets of $2,673,000 with deposits of $2,430.500 at the end of 1965, it had grown to $7,836,189 in assets and $6,761,527 in deposits by 1975, an increase of nearly two hundred percent.[63]

57 Minutes, Board of Directors, Georgia Bank, April 10, 1979, ibid., 13.009.
58 Ibid., 13.027. Ms. Henderson in now Elaine Demarest.
59 Banks could only hold one charter; holding companies, on the other hand, were permitted to hold multiple charters.
60 Ibid., 13.005.
61 Milford B. Hatcher to Officers and Employees of Georgia Bank and Trust Company, December 27, 1978, ibid., 13.006. This was a pleasant reversal since he had told the stockholders a few years earlier that "1974 was not one of our best years. Earnings declined from $2.23 per share to $1.81 per share, a decline of $.44. . . . This was a result of . . . the high cost of funds and the rapid increase of operating expenses (opening two branches and adding on to the main office and consequent personnel increases)." ibid., 13.027. That was one of the very few, if not the only time in which profits per share had failed to increase from one year to the next, but obviously, those infrastructure investments had paid off by 1978.
62 Board of Directors Minutes, April 11, 1978, ibid., 13.010.
63 Report of Condition as of 9/30/75, Thurman Willis, Jr. Cashier, *Monticello News*, October 23, 1975 p. 6, from FNB file, Lewis Archives.

Her meticulously kept ledgers show that as the seventies wore on Dorothy was becoming more active in business in other ways; after several years in which stock entries had primarily involved recording inheritances from her husband and parents, splits and dividends, it is apparent that she began to buy and sell more actively. As before, blue chip companies like IBM, Phillip Morris, Union Pacific, Mobile, and DuPont, predominated, but she also invested in the Georgia-based Scientific Atlanta. Her taste in bonds ran to tax-free municipals—and no wonder. As Charles Grinstead, an accountant then practicing with Sidney McNair pointed out, despite their lower return, when the cost of paying taxes on the higher interest (she was in the seventy percent bracket) was factored in, the net on municipals was significantly more.[64] Letters in her files also document her efforts to ascertain the status of some of the firms for which she still had securities in hand but with which she had apparently lost contact.[65] In addition to the securities, she still owned downtown commercial property, the apartments on Callaway, the timberland in Monroe County, and the "little brown house" on Old Club Road, as well as an assortment of residential lots which had resulted from the division, amongst its principals, of properties remaining unsold when the Idle Hour Development Company was dissolved in 1978. By far the largest portion of her nearly three million dollar net worth, however, was in Mirro[66], Georgia Bank, and Farmers National Bank stock.[67]

Dorothy's confidence in business matters is evident in drafts of two letters to her brother, dated November 1976 and July 1977. Abby had retired from Mirro in 1970 after which he and Flo spent increasing amounts of time in the old Vits home at 1304 Michigan Avenue in Manitowoc and at the family's summer place at Elkhart Lake, both of which were jointly owned by the siblings. Apparently uncomfortable with the joint ownership, Dorothy had offered to buy Abby out or to sell her share to him, to no avail. In October of 1976 he sent a long list of repairs he'd undertaken at Elkhart Lake, as well as those he thought were still needed, by way of requesting her participation in the expense. "I will not comment on the contents of the letter," his sister replied, "as it only emphasises [sic] what I have told you on other occasions, that you don't know

64 Charles Grinstead to Dorothy Lewis, July 25, 1978, Re: Non-Taxable Investments and Yields, Stock Information File, Lewis Archives. Bill Epps, who began assisting Sidney McNair with the Lewis account in 1976 noted that while Mrs. Lewis, like anyone else, did not like to pay taxes, she never engaged in questionable practices to avoid them. Once she was even almost cheerful while writing a large check to the IRS, saying something on the order of "If you make it, you've got to pay it!" Oral Interview, May 31, 2005.
65 For example, State of Colorado Secretary of State to Mrs. Logan Lewis, January 17, 1969, re U. S. Mining and Milling Company, and State of Delaware to Mrs. Logan Lewis, February 3, 1978, re Sunac Petroleum Corporation; in these two cases the certificates proved worthless. Old Stock Certificates File, Lewis Archives.
66 The Aluminum Goods Manufacturing Company changed its name to the Mirro Company in 1957, capitalizing on the popularity of its Mirro line of cookware, especially the 1945 pressure pan known as the "Mirromatic." In 1983 Mirro was acquired by the Newell Company, which in 1985 also bought its longtime Manitowoc competitor, the Aluminum Specialty Company, as well as the WearEver Company in 1989. Dorothy had held a number of shares in her own name before inheriting 1800 shares from her mother in 1967 and receiving another 17,000 from her father's estate when the trust benefiting her mother was dissolved in 1971.
67 Financial papers, Lewis Archives.

anything about selling real estate." Instead of reimbursing his costs she enclosed an agreement drawn by her lawyer showing that she had legally given him her half interest in the cottage; she then admonished him to "Keep this paper in your files" in order to verify his sole ownership in the event of a sale. The second letter was in response to a telephoned request for the cost of stocks "in father's estate." Dorothy was clearly irritated:

> To begin with, you have forgotten that father did not own any Pepsi or Georgia Pacific. Both were owned by mother. At the time of her death we inherited Pepsi, the cost of which is on the schedule I sent you several weeks ago when you requested the cost of Mirro that we also inherited from mother. Georgia Pacific we got through spin off of Bestwall from Certain-teed. Mother gave us Bestwall stock in '58. You have all that info as I find a letter in the files from you dated February 13, 1961 explaining the cost of Bestwall. Then I find another memo of Mrs. Bryant's dated March '75 attached to a batch of papers concerning Certain-teed and Bestwall which she had copied and sent to you at your request. So you have duplications of all that info. Because I needed great sums of money to pay estate taxes, personal taxes and debts I sold about everything including all 3800 shares of Ga Pacific in 1969 . . . . I don't know why I waste my time telling you this as I am sure this is in the Bestwall info sent you in '75. As to Mirro enclosed is a card which explains that—you also have letters from Pat Clark stating same . . .

The tone of the rest of the letter does not change until its last sentence, which reads, in sharp contrast, "This is such a lovely time of year in Wisconsin I hope you can get up there [Elkhart Lake] soon. As always, Do"[68]

As the above copy demonstrates, Anne Bryant had continued to provide significant assistance to her employer's widow, although she worked only part time for an annual honorarium. References to her in notes and letters by both the Lewises, and the kinds of responsibilities she was given, indicate the high regard in which she was held. As her husband might have done, Dorothy had made an interest-free loan to Mrs. Bryant in 1972, funds which in all likelihood went into the small business her husband was struggling to get on solid footing.[69] But in 1975 that business fell on harder times and after having devoted herself to keeping track of the Lewises' multiple financial interests for over twenty years, Anne Bryant needed to put her energies into more financially fruitful endeavors,

68 Both of the letters quoted here were drafted in pencil on yellow legal pads, and both drafts were found in piles of old papers in Mrs. Lewis' kitchen cabinets after her death. While only the drafts were found, other materials give no reason not to believe that both were sent essentially as drafted. A December 28, 1976, letter from John Spindler of Nash, Spindler, Dean & Grimstad in Manitowoc to Dorothy Lewis enclosed a copy of the referenced Agreement and noted that it had been recorded in Sheboygan County on December 7, 1976 as Document 1004722, Volume 792, page 904; Martin, Snow, Grant and Napier File, Lewis Archives.
69 The December 5, 1972, loan is recorded in Mrs. Bryant's handwriting, on a ledger sheet entitled "Notes Receivable-Mrs. Anne Bryant" along with a record of $500 payment toward the principal and the words "PAID IN FULL 1985" in Dorothy's hand. The loans for which interest was collected, notably to Emmett Barnes and Billy Nalls, are recorded on a page headlined "Interest Received." Ledgers, ibid.

taking a fulltime position with the Georgia Railroad.[70] Dorothy did not hire anyone to replace her, however; now certain of her ability to manage her affairs, and doubtless not unhappy to save the modest salary, she took over maintaining the ledgers and files herself. In so doing, of course, she was able to keep even closer track of her business interests.

Just how close is demonstrated by a 1977 letter found in the Mirro file addressed to the company's president. His communication containing news of a twenty-five per cent drop in profits elicited an impassioned response from what was surely one of his larger stockholders:[71]

> What your letter to stockholders . . . portends turns me on to such a degree that my first two replies ended in the wastebasket . . . . When one expends time, money and effort in the pursuit of profit writing it must have been a most unpleasant chore. I found it gratifying to re-read the clippings of your appearances defending the free-enterprise system which you so kindly sent to me just about a year ago . . . Lest you think you are a voice in a tunnel the enclosed I received from another company of which I am a shareholder. Does everyone at Mirro really understand the odds against which they struggle? Perhaps this quarterly report will shake them up sufficiently to make them stop and think. The American Executive is the unsung hero of the world. You have my sympathy! I hope the Lord hears my prayers for each and everyone of you.[72]

In all likelihood the letter she enclosed was one from Donald Kendall of Pepsico lamenting that "The high taxation of the last two decades has taken . . . economic power from the people and transferred it to government. You, as a shareholder . . . know how important the preservation of our free enterprise system is. Unfortunately, there are too few people voicing this sentiment today. We are offering you a way of speaking out for the system," by joining the Political Action Committee the company had decided to create.[73] Mirro was purchased by Newell in 1983 and despite increased competition in a changing market, remained a significant part of Dorothy Lewis' portfolio for the rest of her life.

In 1976, Emmett Barnes's balloon note on the Town and Country Shopping Center came due, and he wrote Dorothy to request that she continue the amortization over the whole fifteen years.[74] She called Sidney McNair for advice as to the tax implications of receiving the entire amount in that year versus the installments she had been getting, reaching his assistant, Gerry Hall, instead; the question was, Ms. Hall pointed out, could she get the equivalent

70 Mrs. Bryant later went to work for Macon Federal Savings and Loan, starting as an administrative assistant and eventually becoming, despite her lack of a college degree, a vice president.
71 At this point Dorothy owned 44,000 shares.
72 Dorothy V. Lewis to Charles W. Ziemer, February 22, 1977, Mirro File, Lewis Archives.
73 Donald M. Kendall, Chairman and Chief Executive Officer, PepsiCo, to Shareholders, June 30, 1976, PepsiCo File, ibid.
74 A. Emmett Barnes III to Dorothy Lewis, September 15, 1976, Town and Country File, ibid.

of a nine and one half per cent return from any other investment? Indeed. In the draft of a letter that looks as though she had typed it herself Dorothy wrote Barnes: "I prefer receiving the full amount of $347,169.34." Nevertheless she was willing to accede to his desire to continue the amortization, but "the interest rate will have to be raised to nine and one half per cent (9 1/2%) for eight years or ninety-six months, beginning in November 1976."[75]

Perhaps nothing illustrates Dorothy Lewis' enterprising use of her assets to augment her capital position better than this loan. Far from having had the funds available to lend Barnes in 1968, a time when both she and Logan, as noted above, had been heavily indebted,[76] she nevertheless borrowed the monies from Fulton National Bank in Atlanta at one-half to three-quarters of a percentage point less than she charged Barnes. In a practice she had followed since first beginning to develop the shopping centers in 1959, she used her securities portfolio as collateral, repaying the loans as she was able.[77] While most widows would have been content just to draw income from their portfolios, Dorothy Lewis was not like most widows.

A New Era in Banking Impacts the Lewis Portfolio

The late seventies and early eighties were an especially turbulent time for banks. Rising energy costs, "stagflation," and heretofore unheard of increases in interest rates made each day a potential pitfall. A memo to lending officers from Georgia Bank's Executive Vice President George Hall noted that

> We have been cautioned repeatedly by all of the regulatory authorities and by our management. I suppose by now, all of you know that Citibank has raised it's *[sic]* Prime rate to 14 1/2 . . . . The problem is . . . the possibility, if not probability, of a serious recession-depression. . . . when . . . you may be sure we will see a great increase in unemployment and decrease in business activity. Consumers will not be able to meet their monthly obligations, and speculative real estate— among other things—will not sell. Needless to say, our delinquency ratios, charge-offs and problem loans will increase dramatically.

Warning his officers to tighten their credit requirements he concluded, "If I sound pessimistic it is because I am pessimistic! And my attitude does reflect the thinking of the Board of Directors."[78]

In addition to these economic perils, the politics of deregulation brought many new opportunities (such as credit cards, certificates of deposit, individual

---

75 Dorothy Lewis to A. Emmett Barnes III, September 22, 1976, ibid. The interest rate had previously been 7 1/2 percent. A copy of the actual letter sent is not in the file but the ledgers indicate that these terms were accepted.
76 She had also given a $150,000 second mortgage to the group that purchased Cherokee Shopping Center in 1965.
77 Receipts for the securities held by Fulton as collateral were found in the file marked "1968"; lists and correspondence relating to the various securities go back to the early sixties.
78 Memorandum to All Lending Officers from George H. Hall, October 9, 1979, Hatcher Papers, 13.011.

retirement accounts, Keogh Plans, etc.) and, consequently, the blurring of lines between financial institutions. Retailing giant Sears Roebuck issued credit cards and got into mortgage banking by buying the nation's largest real estate broker, Coldwell Banker & Co., as well as stocks and bonds when it acquired Dean Witter Reynolds. Brokerage houses and other less regulated operations could pay higher returns on money, and what banks and savings and loans could do was in constant flux as regulators announced policy changes only to reverse their directives, sometimes within weeks. Positioning themselves for this new climate was a challenge for once staid institutions that suddenly found themselves in competition for many of their basic services.[79]

As Dr. Hatcher's remarks to stockholders quoted above suggest, the Georgia Bank had been almost laconic about the 1976 change in Georgia law that enabled banks to establish holding companies so as to operate across county lines. Unlike those of its Tar Heel neighbor to the north, Georgia laws had been fairly restrictive after the spate of Depression-spawned bank failures: it was not until the mid-fifties that banks had been allowed to open even in-county branches. In North Carolina, by contrast, banks had been expanding outside the counties in which they were chartered for years, experience which served them well when deregulation and market pressures brought about the mega-mergers of the eighties and nineties. The change in Georgia law to permit holding companies,[80] regulated under a 1956 federal statute, had been sought primarily by large Atlanta banks which wanted to extend their reach; small banks in small communities lobbied against it for fear they would be swallowed up. Georgia Bank & Trust Company, a medium-sized institution in the state's second-largest city, didn't particularly have a dog in the fight.[81] It was a locally owned bank that had grown big enough to provide customers with a range of services that enabled it to compete with the Atlanta-headquartered Citizens & Southern, and the Trust Company of Georgia-affiliated First National. In keeping with its founding philosophy, it was primarily interested in serving its own community. It had an active, involved board of directors that included some of the city's most energetic and successful businessmen, and that board carried out an aggressive program of soliciting depositors using incentives that ranged from jars of syrup to dinners for two. The effectiveness of those incentives was evidenced by the fact that G. B. & T.'s deposits were fifty-nine percent of First National's and sixty-seven

79 Steve Bills, "Financial Institutions Face Confusion As Deregulation Forces Competition," *Macon Telegraph*, November 8, 1981, p. 6B.
80 Statewide banking had been permitted until the 1920s, when a spate of bank failures led the legislature to tighten the rules. (C & S, already doing business in several counties, was grandfathered.) Even after Georgia changed its laws to allow banks to form holding companies and acquire other banks, however, acquisition remained the only means by which a bank could operate outside its home county, while North Carolina banks were free to open branches across county lines. Philosophically, Georgia believed more banks were better than fewer, and that's what they got: in 1989, more than a decade after the holding company law had been passed, Georgia had about four hundred banking companies as compared to only sixty-three in North Carolina. Erle Norton, "Does Georgia Law Put State's Banks at a Disadvantage?" *Macon Telegraph*, April 10, 1989, p. 11 Business Plus.
81 John F. Rogers Jr., Oral Interview, April 14, 2005.

percent of C & S-Macon's; of the city's $397,364,000 in deposits, third-ranked Georgia Bank had $86,071,024. (The only other banks operating in Macon at that time were Central Bank, the formerly private People's Bank, which Neal Ham had returned to Macon to run,[82] and the newly organized Macon Bank. In addition there were a number of savings and loan companies.)

The environment in which the bank operated, however, had another challenge. Despite the recent success of local economic development officials in attracting new manufacturing facilities,[83] Bibb County was growing at only two per cent a year in the late seventies; if Georgia Bank were to maintain its pattern of accelerated development it would have to expand outside Bibb County.[84] Given a choice between remaining in place or moving forward there was little doubt as to the option Georgia Bank's board and stockholders would select: theirs was an entrepreneurial culture. Don Gordon told the 1978 Annual Meeting that profits through March were more than 10 percent higher than budgeted, and that the trust department had been successfully computerized as well as all teller terminals, reducing check cashing time to eighteen seconds. When local attorney John B. Harris Jr., as was his habit, took the floor to nominate directors for the following year, he used the occasion to express "his great satisfaction as a stockholder in the work of the directors and officers in the progress the bank was making." At the end of the meeting, when Dr. Hatcher asked if there were any other comments to be made, Marvin Coddon offered similar words of praise and appreciation.[85]

Given this store of good will, the directors began to discuss forming a holding company the very next month, and voted to name it "Georgia Bancshares, Inc."[86] By May "a plan of reorganization and agreement of merger" was presented to the board; it called for Georgia Bank & Trust Company to merge into a newly chartered "Georgia Interim Company," a wholly owned subsidiary of Georgia Bancshares, Inc., which would acquire all of the Bank's stock in the process.[87] The Directors selected this merger process rather than a "direct exchange" in the belief that "being satisfied with the present situation might prevent many of the stockholders from exchanging their stock."[88] Dorothy Lewis, one of only two stockholders to own more than five per cent of the shares, was one of the eight directors selected to oversee the conversion.[89] Halstead Anderson, Don Gordon, George Hall, Milford Hatcher, Thomas Shealy, Chris

82 Ham left Georgia Bank in 1969 to become President of the Farmer's Bank in Monroe, Georgia. "As our younger officers develop, we will always be vulnerable to these hazards," Dr. Hatcher had told the 1970 Stockholders Meeting, by way of expressing regret at Ham's loss. Hatcher Papers, 13.027.
83 YKK, Texprint, and Brown and Williamson opened plants at the Ocmulgee East Industrial Park, and GEICO built a pink-collar back office operation there in the early seventies.
84 Herbert F. Ponder, Oral Interview, ibid.
85 Minutes, Annual Stockholders Meeting, March 30, 1978, Hatcher Papers, 13.027.
86 Board of Directors, Georgia Bank & Trust Co., Minutes, April 11, 1978, ibid., 13.010.
87 Board of Directions, Georgia Bancshares, Minutes, June 27, 1978, ibid.12.005.
88 Cubbedge Snow Jr. to Board of Directors, Georgia Bank & Trust Company, May 15, 1978, ibid., 13.006.
89 According to the Registration Statement filed with the Securities and Exchange Commission she owned 22,542 shares, or 7.2% of the stock; A. Emmett Barnes, III, whose son, Emmett IV sat on the board, was the other, with 16,040 shares, or 5.13%. The principal officers and directors owned 92,285 shares, or 29.5% of the stock. ibid., 12.012.

Sheridan, and David Zuver were the other "Bancshares" directors. Don Gordon filed Articles of Incorporation for the new firm with the Georgia Secretary of State on June 14; they were accepted the next day. On the twenty-seventh, the eight directors/stockholders met to organize, adopting by-laws, electing officers, accepting subscriptions for shares, and directing the officers to proceed to file applications for the necessary approvals. The regulatory hoops were not inconsiderable: in addition to the Georgia Department of Banking and Finance, and the Federal Reserve Board of Governors, the bank's lawyers had to submit its plans to the Securities and Exchange Commission (for issuing shares), the Federal Deposit Insurance Corporation, and the United States Justice Department. The plan also had to be published in the Federal Register, and attorney Jerry Harrell recommended seeking a prior ruling on the tax-free status of the transaction from the Internal Revenue Service. In an easily overcome snag, the application to the Federal Reserve Board of Governors had to be amended in October when one of its lawyers pointed out that between the time Georgia Bank's application had been submitted and the agency's anticipated response, Congress had passed the Financial Institutions Regulatory Act of 1978 which prohibited "director interlocks," i.e., persons could not serve on the board of a holding company if they were directors of another financial institution within the same Metropolitan Statistical Area. Seven Georgia Bank directors fell under this prohibition, all of whom agreed not to stand for the Bancshares board. The rule did not affect Dorothy Lewis, sitting on the Farmers National Bank board, or Lee Newton, with the Citizens Bank, because Monticello and Forsyth were outside the Macon MSA.[90]

Once the required waiting period had elapsed, the stockholders cast 75.58 percent of their shares in approval of the conversion, well in excess of the required two-thirds, at a called meeting.[91] On March 30, 1979, shortly before beginning its twentieth year, Georgia Bank & Trust Company became a wholly owned subsidiary of Georgia Bancshares, Inc., with the 312,500 shares of common stock automatically converted. Thus restructured, "the only bank in the world headquartered in Macon, Georgia," was ready for the challenges of a new era in banking, and its final spurt of growth.

Which wasn't long in coming. In May the directors began discussing the acquisition of the First National Bank of Houston County, the correspondent it had helped to organize in 1964, which by then had branches in Perry, Warner Robins, and Centerville.[92] Located just south of Bibb, and anchored by the huge air logistics center that Macon business leaders had worked with Congressman Carl Vinson to launch during World War II, Houston was one of the fastest

90 George Pieler to Edward J. Harrell, October 25, 1978, ibid., 12.007.
91 Minutes Stockholders Meeting, January 11, 1979, ibid., 13.027.
92 That same month the directors declined an overture from C B & T Bancshares of Columbus. Minutes, May 8, 1979, ibid.

growing areas of the state, its population having increased a whopping 22 percent between 1970 and 1980. It was an ideal place into which to expand. Don Gordon told the directors in August that "he felt it would be necessary to pay approximately $90 per share" or twice book value. Pink Persons, expressing confidence in the proposal, moved that the board endorse a plan whereby Georgia Bancshares would offer a cash purchase of at least 80 percent of the stock, covering half the cost with a Georgia Bank dividend and borrowing the rest of the funds; the motion passed unanimously.[93] By the December meeting, attorney Harrell was able to report that both the Georgia Department of Banking and Finance and the Federal Reserve had approved the acquisition.[94]

In celebrating its twentieth anniversary in July of 1980, the company newsletter could be forgiven its pride in exulting that as of the close of business December 31, 1979, Georgia Bank had grown from a $6 million operation at the end of 1960 to a full service financial institution of over $100 million, and was "Macon's third largest bank, home-owned and operated."[95] In his column in the same newsletter, newly designated President George Hall noted that the Bank's $476,957 year-to-date earnings had increased slightly over 1979's year-to-date figures "despite the fact that approximately $2 million in earning assets were transferred to Bancshares, Inc., on March 30, 1980, to acquire First National Bank of Houston County." Average deposits were up nearly $10 million from the previous year, and though he expressed concern with maintaining the bank's net interest margin due to "the dramatic decline in the prime lending rate over the past two months," he anticipated an end to that trend "as the high-rate money market certificates start rolling off and are replaced by lower yielding" ones.

By most accounts, Dorothy Lewis' role on the board of the Georgia Bank was not unlike the one she played at the Farmers National Bank in Monticello, with the exception that she does not seem to have solicited business for Georgia Bank as she had for FNB when she recruited Georgia Pacific. Impeccably dressed, with each naturally graying hair in place,[96] she came to everything to which she was invited, from committee meetings to board meetings to social events.[97] She was cordial but not chatty. Not at all meek, and, as her knowing nods made clear, perfectly cognizant of what was being discussed, she nevertheless said little, only rarely inserting herself into the give and take. Sensitive to appearing heavy-handed, she did not interfere in day-to-day

93 Minutes, Board of Directors, August 14, 1979, ibid., 13.011.
94 Minutes, Board of Directors, December 11, 1979, ibid.
95 "Georgia Bank Celebrates 20th Anniversary," B-Bit, July-August, 1980, Newsletters, ibid., 13.021.
96 Having been considered "stunning" as a young woman, one who set styles and enjoyed expensive jewelry, it is worth noting that Dorothy Lewis aged gracefully. She was not vain; she never dyed her hair, eschewed glasses, or struggled to shed the expanded girth that usually accompanies an increase in years. But she was always well dressed and poised. Sister Fidelis recalls wondering "who that very attractive, stately woman" was before being introduced; Pink Persons described her as "a great dresser; she always wore great clothes and looked good in them." No one, not even her close friend Betty Curtis, seemed to know that she made many of her outfits herself.
97 There is not a single set of minutes for either Georgia Bank or Georgia Bancshares in Dr. Hatcher's files that does not list Dorothy Lewis as present. Testimony as to her faithful participation in other events came from numerous interviewees.

operations or make suggestions about things that weren't on the agenda, habits that won respect from those aware of how much stock she owned. Actually, her most hands-on project may have taken place before she went on the board: she had decorated the bank's board room in honor of Logan—complete with an Oriental rug, his portrait and the framed ribbons and medals he had won in World War II. But while her interest in and appreciation of the bank was associated with memories of her husband and his role in it, she was also a business-minded stockholder. She became close to Don Gordon, Logan's successor as president, and she let him and, occasionally, other officers know how she felt about what went on in the meetings. She did have, after all, a substantial investment to look after.

There was one area in which she took the initiative, however, and it had a powerful impact on the eventual value of her holdings. Perhaps it stemmed from having been one of the eight original directors of Georgia Bancshares who met regularly over the year it had taken to complete the reorganization; perhaps she had visualized the possibility even earlier than that. In any event, once the holding company was up and running and had completed its purchase of the Houston County bank, Dorothy approached Don Gordon, then President of Georgia Bancshares (and Vice Chair of the Georgia Bank board) with an offer to sell her interest in the Farmers National Bank. Monticello and Jasper County, located in the middle of a rural area primarily devoted to timber, were not on the same growth track as Warner Robins and Houston, but FNB was a solid bank and a good investment for the Macon firm. On the basis of deposits it was the larger of the two banks operating in Jasper, and the modern facility Logan had put in motion in 1966 was still in good condition, expected to meet anticipated needs for the foreseeable future. The bank's net income had increased 31 percent over the previous five years and its return on assets for 1979 was a healthy 1.57 percent.[98] With total assets of $14,227,000, it was approximately half as large as the Houston County bank, but Dorothy's majority ownership gave Bancshares the opportunity to acquire it through an exchange of stock rather than a cash purchase. There were several advantages for Dorothy. While she had been a loyal supporter of FNB and its president, she had neither the expertise nor the proximity needed to exercise the control having such a substantial part of her assets tied up in its holdings might warrant. Moreover, transferring that responsibility to the officers of Georgia Bancshares gave her greater liquidity as well as protection from a variety of exigencies. Realizing that he would lack the autonomy he had enjoyed as an independent banker, then-president Billy Nalls was not happy with the proposed sale, and discouraged her proposal. Nevertheless, once Don Gordon and George Hall had made a slide presentation on the merger's benefits in Monticello, and Dorothy had spoken on its behalf,

---

98 Figures extracted from Draft of Letter of Intent for Georgia Bancshares offer to Farmers National Bank, ibid., 12.008.

the board voted to accept the offer, and the transfer was completed on June 9, 1981. Jerry Harrell remembers being impressed that, thanks to Dorothy's influence, every single share of the bank's stock was exchanged.[99] When, a year and a half later, Georgia Bancshares acquired the Tennille Banking Company in Washington County, George Hall (who had taken over the Bancshares presidency at Don Gordon's retirement) tapped Nalls to head that firm, with Dorothy Lewis, who had remained on the FNB board, nominating Thurman Willis, Jr., to take his place.[100] "I give her credit," Willis said in an interview. "She saw the way banking was headed. She knew that consolidation was the avenue that banking was taking and she wanted to be sure that this community was part of it."[101]

It was not surprising, according to Betty Curtis, that Dorothy stayed busy going to bank meetings; she concentrated on business because "what else did she have to do?" It was certainly what seemed to give her the most pleasure, and perhaps that is why, much to the suppressed amusement of her colleagues, she turned a blind eye to the Georgia Bank bylaw stipulating that directors must retire when they turned seventy. Former Georgia Bank personnel chuckled in recounting her recalcitrance to this writer: every year Chairman Hatcher would remind the board of the bylaw, and ask anyone who would reach the age of seventy in the next twelve months to let him know so that a replacement could be sought. The "retirement" clause had not been part of the original bylaws, having been added in the late sixties, with those it immediately affected grandfathered until 1970. Still, that was long before Dorothy came on the board. Conscientious attorney/secretary Cubbedge Snow, who, as noted above, had declined to serve on the board while representing the bank, sent a poignant reply to Dr. Hatcher when he was invited to take a seat after giving up his legal role in 1976:

> Believe me I was flattered by your call last week that the Georgia Bank Board had elected me a director, notwithstanding my age, and it was up to me to work out the legality of this action . . . . Joe Timberlake tells me that I am indebted to you for this very gracious action, and I do appreciate it most deeply. I have spent many hours since our conversation trying to carry out my part of the resolution, but I regret to say that there is no way . . . . Our Supreme Court has held that a bylaw of a corporation is a rule of law . . . [that] cannot be ignored or evaded . . . . I am sure that you will see if retirement at age 70 is mandatory, it would be a flagrant evasion of the law to elect me, now 74, to serve even one day on the board . . .[102]

99 Edward J. (Jerry) Harrell, Oral Interview, June 9, 2005.
100 Ponder and Hall, Oral Interviews.
101 Interview # 2.
102 Cubbedge Snow to Milford B. Hatcher, May 20, 1975, Hatcher Papers, 13.005

Perhaps it wasn't as "flagrant" just to stay on after one already held a seat; in any event Dorothy Lewis didn't seem to mind skirting the requirement. It was not as though retired directors were cast aside with no further connection to the bank. They moved into honorary status, were listed with the board on annual reports, and encouraged to attend whatever meetings they desired. When Dr. Hatcher and Halstead Anderson turned seventy in 1979, they left the active board, and minutes show they frequently showed up for meetings. Dorothy Lewis, however, who reached the same age in the same year, remained silent whenever Dr. Hatcher or his successor brought up the issue. There were only two bank forms found in Mrs. Lewis' bank files noting her date of birth: the first was a Financial Report submitted in 1977 that claimed she had been born in 1912. Another, done in 1986, also listed her birth date as 1912—and it had been filled out four years after such a birth date would have made her ineligible to continue in service! The bank did not blow her cover—using a date from some other, unknown source, it put her age as "63" on a board list that accompanied the notice of a substitute annual meeting on July 5, 1979.[103] One year stockholder Crockett Odom, who had heard Abby Vits announce his sister's age at her Manitowoc wedding, and who further knew that she had been Bib Hay's classmate and must therefore be her contemporary, age-wise, showed up early at an annual meeting to complain to anyone who would listen that Dorothy Lewis was lying about how old she was and should be forced to step down from the board. The conversation came to an abrupt end, however, when the elevator doors opened to reveal that the lady in question had arrived.[104] After that, when anyone brought the problem to George Hall's attention the only response they got was, "You tell her." She did not step down from the active board until 1987.

Georgia Bancshares' ongoing success made it a likely takeover target itself. Its directors had rebuffed a 1979 overture from C B & T Bancshares of Columbus, asking Don Gordon to "politely decline" it.[105] In 1981 they gave more serious consideration to another offer, hiring a nationally respected financial consultant to study a proposal from First Atlanta Corporation. First Atlanta, already the second largest banking organization in Georgia, wanted to establish a presence in counties representing 70 percent of the state's market. Acquiring Georgia Bancshares, fourteenth in size, which was located in the only part of the state in which the Atlanta bank lacked a "presence," would meet that objective. The price offered was $58.50 per share. After carefully evaluating the two banks' assets, deposits, loans, investments, earnings, and return on assets over the previous decade, however, W. T. Grimm's thirty-eight page analysis

103 Ibid., 12.007.
104 Jerry Harrell, Oral Interview #2.
105 Minutes, Board of Directors, Georgia Bank, June 12, 1979, Hatcher Papers, 13.009.

concluded that the price should be closer to $71. The study also contrasted the differing business styles of the two financial institutions, with First Atlanta's more aggressive, consequently more volatile posture coming off less positively than Georgia Bancshares' conservative approach, with its yield of steady, predictable, growth. In a sentence that may have doomed the deal, the consultants noted that "If Georgia Bank had been acquired for first Atlanta stock in 1973, the shareholders would have suffered a 75% decline in market value in the next two years." This would be so, they explained, because

> In exchanging Bancshares' stock for First Atlanta's stock, the stockholder is acquiring a different kind of stock involving an exposure to new risks inherent in First Atlanta's more aggressive management style. An immediate paper profit of $29 per share could eventually disappear.[106]

They further wrote:

> In our opinion, the earnings of Bancshares are distinctly higher quality than the earnings of First Atlanta. By exchanging Bancshares' stock for First Atlanta stock, the Bancshares' stockholder is receiving a lower quality, more volatile, more speculative stock.[107]

Yet there were strong advantages to such an exchange. The marketability of Bancshares' stock was limited, and coping with the intensifying competition brought about by deregulation and the multiple new products then "revolutionizing the banking business" could be accomplished "more economically by larger banking units." In evaluating other potential suitors the consultants concluded that none offered the liquidity, size and interest of First Atlanta.[108] Prophetically, however, they noted that "it is possible that within the next year or two the banking laws will be changed to permit bank holding companies to purchase banks in adjacent states," opening up a whole new set of options. Even when First Atlanta raised its offer to $65, Bancshares rejected it.[109] As a result of that decision, the Atlanta behemoth made its entry into the Middle Georgia market by acquiring the city's newest, and smallest, "local" bank, seven-year-old Macon Bank.

Georgia Bancshares, meanwhile, proceeded to follow its path of steady growth. When Don Gordon retired at the end of 1982 after sixteen years at the helm, he could tell the *Macon Telegraph*.

> We've never had a loss month since the bank was formed in

106 W. T. Grimm & Co., Valuation Study for Georgia Bancshares, Inc., p. 25, ibid., 12.015.
107 Ibid., p. 33.
108 The others were Bank South, the fourth largest bank in Atlanta which had no interest, and C B & T in Columbus and First Railroad and Banking Co. of Georgia in Augusta, which were interested but lacked liquidity and size. ibid., pp. 28-9.
109 The First Atlanta proposal letters, the one offering $58.50 dated July 23, 1981, and the second offering $65 dated September 8, 1981, are both in Hatcher Papers, 12.008.

1960. There have been lots of institutions that made more money than we have, but we've been consistent—a consistent uptrend. We'll end the year with the best year we've ever had in 22 1/2 years, and the largest asset base.[110]

In the same interview Gordon disavowed any interest in big changes for the bank: "We have no ambitions to be a big statewide holding company." Nevertheless *Telegraph* business writer/reporter Steve Bills opened another news story the following September by writing "Georgia Bancshares, Inc., a small Macon-based bank holding company, is starting to act like one of the big boys."[111] The company, he said, wanted to grow and to increase the activity of its thinly traded stock; it had agreed the previous week to buy the First State Bank of Fitzgerald, after having acquired the Tennille Banking Company the previous April. The additional purchases had put Bancshares in a still stronger position. At the end of the bank's second quarter, President George Hall had reported record profits for the first six months of 1983, along with the Directors' approval of a 100 percent stock split in the form of a dividend to be paid July 29. Assets had grown to $220,229,000, a 30 percent increase over 1982. The bank was continuing "to develop innovative new services and enhance existing ones" including a discount brokerage (in which its largest stockholder immediately opened an account![112]) and bonus banking for personal transaction accounts.[113] In a news story reporting these successes Senior Vice President Pete DuBose noted that the corporation had attracted new customers to its other operations (in Houston, Jasper, and Washington counties) by adding services that had not been available there before, such as trust, money market accounts, etc. For his part, Hall told the newspaper that he hoped the stock changes would result in "more interest and more trading in our stock."[114]

By September the holding company had also decided to offer stockholders a chance to buy 200,000 new shares for $13.50 a share.[115] "They're very aggressive," Interstate Securities broker Rick Johnson had been quoted as saying in the story cited above.[116] And Hall himself, in mentioning ongoing talks about other acquisitions, said "It is our intention to be active in the acquisition market, primarily in Middle Georgia." The reporter, however, could not resist offering a caveat:

> But for a banking organization trying to break into the first tier of
> Georgia institutions, the Macon-based company has a problem. There
> is very little trading interest in the stock. There are prospective buyers,

110 Steve Bills, "A Lot to Be Said for Being Small," *Macon Telegraph,* January 2, 1983, p. 9B.
111 Steve Bills, "Georgia Bancshares May Be Takeover Target," *Macon Telegraph,* September 7, 1983, p. 5C.
112 Lewis Archives.
113 Georgia Bancshares Second Quarter Report, June 30, 1983, Hatcher Papers, 13.023.
114 "Georgia Bancshares Directors Announce Plans for Stock Split," *Macon Telegraph,* July 15, 1983, p. 3B.
115 Dorothy Lewis bought 25,264 of these 200,000 shares, at a cost of $341,064. Ledgers, Lewis Archives.
116 Steve Bills, "Georgia Bank May Be Takeover Target," ibid.

but stockholders don't want to sell. "We're going to get some activity in our stock," Hall vowed Tuesday. Bancshares officials hope the current subscription offering will encourage stockholders to trade more. If not, the company might issue another 200,000 shares, Hall said. "We can use the money well," he added. "There are an awful lot of banks that are available."

Since organizing the holding company in 1979 the firm had grown 75 percent. The Fitzgerald merger was expected to push Georgia Bancshares above $250 million in assets and into tenth place among the state's holding companies. It would also interest brokers who had paid little attention to Bancshares both because of the scarcity of stock available and because of its small size.

Unbeknownst to Reporter Bills, the successful suitor was already polishing a ring. Fulton National Bank had been Logan Lewis' Atlanta bank. He owned a few shares of its stock; it had loaned both him and Dorothy funds for various business ventures, most notably Logan's purchase of the Farmers National Bank and Dorothy's development of the shopping centers; its Trust Department had handled the details of settling Logan's estate; and its president, Gordon Jones, was a good friend. Furthermore, it had bankrolled eager stockholders when Georgia Bank was organized in 1960, and been the new bank's primary correspondent, all the while growing in the same steady, conservative fashion as its Macon colleague. It had bought a small Forest Park bank with the appealing appellation "Bank of the South" some years earlier, for its name, not wanting metropolitan Atlanta nomenclature to impede its plans for statewide expansion.[117] Having then become "Bank South," it was now the state's fifth-largest banking network with $1.8 billion in assets and subsidiaries in five metro Atlanta counties as well as Athens, Columbus, and Savannah. According to the 1981 Grimm Valuation Study, it had been a good match for Bancshares at the time First Atlanta made overtures, save for the fact that it just wasn't interested. Three years later, it was.

The Telegraph announced the pending merger on May 11, 1984.[118] "We have been real close with Bank South for twenty-four years," George Hall is quoted as saying, "so they were the logical folks for us to marry." Bank South's president Robert P. Guyton, acknowledging that this was not the first time the two financial institutions had considered getting together, said "When we looked before, the timing just was not right for one or the other of us." The advantages of merger cited by Grimm were still present: the additional services necessitated by increased competition could be met most economically by larger banking units, and, naturally, stockholders' investments would be far more liquid. Furthermore, Bank South's terms were much more compatible than First

---

117 Ponder Interview, ibid.
118 Steve Bills, "Last Locally Owned Bank To Merge With Bank Firm," *Macon Telegraph,* May 11, 1984, p. 1A.

Atlanta's had been: while Bancshares would change its name to Bank South-Macon, it would operate as an independent, autonomous subsidiary, with the same directors, officers, and employees. In turn, each of its subsidiaries would continue its independent operation. Under the proposed agreement Bancshares stockholders would receive 1.1 shares of Bank South for each share of the Macon company they owned; two Bank South executives would join the Macon board; and George Hall would become a member of the Bank South board.[119] Stockholders approved the deal by a ninety-nine per cent vote the following November.[120]

It would be hard to overstate the impact of this merger activity on Dorothy Lewis' portfolio; the value of her stock in both the Farmers National Bank (which became Bank South Jasper County) and Georgia Bancshares (Bank South Macon) were substantially enhanced by their conversion to Bank South stock. Following Logan's 1966 death, his and Dorothy's combined holdings in the two banks[121] had been worth just over half a million dollars using the upwardly revised price the Internal Revenue Service placed on them. After Georgia Bancshares was formed in 1979 their value doubled to slightly more than a full million. In 1983, immediately prior to Bank South's acquisition of Georgia Bancshares, they had increased to $2 million; that included the additional 25,264 shares (of the 200,000 offered in September of that year) that Dorothy was eligible to purchase (so as to keep her holdings proportionate), and did. In 1984, the first year after the Bank South buyout, their value had increased to $5.25 million.[122] But just as significant as the bank's appreciation in value was its potential interest to even bigger banks—the merger frenzy was far from over.

At the time of its 1984 merger with Bank South, Bancshares had been on the verge of acquiring First Citizens Bank in Forsyth, and Bank South had been about to buy the Bank of Cumming; both deals went through concurrently. Other local banks were undergoing similar consolidation: First National joined with the Trust Co. affiliate in Warner Robins to become Trust Company Bank of Middle Georgia, N.A.; Macon Bank had already been acquired by First Atlanta. Benefiting from a strong regional economy, Georgia's banks and savings and loan associations outpaced their national counterparts in the mid-80s; their growth and greater levels of efficiency led to higher profits.[123]

119 Agreement and Plan of Merger, with Memorandum from Pete DuBose to Directors of Georgia Bancshares, Hatcher Papers, 12.009.
120 Steve Bills, "Georgia Bancshares Merger Into Bank South Corp. OK'd," November 14, 1984, *Macon Telegraph*, p. 5D.
121 Logan left 4312 shares of Georgia Bank, and 5395 shares of Farmers National Bank; Dorothy owned 2100 of Georgia Bank herself, and continued to buy (and sell) small numbers of both bank stocks in subsequent years. She exchanged 14,550 shares of FNB for 1.5737 per share of Georgia Bancshares, equaling 22,897 shares, which split, eventually totaling 90,878. In 1983, when Georgia Bancshares made another stock offering she was eligible to increase her holding proportionately, and she did, buying 25,264 of the 200,000 offered. Logan also left 130 shares of Fulton National Bank, which split in 1973 and issued stock dividends in 1980 and 81, so that Dorothy also held 357 shares of the buying bank before the merger.
122 Figures drawn from Financial Reports Dorothy Lewis filled out in fulfillment of her responsibility as a bank director. Financial Statements File, Lewis Archives.
123 Associated Press, "Georgia Financial Institutions Outpacing Other Banks," *Macon Telegraph*, November 17, 1986, p. 2C.

The 1981 Grimm study had predicted that "with the trend toward deregulation . . . laws will be changed to permit bank holding companies to purchase banks in adjacent states." The prediction proved accurate. Regional banking came to Georgia in 1985 when the Trust Company merged with Sun Bank of Florida and the Citizens and Southern Georgia Corporation acquired Florida's Landmark Banking Corporation, adding South Carolina banks the next year. North Carolina's Wachovia Bank & Trust announced a "merger of equals" with First Atlanta in 1985, creating what was for a time the largest banking company in the Southeast at $15.5 billion.[124] Another North Carolina powerhouse, First Union, bought Macon's Central Bank. As the merger mania picked up steam, the courtship was not always mutual. "The once genteel arena of bank buyouts has become a battle zone," [125] the *Telegraph* reported late in the decade. NCNB Corp. of Charlotte, led by hard-charging ex-Marine Hugh L. McColl Jr., shattered tradition when it made an unsolicited bid for the by-then $21.1 billion C & S in 1989; rebuffed at first, the merger succeeded two years later, with the resulting new entity, NationsBank, boasting 1900 branches in nine states from Maryland to Texas. Big, regional banks were well-positioned to meet the challenge of non-bank competitors by offering additional services while spreading out their fixed operating costs; reducing the percentage of revenues absorbed by overhead enabled them to dominate the industry.[126]

Meanwhile Bank South continued to take the scrappy, customer-oriented approach to business that had made it such a good match for Georgia Bancshares. In 1988 it expanded its reach and appeal by opening branches in Kroger grocery stores, a move which enabled increasingly time-pressed consumers to manage their money and provision their families in a single stop-during night and weekend hours. Its people-friendly network of 267 automated teller machines grew to be the largest in the state. Announcing that its first quarter net income had risen 8 percent while earnings per share climbed 11 percent, an April 1989 press release quoted President Guyton as saying, "We are continuing the aggressive sales and service efforts which have attracted higher loan and deposit volume, while also emphasizing the need to control expenses and further develop deep specialties in services which generate non-interest income."[127] Tellingly, the company added that it had changed its policy regarding rumors of impending buyouts; having previously denied them, the firm had decided, on advice of attorneys, to adopt a "no comment" position.

Unfortunately, there was a bit of bravado in Guyton's good news—by fall the word from Atlanta was "restructuring" as the company sought to cut

124 Ross Yockey, McColl, *The Man with America's Money*, Longstreet Inc., Atlanta, 1999, p. 298.
125 Erle Norton, "Bank Battle Zone," *Macon Telegraph*, April 10, 1989, p. 1S.
126 Mike Billups, "The New Shape of Banking," *Macon Telegraph*, September 11, 1995, p. 1E.
127 "Bank South's Net Income Increases," *Macon Telegraph*, April 18, 1989, p. 6A.

costs by $15 million a year.[128] That meant eliminating jobs, plus, in a move that frustrated its Macon contingent, pulling independent charters in order to improve the company's capital position. The local board, no longer setting policy for the Macon branches, became as toothless as the old C & S advisory board on which Logan Lewis had chafed in the 1950s, its frustration only partially abated by rising stock prices. Dorothy Lewis had stepped down from the active board two years earlier, and begun attending the luncheons for honorary directors, but in the fall of 1989 she quit even the luncheons. At Thurman Willis's urging, she had stayed on the Jasper County board; in the fall of 1989 she resigned from it as well. Nevertheless, the retrenchment was only partly successful. After a $55 million loss in 1991, former C & S executive Patrick Flinn replaced Guyton as chief executive, and the bank began to pressure market leaders with aggressive promotions like six months worth of free checking for new customers. Capitalizing on its local, Georgia-based "little guy" status behind NationsBank, (formerly C & S), Wachovia (First Atlanta), First Union, and SunTrust, its ads lampooned out-of-state mega-banks, featuring, for example, a customer whose life had been turned upside down by faceless bankers in North Carolina.

Was the bank grooming itself for sale? It certainly set the stage for the next merger, which came in the mid-1990s. Dorothy Lewis was no longer well by then, though she continued to hold onto the stock and was surely enjoying its dividends. As Bank South cut expenses and consolidated operations, it became increasingly competitive in Atlanta, fueling months of buyout rumors, which ran its stock up 30 percent. The speculation finally ended in 1995 when NationsBank, feeling threatened in what had been C & S's primary market, and wanting a major Atlanta presence during the Olympics to enhance its international banking efforts, put an end to the competition by buying its competitor. "NationsBank gobbles up the South," blared a four-column, page-one headline in the *Telegraph*.[129] "Merger with Bank South cements bank's place in Atlanta market," a large subhead added. Would customers drawn by Bank South's "smaller-is-better" posture be turned off by another consolidation? NationsBank President Ken Lewis claimed the merged bank would be able to offer the best of both: "We'll emphasize convenience and breadth of service," he said. Macon customer Curtis Stevens, interviewed while waiting in line at the Baconsfield Kroger seemed to agree: "I was with them when they were the Georgia Bank," he said. "If anything they got better after Bank South came in, opening these supermarket branches." Stockholders were equally pleased. Following the announcement, Bank South was the most active issue on U.S. markets, moving from 22 13/16 on September 1st to 26 5/8 two weeks later. NationsBank, third largest in the country with assets of $184 billion nationwide

128 Erle Norton, "Bank South to Cut 300 Jobs in Restructuring Plan," *Macon Telegraph*, September 7, 1989, p. 5C.
129 Marc Rice, "NationsBank Gobbles Up the South," *Macon Telegraph*, September 6, 1995, p. 1A.

and $18 billion in Georgia, barely burped as it swallowed $7.4 billion Bank South. In fact, Chairman McColl was so pre-occupied with the possibility of a much larger merger—with the country's second-largest bank—that summer, that he left Atlanta-based Ken Lewis to manage the Bank South initiative by himself; the name "Bank South" does not merit even a mention in the North Carolinian's authorized biography.

Still, the consolidations sending Dorothy Lewis's bank stocks skyward were not yet over. In 1999, in a deal that culminated thirty years of breaking boundaries for the now near-legendary McColl, the Charlotte-based behemoth bought California's Bank of America to become the largest bank in the country. Share prices soared, quadrupling in eighteen months.

In Macon, the "Bank South" signs, like those that had read "Georgia Bank and Trust Company," came down, replaced first by "NationsBank," and then, just a few years later, by others reading "Bank of America." In Monticello, where Thurman Willis Jr. had written enthusiastically to customers to endorse the 1984 Bank South merger, extolling Farmers National Bank's "warm, fifty-year relationship" with Fulton National,[130] and pointing out the new services and technology to be offered by this still "independent" bank, things were different. As Logan Lewis would surely have agreed, a huge national conglomerate was no place for a small country bank, and Willis was worried about his employees, some of whom had been with the bank twenty or thirty years. He consulted his brother-in-law, who was president of the McIntosh State Bank in Griffin; as it happened that firm had been considering acquiring another bank. They decided to put the two banks together and Willis then negotiated the buy-back from NationsBank, long before the Bank of America merger took place. His mentor, the bank's onetime majority stockholder, was as supportive as her husband would have been, confident that a small bank in a rural community would fare better under local management. "Good for you," she responded as he reported what he had done.

Dorothy Lewis's stock, however, stock that her husband had acquired when he bought the small country bank in 1965, along with their joint holdings in the local bank he had founded in Macon in 1960, had been mergered into 254,034 shares of the largest bank in America, with a combined market value of $19,418,000. Stockholder Dorothy Lewis was a multimillionaire.

Preparing To Exit

Having spent many years husbanding her assets, it behooved Dorothy

130 Thurman Willis, Jr. to Valued Customers, November 15, 1984, FNB File, Lewis Archives.

Lewis, as she faced her seventieth birthday, to consider their ultimate disposition as carefully as she had their accumulation. Longevity ran in her family, her father having lived until his eighty-fifth year, her mother until her ninety-fourth; at the same time her mother and aunts had endured severely diminished capacities in their last years, and pragmatic as she was, Dorothy must have foreseen the possibility of a similar end to her own life. She was not close to her brother, she had maintained regular contact with only one of her cousins, and of course she had no children to provide for or to lean on. In any event, near the end of 1978 she decided to make a new will. As she had when deeding her half of the Elkhart Lake house to Abby, she consulted the attorneys then busy guiding the establishment of the bank holding company.[131]

She made an appointment with Cubbedge Snow Jr. early in the winter of 1979, telling him she wanted to discuss estate-planning issues. Snow, who had grown up on Callaway Street, just behind Tero Amos's Vineville Avenue-facing home, was delighted to help; apparently his former neighbor had not held a lasting grudge about all those times he and his tricycle trespassed on the Lewis driveway. Being primarily a litigator, however, he asked his young associate, Jerry Harrell, to sit in on the session.

Mrs. Lewis had not decided exactly how to implement her intentions; she was interested in options, and advice on those options. After listening to her concerns, Harrell suggested a private foundation as the best vehicle to accomplish her objectives. She wanted the bulk of her estate to go to various charities she had supported, primarily Catholic missions and schools, but she wanted to exercise some control over how her gifts were spent. Setting up a private foundation was both practical and effective. The foundation could have a focus but would not be restricted, thus ensuring that no matter what happened to the particular charities in which she was interested, the charitable assistance she envisioned would go on in perpetuity. In addition, she would get an immediate deduction against current income, which was then rising as dividends from both banks increased dramatically. She was aware, of course, that the Hay family had donated the family's antebellum Italianate mansion atop the Spring Street hill to a private foundation in order to preserve it for the future, and would support that venture herself in a few years, but she had not mentioned establishing something similar to either Bib Hay Anderson or Betty Hay Curtis. Frank Jones remembers having discussed foundations with Logan, even sending him information on Macon's Porter Fund, but his last will, signed in 1963, left his entire estate to Dorothy, and, should she not survive him, to a trust defined in a letter which he

131 While Frank Jones had left Macon and the firm that continued to use his family's name, moving to Atlanta to join King and Spalding in the mid-seventies, the change to the Martin, Snow firm was more likely precipitated by that firm's connection to the Georgia Bank.

had placed with the Georgia Bank.[132] While Dorothy's net worth in 1978 was modest in comparison to what it would become after the multiple bank mergers ran up the value of her bank stock, and her charitable donations had been modest in comparison to her income, Harrell's suggestion that she establish the foundation and make contributions to and through it, in effect giving it a dry run, proved appealing. As he pointed out, she could "kick the tires and drive it around" for awhile; in short, set it up and see how she liked it, knowing that she could alter the plan if she desired.[133] Including her husband's name in its title was both appropriate and gratifying.

The Dorothy V. and N. Logan Lewis Foundation was chartered in February of 1979, and held its first, organizational meeting February 16. Dorothy had selected the directors of what was to become, according to the bylaws, a self-perpetuating board, whose members were appointed for life. In addition to herself, they were her attorney, Cubbedge Snow Jr.; her pastor, Father John Cuddy; her dentist, Dr. James L. Cassidy (who was active at St. Joseph's); and another St. Joseph's parishioner, Ralph Lane Williams. Snow was elected to chair the first meeting and presided over the business of adopting by-laws and electing officers, which were Dorothy as president and himself as secretary/treasurer. Dorothy was also named investment advisor and bookkeeper. Sidney McNair was chosen to prepare the tax returns, and Jerry Harrell to oversee legal requirements such as annual reports to the Secretary of State, legal ads, preparation of minutes, etc. The Foundation's accounts were placed, naturally, at the Georgia Bank. Dorothy launched the project in June by contributing $2500 in cash and four hundred shares of IBM stock. In December she added another $3500 to maximize the allowable deduction for that year. In January the organization met again (with Snow presiding at the request of President Lewis), to make its first gift of $1000 to St. Joseph's Catholic Church "to be used . . . for the enrichment of the educational processes at St. Joseph's Catholic School."[134] The church was asked to report back on the disposition of the funds. Despite the necessity of giving public notice of the foundation's activities, all involved kept a low profile in an effort to prevent potential grant-seekers from imposing on the donor.

The next month Snow wrote to let his client know that the last thing in connection with her will—getting a commitment from the Georgia Bank as to its charges for serving as executor—had been completed. Enclosing a letter from Trust Officer Charles Rehberg he said "I think that it does show a substantially decreased rate from the rates that both the Georgia Bank and other banks charge."[135] Dorothy may have been devoted to the bank but she did not intend to

---

132 Oral Interview, November 11, 2003; the will is recorded in Book BB, Folio 47, Bibb County Courthouse.
133 Harrell Interview #2.
134 Minutes, January 23, 1980, from the official minute book of the Dorothy V. and N. Logan Lewis Foundation.
135 Cubbedge Snow Jr. to Mrs. Logan Lewis, February 11, 1980, Foundation File, Lewis Archives.

burden her estate with unnecessary expense.

That December Dorothy gave another $39,500 to the Foundation and decided that it should donate $1500 to St. Joseph's for the orphanage in Savannah, an action that was approved by the circulation of signed minutes amongst the directors, without the formality of a meeting. In 1981, she contributed $35,000 to the Foundation, after which, again without a formal meeting, the Foundation donated $1,000 to St. Joseph's, $1,000 to St. Mary's Home for Dependent Children, and $8,000 to St. Joseph's Catholic School for "special education."[136] In 1983, however, the directors met in Father Cuddy's office. They discussed St. Joseph's expenditure of its grant for computer equipment, with Director Cassidy speaking enthusiastically of its success. President Lewis reported a gift of $5,000 to St. Peter Claver and the directors authorized her to make such additional gifts to the Catholic schools as she saw fit, as well as reviewing the investment portfolio and ratifying the management of funds to date.[137]

The financial pressures Dorothy Lewis had felt immediately following her husband's death, coupled with her desire to keep her money working, may explain why her charitable gifts had not kept pace with the growth of her income. In the decade since the transfer of her parents' assets she had made only six four-figure donations,[138] even as she continued to provide nominal support to a number of civic, cultural, and religious organizations. Once the foundation was up and running, however, her giving increased—primarily to the foundation, of course, but outside the foundation as well. She sponsored several Youth Concerts for the Macon Symphony, contributed to the capital funds drive at the Hay House, helped the Museum of Arts and Sciences wind up its endowment campaign, participated in the Jasper County Friends of the Library effort, and made substantial gifts to St. Joseph's, the Confraternity of the Laity Drive, the Cathedral Development Fund, and St. Mary's Home for Dependent Children, all fully deductible. Meanwhile she contributed the maximum 20 percent of her income that was eligible for a tax deduction, to the Foundation. As the foundation grew, the gifts it made grew as well, encompassing all of the Catholic schools in Macon, in increasing amounts. Richard C. Keil, at that time pastor Father Keil of St. Peter Claver, remembers looking up one day and seeing "an older lady" outside his office door; she wanted to know what his school needed to enrich its students' educational experience. He suggested a set of encyclopedias, to which she replied that she had something more substantial in mind: "I'll give you a figure—I'll give $5,000."[139] Sister Fidelis Barragan, then

136 Minutes, December 23, 1981, from the official minute book of the Dorothy V. and N. Logan Lewis Foundation.
137 Minutes, January 27, 1983, ibid.
138 They went to the Holy Family Hospital in Manitowoc where Anne Vits had been cared for, the Holy Spirit Catholic Church in Warner Robins, the Mt. De Sales library fund, the Jesuit Missionary Fund, St. Joseph's Catholic Church, and the Museum of Arts and Sciences Expansion Fund. Ledgers, Lewis Archives.
139 Richard Keil, Oral Interview, February 17, 2005.

principal of Mt. De Sales, used Lewis monies to add reference volumes and a coin-operated copying machine to the library, equip a computer laboratory, and buy tapes and tape players for the Foreign Language Department.[140] At St. Joseph's School the Lewis gift challenged supporters to raise $100,000 in endowment. And, as Harrell enjoyed pointing out to the benefactress, "When you consider that over half of this money would now be in the hands of Uncle Sam had we not sheltered it, I believe the foundation has been a tremendous success."[141]

As Dorothy approached her seventy-fifth birthday she also began to make non-cash gifts, both to appropriate individuals and to recognized charities. Some of the Logan, Lewis, and Callaway heirlooms whose provenance Johnnie Logan Lewis had painstakingly documented in the little composition book in 1939 had been given to Helen Clisby, Martha Kaderly, and Katie Mae Hardin, respectively, in 1968. In 1985, as Dorothy noted next to descriptions of various objects described in the book, other Callaway things went to Hazel Hardin Wright and Katherine Hardin Newton, additional Logan things to Helen Clisby Barfield, and more Lewis things to Martha Kaderly Zebrowski.

The largest number of Callaway objects, however, was donated to the Callaway Plantation, the Callaway family seat in Wilkes County that had been converted into a "working plantation" museum. The property had not been out of the family since Job Callaway's arrival in the late eighteenth century, passing from one generation to another. Carleton Callaway's younger brother, Aristides, built a Greek Revival home on the place in 1869, and it was to that house, the focal point of what was intended to be a living heritage museum, that Dorothy contributed more than a dozen pieces of the furniture[142] that Johnnie Lewis had attributed to "Grandmother Callaway." Her interest in the place had doubtless been sparked by Nat Hardin, whose family had donated the house and subsequent parcels of land (along with an endowment) to the Washington Wilkes Historical Foundation and the City of Washington beginning in 1967.[143] (His mother, Katie Mae Arnold, who had been in Johnnie Lewis's 1906 wedding and remained a close friend throughout her life, was a granddaughter of Aristides Callaway, hence also Johnnie's second cousin.) Dorothy's gift was well-received: "There is no way to express the excitement the van load of furniture created at Callaway Plantation yesterday," wrote Aveola Callaway, chairman of the committee to furnish the site. "My committee was beside themselves, so excited that one of the men forgot to take time out for lunch."[144]

140 Series of letters from Sister Fidelis Barragan and Sister Mary Edward Cassidy to Dorothy Lewis, Foundation File, Lewis Archives.
141 Edward J. Harrell to Mrs. Logan Lewis, January 23, 1985, ibid.
142 Included were a Victorian sofa and chairs, Empire crotch mahogany chest, bureau and table with marble tops, a mahogany wardrobe and a Federal secretary, the total value of which was $35,000. From the Appraisal done by Dolores McLean, September 26, 1986, Callaway Plantation File, ibid.
143 Several letters from Hardin, ibid., kept her apprised of his family's efforts on the project's behalf.
144 Aveola Callaway to Mrs. N. Logan Lewis, October 29, 1986, ibid.

Valuable objects with shorter family histories also found their way into other museum collections. The charming pastel depicting an African American woman by Charleston artist Elizabeth O'Neil Verner that Dorothy and Logan had purchased on their wedding trip, was given to founder Richard Keil for the newly forming Harriet Tubman Museum;[145] a Steuben vase and a Lalique crystal bowl, both signed, that had belonged to her mother were given to the Museum of Arts and Sciences.[146] Several sets of Ironstone China, a c. 1793 pair of Worcester porcelain coolers, and a large selection of silver hollowware went to the Hay House. A sense of the donor's concerns can be gleaned from the terms of one of these gifts, as detailed by the then-chair of the Hay House Board of Directors, Gene Hatcher: "If the museum should cease to exist as an historic house museum, the Directors . . . will notify Dorothy V. Lewis in her lifetime, or the Executors/Trustees of her estate or such foundation as she may have established for the administration of her estate . . ."[147] (The existence of her then six-year-old Foundation, obviously, was still being kept very quiet.) More typical is the sentiment verbalized in a handwritten note to Sidney McNair on the envelope conveying Cecil Coke's photographs of the donated silver for the IRS: "Is the cost of these photos deductable [sic] $127.23. DVL"[148]

Georgia Bank had formed a Trust Department in 1967, and worked to develop it during the seventies. It had grown substantially, as Dorothy was well aware, having been a member of the Trust Committee since joining the board in 1975. In December of that year Trust Committee Chair Robert McCommon had reported that the bank had $10,305,000 under management in 206 accounts, an increase from $8,688,000 and 189 accounts the previous year.[149] Four years later there was $22 million under management in 338 accounts, and the bank had been named executor in four wills.[150] But by the time the 1983 Prospectus for the 200,000-share stock offering was published, that total had shot up to nearly $37 million. Physically, the Department was located near the room in which the Board met and Dorothy had gotten in the habit of stopping by to visit with new trust officer, Dave Jeffords,[151] about various investments, and hers in particular. Over time, as their camaraderie grew, Jeffords pointed out to her how the bank could help her collect her dividends and interest, and keep up with the nearly fifty separate securities she had been maintaining in her safe deposit box. Shortly after the May 1984 announcement of Georgia Bancshares' merger with Bank South, the former Fulton National Bank whose Trust Department had helped to settle Logan's estate, Dorothy went back to Harrell and had him

145 Father Richard C. Keil to Mrs. N. Logan Lewis, July 2, 1984, Foundation File, ibid.
146 Deed of Gift signed August 1991, per Museum of Arts and Sciences Director of Collections Alexandra Klingelhofer, June 27, 2005.
147 Eugene S. Hatcher to Dorothy V. Lewis, February 27, 1985, Hay House File, ibid.
148 The photographs were in a previously used Farmer's National Bank envelope that had a June 8, 1984 postmark, ibid.
149 Minutes, Georgia Bank Board of Directors, December 8, 1975, Hatcher Papers, 13.009.
150 Minutes, Georgia Bank Board of Directors, September 11, 1979, ibid.
151 Jeffords joined Georgia Bank in 1982.

draw a revocable trust agreement by which the bank became custodian of her assets, greatly facilitating the collection and documentation of her increasingly substantial dividends. After a year of seeing how that worked, she stopped keeping her double entry books.

She did not, however, stop the active management of her investments—while the bank made some recommendations, she continued to decide on what and how much to buy, and the Trust Department bought pursuant to her instructions. She was in the bank weekly for meetings and other events, and made a practice of dropping in to go over the reports, discussing whatever needed discussing. Jeffords found her very astute. One day she asked him to buy ten shares of Berkshire Hathaway. Being unfamiliar with the Warren Buffet conglomerate at the time, he was startled when he called the broker to find how expensive the shares would be; nevertheless the purchase was made, after which their value grew. The bank did encourage her to diversify since she had so much Mirro (which by that time had been purchased by Newell), and she gradually did so, replacing the old Vits stock with tax-free bonds. Typically, according to Jeffords, she never mentioned her familial connection to the security.

The new arrangements must have suited her. By 1985, when the Foundation's assets had grown to $300,000, the minutes of an annual meeting at which every director was present described the handling of investments as "a burden to Mrs. Lewis." The solution proposed was the establishment of a custodian account at the Trust Department of Bank South. "Bank South Macon is hereby directed and authorized to rely on instructions from Mrs. Dorothy V. Lewis in making investments," while holding assets and maintaining the accounting records.[152] As for the distributions made that year, "It was basically the feeling of the directors that it would be in the best interest of the schools for the foundation to make unrestricted annual cash grants to be included in their operating budget," so as to give the recipients the most flexibility. However the funds were to be used to "enhance educational programs not to fund brick and mortar projects." The three schools were each awarded $10,000.

In 1977 Dorothy had followed in another set of her husband's footsteps by joining the Board of Managers of Riverside Cemetery, perhaps the only non-profit organization in which she played any administrative role prior to setting up the Lewis Foundation. Established as a private entity in 1887 by people unhappy with the upkeep of city-owned Rose Hill, the cemetery had never made money, and in recognition of that fact it was re-organized as an eleemosynary organization after World War II. The board only met once a year but Manager Cecil Coke Jr. occasionally reported to or consulted with the

152 Minutes, December 6, 1985, Lewis Foundation.

group by mail. Such an instance provides one of the few surviving examples of words in Dorothy's own voice, amply demonstrating her no-nonsense, practical side. Coke had asked for solutions to the increasingly frequent instances (and consequent complaints from lot-owners) of stolen floral tributes. One lot owner had called "to inform me that she was placing three new silk flower arrangements on her husband's grave and would guard them Saturday and Sunday with her gun, shooting anyone trying to steal them."[153]   In the penciled draft of her reply Dorothy seems to be thinking out loud:

> Those who complain must be young or naïve or both. Stealing from cemeterys [sic] is as old as time. The lady with the gun—anyone putting expensive arrangements at a grave should take the responsibility of safeguarding them. This is a NONSENSICAL, unrealistic tribute in a time of economic uncertainties. I agree guards and gates are useless. You've already done all that can be by informing the lawyer and police. As I see it it's our only recourse. Perhaps a sign notifying of prosecution if caught stealing. Or an item in the paper telling of our concern and cooperation with authorities. Have you discussed this with your friends at other cemeterys? [sic] What do they do? Unfortunately I don't think there is cemetery in the world that has definitely solved the problem. I wish I could be more helpful. I know it must be a pesky annoyance. Just remember the solution doesn't require you to put yourself in an unsafe position—would it be of any advantage to deputize you? The increased thieving is in part due to drugs and inflation. Patience, sympathy and tact are the best tools until the economy gets back on track—especially patience![154]

She served on Riverside's Finance Committee. Although Coke remembers her being, as was her wont, a reserved member who had little to say, it must have been a pleasant association because she remained thirteen years, resigning only after suffering her first stroke.[155]

Since the death of Logan's aunt, Martha Lewis Kaderly, in 1967, Dorothy had acted as the representative payee for her younger sister, Mary Jelks "Jelksie" Lewis. In 1981, at age ninety, by this time a resident of the Town and Country nursing home, Jelksie died of a stroke. Despite her own religious scruples against cremation,[156] Dorothy made the arrangements for Hart's Mortuary to perform the requested service, and she and Buster Hart drove down to place the cremains in the Lewis plot in Hawkinsville. She completed her responsibilities by sending the few funds remaining in Jelksie's account to her two nieces.

153 Cecil Coke, Jr. to the Board of Managers, April 19, 1983, Riverside Cemetery File, Lewis Archives.
154 Handwritten draft, ibid.
155 Riverside Cemetery Board of Managers Meeting Minutes, June 18, 1990: "Mrs. F. M. Houser was approved to serve on the Finance Committee to fill the vacancy created by the resignation of Mrs. Logan Lewis." Provided by Cecil Coke Jr. Winburn Stewart was President of the Board of Managers at that time.
156 O'Callaghan Interview, June 2, 2005.

Abby Vits died at the end of May 1986, his wife, Flo, surviving. Doubtless feeling flush after the Bank South merger and unwilling to undergo the hassle of changing planes to get to Manitowoc on a trip that cannot have held any pleasure for her, Dorothy asked Jeffords to charter a Lear jet, and he did. She was there for six weeks settling affairs, the last time she would ever set foot in the city of her birth. Abby's will left everything to Flo or to the trust he had established for her, and specifically pointed out "I have knowingly and intentionally made no provision for my sister, Dorothy Vits Lewis, since she is amply provided for."[157] But his and Dorothy's joint ownership of 1304 Michigan Avenue, where he and Flo had been living in retirement for several years, had to be sorted out. The house and its contents were still essentially as they had been at Anne Vits's death; Abby's attorney and executor John Spindler, cognizant of his client's desire that nothing be sold in Manitowoc, helped Dorothy and Flo obtain an appraisal of the furnishings from a Milwaukee gallery to aid in their division and sale. A note in Dorothy's hand on a copy of Spindler's memo setting out options for handling the situation reads "Ask about giving house to City, Church, etc." Eventually it was agreed that Dorothy would sell her undivided half interest, minus the value of the furnishings she selected, to Abby's estate, which enabled Flo to remain there until a buyer was found, a considerable uncertainty given the limited market for a house and yard of that size in such a small city. On the same day the papers were executed, movers packed up the things to be sent to Macon[158] and Dorothy signed a record documenting her gift of the Edwardian bedroom set and Lincoln Rocker that had been in the maid's room to Olive Suchomel, the longtime Vits housekeeper, "out of love and affection for the many years of help and kindness [she] has given to me and my family." Her work done, she asked Jeffords to send the plane back to get her, and returned to Macon. Once home, she thanked those in Manitowoc who had helped her complete the tasks in familiar fashion, by sending them pecans.[159]

Dorothy attended her foundation's annual meeting in December 1987, the first scheduled after the custodial agreement with the bank had taken effect. Dave Jeffords was there to review the Foundation's assets and report that Dorothy Lewis would make a $60,000 gift that year; Jerry Harrell attended as attorney. It was noted that the Foundation could not maintain the level of giving the board had been approving ($15,000 to each of the three schools for several years) and continue to grow, because the distributions exceeded the income. Nevertheless, the board voted to continue for the present with the caveat that it might not be possible to continue.[160] That was the last Foundation meeting its founder would ever attend.

157 Last Will and Testament of Albert J. Vits, Jr., dated May 17, 1985, copy in Lewis Archives.
158 Among them were bedroom furnishings that may have freed up the Callaway pieces to be given to Callaway Plantation later that fall.
159 John Spindler, Oral Interview, October 19, 2000.
160 According to Holst Beall, who was actively involved with the Catholic schools in those years, Dorothy's loyalty was sorely tried by the fact that Sister Mary Edward insisted on keeping her accounts at C&S where she could deal with a St. Joseph's parishioner; it apparently pained the Bank South stockholder to see the C&S logo on the backs of her returned checks.

During all this time Dorothy had continued her active participation in the board work of both Bank South Macon and Bank South Jasper County, especially the latter. Her calendars show that she attended meetings of the executive committee during her assigned quarter, committee meetings, meetings of the full board, and social events in Macon. In the spring of 1987, however, seven and a half years after policy mandated it, she stopped attending the Tuesday afternoon Macon board meetings and began going to the Thursday luncheons for the honorary directors. She also tried to step down from the Monticello board, but Thurman Willis, believing her participation was still useful to his board, refused to accept her resignation, and she continued driving to Monticello on the fourth Mondays. Unfortunately, in what may have been a harbinger of what was to come, she had an accident there in June of 1987: leaving the meeting, she fell as she started down the steps, opening a gash in her forehead. "I've caught my heel and stumbled," she said when the gentlemen rushed out to help her, but Willis wondered whether a small stroke had caused her to lose consciousness. A trip to Charter Northside Hospital and six or seven stitches by a plastic surgeon accomplished her recovery, and Monticello was back on the calendar for the fourth Monday of July. It wasn't until the fall of 1989 that she finally prevailed upon Willis to accept her resignation. In acquiescing he insisted on presenting her with a Resolution from the Board of Directors acknowledging the role both she and Logan had played in the bank's history: "Mrs. Lewis carried out the dreams of her husband by giving leadership as our bank grew from $5 million to $40 million in assets,"[161] the document read. That same month her calendars indicate that she also gave up her honorary membership on the Macon board.

Meanwhile a man named Arlan Ettinger had made her acquaintance via the telephone. The founder and president of Guernsey's Auction House in New York City,[162] Ettinger suffered from "a longstanding love affair" with 1950s sports and racing cars that had begun in his teens. Having heard that an older woman in Georgia owned a vintage Maserati, he tracked her down and called her up. A major auction was coming up he announced, after introducing himself; was she interested in selling? While extremely courteous and polite, she said no; she had not seen the car, which was parked in a small barn near her home, she added, since her husband's death. She had no clue as to its model or condition but thought that it was made in 1953. Ettinger's heart leaped: pre-1960 models are far more significant than those made after that date because there were so few manufactured. But it seemed he had discovered a treasure only to find

161 Copy of Resolution (which was hanging on Board Room wall at the McIntosh State Bank in Monticello in the summer of 2000) provided by Thurman Willis, Jr.
162 Ettinger and his wife, Barbara Mintz, had seen a niche for an auction house devoted to unique twentieth century objects of value and potential interest to a wide variety of collectors-were they aggressively marketed. They started Guernsey's in 1975 and Ettinger's passion for cars soon led them to focus on that genre, among many others. A photograph of the Lewis Maserati graced the Guernsey's website in 2005, though the car had been sold some years before. The story of Ettinger's purchase of the Maserati was obtained in a telephone interview with the subject on July 18, 2003, and an in-person interview in New York City, October 2003.

it unobtainable. He pursued her for weeks, calling intermittently to chat and see whether she had changed her mind, but when she appeared to be standing fast, he gave up. Then several months later she called him. Explaining that she had moved to Georgia as a young woman and had come to enjoy their "conversation with northern intonations," she said she'd just like to talk. So they talked, becoming friends in the process. Finally one day she uttered the words he'd been longing to hear. "Look, if you're still interested, come down." He did; she pointed him to the barn with instructions to "dig it out." Ettinger found the car "stunningly beautiful—put away in a caring manner with an extra engine and parts . . ." It was an A6GCS, of which only twenty were built and only four known to still exist. When the awed collector went back to the house Dorothy asked, "So what do you think?" "Forget the auction," he remembers blurting, "I want it myself." Guernsey's had done well lately. "You'd really give me that much?" she said, after he named what he thought was a fair price. She turned to his wife: "Is your husband crazy?" It was an excellent return on Logan's investment. Meanwhile Ettinger was so excited he had the money wired to Georgia, rented a U-Haul truck and drove his prize back to New York himself. An envelope full of snapshots of Dorothy Lewis posing with the couple in front of 455 Old Club Road as the car was being loaded was still in her desk after her death, along with articles about Guernsey's, its auctions, and the Maserati, once Ettinger restored and began racing it.

Just a few months later, in late winter 1990, Dorothy Lewis "suffered a severe cerebral hemorrhage."[163] She had been working in the yard, apparently without the faithful presence of Gene Chambliss, when she was stricken, unable to get up. Two golfers coming up on the 14th green noticed her hand waving from behind some shrubbery, and called for help. Although she had never been to his office, she told hospital staffers that internist John O'Shaughnessey, a prominent member of St. Joseph's, was her physician. In fact, she had not seen any doctor, save the plastic surgeon who stitched her head after the Monticello fall, for many years, although she did regularly visit her dentist, Jimmy Cassidy.

The attack was massive and she was not, at first, expected to survive. Bib Anderson remembers pleading with her to get well, only to worry later whether that had really been in her friend's best interest. Trying to increase Dorothy's comfort, she carried her own sheets and pillowcases to the various hospitals in which she recovered over several months. Once when she declined to eat, the staff called on Bill McCowen for help. Addressing the situation as forthrightly as the patient might have herself, he fetched halibut from the S & S Cafeteria and "hand fed" it to her: "It was a Friday and I never knew a Catholic

---

163 From the "To Whom It May Concern" letter written by her doctor, W. John O'Shaughnessey, Jr., June 2, 1992, which Dorothy took to Europe in 1992. Personal File, Lewis Archives.

who could refuse fish on Friday." Still hospitalized on the Fourth of July she gave him the keys to her house and asked him to be sure the flag was displayed for the holiday, a practice she had followed for years. She spent many weeks in the rehab hospital but when a full recovery proved impossible she was finally dismissed with the expectation that she would be wheelchair-bound for the rest of her life. In an unfortunate after effect, she suffered seizures that were exacerbated by her refusal to take the medicines O'Shaughnessey prescribed for her. Jeffords arranged for care in her home around the clock: a nurse plus an aide at all times of the day or night, and eventually, a van to accommodate her wheelchair so that she could continue going to church. Taking part in the Mass was a most important part of her life and she kept it up as long as possible. For a time she sat in the "Cry Room," a space to the right of the altar which was separated by a glass wall so that mothers with babies could share the service, but later moved to the Sacristy on the left side, in order to have more privacy.

Dorothy was not able to attend when the directors convened for the Lewis Foundation's annual meeting that December of 1990, nor was Dr. Cassidy, whose health was also in decline. Income from the corpus was about $30,000 and the board decided to divide that amount between the schools pending any further donations. Lane Williams then moved, seconded by Cubbedge Snow Jr., that Mr. Jeffords should express to Mrs. Lewis "the deepest gratitude for her generosity on behalf of the schools receiving her charity, and also . . . the personal sympathy and best wishes of all the Directors in this trying time."[164] In February the board responded to the changed circumstances without meeting, all five directors signing the document that recorded their action.[165] First, it decided to enter into an agency agreement with Bank South Macon since Mrs. Lewis was no longer able to hold or direct the Foundation's investments "due to her health." In addition the charter was amended to increase the number of directors from five to seven, and Dave Jeffords and Jerry Harrell were elected to five-year terms. At the annual meeting the following December, Mr. Jeffords reported that Mrs. Lewis sent her regards and thanks to the board, but was not able to attend.

In January of 1992, having been found to have a malignancy in her breast, Dorothy underwent mastectomy surgery. Finding that she had accepted Part A of Medicare, but not Part B, which required a monthly payment, Jeffords and the Bank South Trust Department arranged with the Social Security Administration to pay the back premiums in order to make her eligible for the additional coverage. It was a wise investment given the decade of health problems their charge faced.

Despite—or perhaps because of—her declining health, Dorothy decided

---

164 Minutes, December 4, 1990, from the official minute book of the Dorothy V. and N. Logan Lewis Foundation.
165 Action, February 25, 1991, ibid.

to return to Paris in the summer of 1992. Ship & Shore Travel owner Dixie Stewart remembers wheelchair-bound "Do" arriving at her office, beautifully outfitted, as always, with the characteristic bow in her hair, caretakers in tow, to make the arrangements. Of necessity they were elaborate. There was no budget. Betty Curtis had described her pleasure at going to Europe on the supersonic Concorde from New York, and returning on Queen Elizabeth 2, and that is how Dorothy chose to travel. They were met at the airport by a limousine and driver, a handsome young Frenchman who took them wherever they wanted to go, whenever they wanted to go there. Breaking tradition, Dorothy sat in the front with the driver, while the caretakers rode in style in the back. They stayed in the Ritz Hotel and "did everything,"[166] including Versailles, where Dorothy had spent the year following her graduation from Finch. Dorothy wanted to go to the Folies Bergere, the Moulin Rouge, and many of the restaurants she had enjoyed on her trip with Logan. An album of photographs taken by the caretakers documents their elegant hotel room, the sights they saw, and the ship they sailed on; in some of them Dorothy is clearly enjoying herself. If it was stressful to undertake such a journey in her fragile physical condition, she did not show it; in fact she had planned for it. To break the long trip from Paris to Cherbourg, where the group was to board the QE2, Ms. Stewart booked a room at the Lion d'Or for a few hours. Dorothy carried one letter from her doctor, with information about her medical situation, and another from Bank South Macon Chairman George Hall, vouching for the bank's support:

> Mrs. Dorothy V. Lewis' late husband was the founder of our bank 25 years ago. Mrs. Lewis was one of the largest stockholders of our bank, and is now one of the largest stockholders of Bank South Corporation. For many years she was on the Board of Directors. She is a lady of substantial means and our bank will do anything in our ability to make her trip pleasant. We would appreciate you calling us collect, any time day or night, should Mrs. Lewis need our assistance.[167]

The success of that trip led to another the next November, this time to Rome, Florence, and Venice. The letter from Dr. O'Shaughnessey has the June date crossed out and 10/23/92 handwritten over it. James Madison, who had caddied for Logan at Idle Hour, drove them to Atlanta to catch their flight; Massimo, the driver who looked after them in Italy, was strong enough to move his charge from car to chair in comfort. Again they bunked in luxury at the Grand Hotel at the top of the Spanish Steps. The highlight, however, was a special audience with Pope John Paul II. Dorothy and her caretakers, with other disabled persons, were allowed in a side entrance and welcomed into a special

166 Dixie Stewart, Oral Interview, September 28, 2005.
167 To Whom it May Concern from George H. Hall, June 8, 1992, Personal File, Lewis Archives.

room in which she was able to receive a personal greeting and blessing from the Holy Father. Vatican photographs of the encounter (one of which she later gave to Sister Rosina Bayliss, who had succeeded Sister Fidelis as principal of Mt. De Sales) witness the powerful import the exchange had for her. Then, in a strange world coincidence, she ran into Georgia Bank executive Buddy Ponder and his wife Saynor, and John and Margie O'Shaughnessey at the Vatican; she laughed at the happenstance, telling Dr. O'Shaughnessey later that when she looked up and saw her banker, her doctor, and the Pope all together she thought she must have died and gone to heaven. She had insisted to Ms. Stewart that she wanted to see a particular sight in Venice of which Bill McCowen had a painting, and she did, bringing his wife, Virginia, a scarf to celebrate having found it. Later she and the caretakers went to California by train, to another elegant hotel she and Logan had visited. Despite enjoying the spa treatments offered by the resort, that trip proved disappointing: the train facilities turned out to be less accessible than advertised, making the transfer from one train to another in New Orleans awkward and difficult, service was in short supply, and the only thing she recognized at the hotel was the chandelier.

Once back in Macon, Dorothy's health continued to decline. In June of 1993, unable to attend in person, she sent a formal communication to her Foundation's Board of Directors.[168] "I have, during the past several years communicated my wishes to you through my trust officer, Dave Jeffords. All of you are aware of my disability, and it is for that reason that I now desire to resign as President of the Foundation. I would like for Dave to succeed me as President. I would like for this change to come about at the next meeting of the Board." Further noting that she had "set out my general thoughts on the Foundation in my Will," she said she had also discussed them with Jeffords, who was best qualified "to lead the Foundation into the future." She signed her name in a manner that, while it bears a resemblance to the hand that she had affixed to numerous previous documents, was obviously that of a physically enfeebled person. When the Board met the following December it accepted her resignation as President but asked her to continue serving as a Director; in December 1994 Jeffords "reported that he had advised Mrs. Lewis [of that fact and] she graciously accepted."[169] The Foundation's assets, as reported at that meeting, were $572,389.

Coming home from a weekend at the beach on Labor Day, 1995, Dave Jeffords was notified of an important meeting at Bank South Macon the next morning. With a series of telephone calls he was able to ascertain that

---

168 Board of Directors, Dorothy V. and N. Logan Lewis Foundation, Inc., from Dorothy V. Lewis, June 18, 1993, from the official Minute Book. Jerry Harrell confirmed (6/16/05) that his office had prepared the letter for Mrs. Lewis' signature, at her direction.
169 Minutes, December 10, 1993, and December 12, 1994, ibid.

NationsBank, the premier example of a go-go bank in the era of go-go banking, had set its sights on Bank South. The purchase was announced that Tuesday. With stock prices set to soar, Jeffords and Harrell became concerned about their client's heavy concentration in bank stock and suggested to Mrs. Lewis that diversification could be facilitated by the transfer of some of that stock to the Foundation. She agreed. In November the Foundation directors were summoned to a special meeting; all save Dr. Cassidy and Mrs. Lewis were present. President Jeffords reported that Dorothy Lewis had donated 300,000 shares of Bank South common stock to the Foundation. The directors passed a resolution expressing their sincere appreciation for "her large and generous gift" and extended "to her the heartfelt thanks of the Board for her financial and personal support of the Foundation and its charitable works." They also decided that Jeffords and Harrell, who were to become the investment committee, should be elected to additional five-year terms, and garner advice from Bank South financial advisors. The session was then suspended to allow the group to proceed to 455 Old Club Road so that Dorothy Lewis could join the meeting. They "collectively and individually thanked Mrs. Lewis for her generosity, and the ideas of the Foundation going forward were discussed among the Directors with Mrs. Lewis. Mrs. Lewis extended to each Director her personal thanks for their service." The meeting concluded with a prayer by Father John Cuddy.[170] The value of the shares at the time Dorothy donated them was $8,850,000; when the directors met in 1996, six months after the NationsBank takeover had closed (and after some diversification had taken place) the Foundation's assets totaled $12,989,740.

In addition to her gifts to the Foundation, Dorothy made two gifts in recognition of special relationships. In consideration of her "friendship and affection" for Bill McCowen, the longtime property manager who had handled its rental for nearly forty years—who was also the solicitous neighbor who had installed a flagpole in her back yard to welcome her home from the hospital— she deeded title to 441 Old Club Road, the "little brown house" that Logan had bought from Hiram Manning in 1955.[171] She gave bank stock to her friend and mentee, Willis Thurman Jr.

The remaining years of Dorothy's life were difficult. Her health continued to decline and by the late 1990s she no longer left home, save for infrequent hospitalizations, being completely bedridden. "Client informs 'I'm DEAD. What time are we having the FUNERAL?'" one of her caretakers wrote cryptically in the log the women kept of their patient's day, on February 20, 1997. "Appetite fair. Wanted to see Fr. Cuddy," it continued. Unhappy in and

170 Minutes, November 21, 1995, ibid.
171 Deed dated June 13, 1996, recorded in Book 3014, folio 26, Bibb County Clerk of Court.

with her condition and appearance, she kept the house dark and discouraged friends from visiting. She told Pink Persons she wanted to die, to which he responded "Dorothy, the Lord will get you when He wants to." She finally asked him not to come any more, saying she preferred for him to remember her the way she had been rather than the way she was. Bib Anderson and Betty Curtis, as devoted as they were, also stopped going as their old friend declined to converse, keeping her attention focused on the television set during their visits. Sister Rosina Bayliss, as had Sister Mary Sheridan before her, came once a week to celebrate a Communion Service, bringing the Holy Eucharist and providing the spiritual comfort that had been such an important part of Dorothy's existence. Neighbor Bill McCowen dropped in to check on her and the caretakers often, keeping Dave Jeffords apprised of household matters. Still, it was a bleak time. Jane Protz, who called every few months to ask about her cousin, prayed that God would spare Dorothy from further misery.

Finally, on July 29, 2002, He did. After years of separation she took her place by Logan's side in Riverside Cemetery.[172] Following the terms of her will, Jeffords arranged a graveside Roman Catholic burial; as specified, the only jewelry adorning her body was her "silver wedding band with gold lining and inscription." Also as requested, the gold rosary that had been a gift from Logan was placed in her hands.[173]

When the directors of the Lewis Foundation met that December they recorded their "joy that [Dorothy Lewis] was relieved from her suffering." As a group they noted their "sincere appreciation for the faithful service, keen insights and never wavering support for the mission and work of the Foundation," as well as their "regret for the loss to the Foundation, her Church, family and community," even as they "celebrate[d] the joy of the beginning of her new life."[174]

The End

---

172 Cecil Coke reported discussing the placement of those graves with Dorothy Lewis many years before her death. Traditionally, he told her, the wife lies at her husband's left, but the layout and placement of graves already in the Lewis plot meant that Dorothy would have to be on Logan's right, unless all the remains were rearranged by disinterring and replacing them-thus incurring an additional expense. "Well, just bury me crossways, it doesn't matter," Dorothy had told him when Coke suggested the re-arrangement. Oral Interview, April 14, 2005.
173 Minute Book 36-W, p. 274, Bibb County Probate Court.
174 Minutes, December 3, 2002, ibid.

Gene Chambliss, who began working for the Lewises in the early 1960s, remained in Dorothy's employ until his death. Courtesy Mary Anne Berg Richardson.

This Drinnon photo of Dorothy Lewis was taken in 1969, three years after Logan's death. Courtesy Middle Georgia Archive, Washington Memorial Library, Macon, Ga.

Arlan Ettinger, car buff/auction house owner from New York, courted Dorothy for years before convincing her to sell him Logan's Maserati-a "fantastic" vehicle that won a *Road and Track* trophy as "the car we'd most like to drive away" when he took it to the Pebble Beach Concours in 1994. After she finally said "yes" in 1989 he and his wife rented a truck to get it home. Here Ettinger, left, and Dorothy Lewis inspect the loaded sports car before its trip north. Lewis Archives.

Left: Two years after her stroke, wheelchair-bound Dorothy Lewis arranged not one but two trips to Europe, accompanied by two caretakers. This photo shows her with one of the caretakers and their Italian guide. Lewis Archives.

Bottom: The highlight of the trip to Italy was this special audience with Pope John Paul II. Dorothy gave this picture, taken by a Vatican photographer, to Sister Rosina Bayliss, who gave permission for it to be reproduced here.

Dorothy gave this delicately beautiful statue of the Virgin Mary, which had belonged to her mother, to Mt. de Sales principal Sister Rosina. Courtesy Sister Rosina Bayliss, R.S.M.

When a hospitalized Dorothy Lewis asked Bill McCowen to be sure her flag was out for the 4th of July, he did one better, contacting a local sign company to have a flag pole installed in the back of her house-where the banner flew continuously until her death.

Epilogue

Though she had two Rolls Royces parked in her garage, Dorothy Lewis did her own housekeeping and sewed many of her own clothes. Pragmatic, independent, straightforward to the point of bluntness, a devout Catholic in a Protestant city, she was a woman who forged her own path.

No one in mid-twentieth century Macon would have been surprised if she had had chosen a life of sheltered comfort after her husband's death. She could have left the management of her assets in the hands of trusted fiduciaries and played bridge between rounds of travel or volunteer work. That was usual for women of her age and class. It was not her style.

With Logan Lewis's help she had been using her money to make more money for nearly two decades, and the loss of his assistance did not break the pattern. It may actually have given her the freedom to become even more involved in shepherding her resources.

Certainly she built on her family's financial success, which came primarily in the form of Aluminum Goods Manufacturing Company stock, just as Logan used the real property he inherited as the foundation for further business ventures. But experience had taught them that an untended garden would wither; rather than simply harvesting their fruits, they increased future harvests by planting more seeds.

Over the years Mrs. Lewis's astute husbandry will have a profound impact on her adopted city. No fiduciary could have been more successful in developing the substantial estate that became the Dorothy V. and N. Logan Lewis Foundation, than its founder.

Vits Family

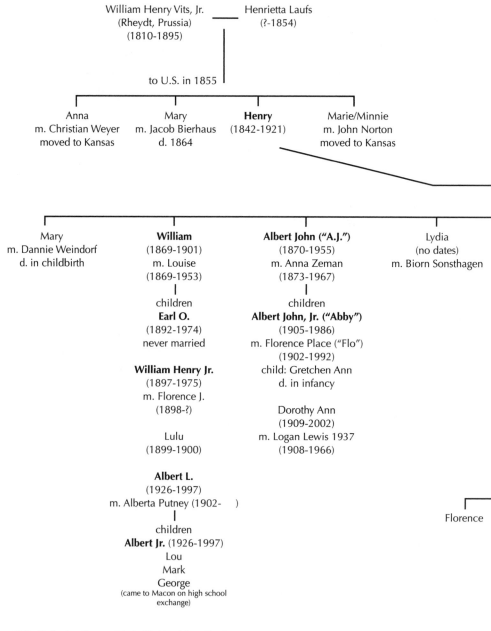

William Henry Vits, Jr. ——— Henrietta Laufs
(Rheydt, Prussia)   (?-1854)
(1810-1895)

to U.S. in 1855

Anna	Mary	**Henry**	Marie/Minnie
m. Christian Weyer	m. Jacob Bierhaus	(1842-1921)	m. John Norton
moved to Kansas	d. 1864		moved to Kansas

Mary	**William**	**Albert John ("A.J.")**	Lydia
m. Dannie Weindorf	(1869-1901)	(1870-1955)	(no dates)
d. in childbirth	m. Louise	m. Anna Zeman	m. Biorn Sonsthagen
	(1869-1953)	(1873-1967)	
	children	children	
	Earl O.	**Albert John, Jr. ("Abby")**	
	(1892-1974)	(1905-1986)	
	never married	m. Florence Place ("Flo")	
		(1902-1992)	
	William Henry Jr.	child: Gretchen Ann	
	(1897-1975)	d. in infancy	
	m. Florence J.		
	(1898-?)	Dorothy Ann	
		(1909-2002)	
	Lulu	m. Logan Lewis 1937	
	(1899-1900)	(1908-1966)	

Albert L.
(1926-1997)
m. Alberta Putney (1902-   )

children
Albert Jr. (1926-1997)
Lou
Mark
George
(came to Macon on high school exchange)

Florence

(BF) = Professionally associated with Aluminium Goods
Manufacturing Company at one time or another.

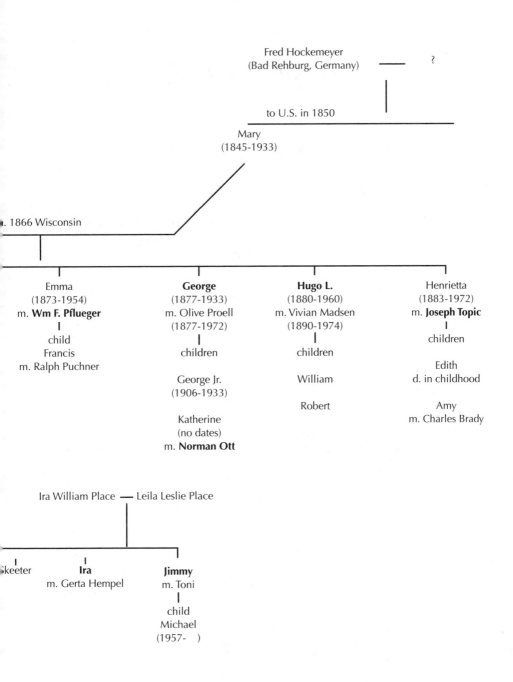

Fred Hockemeyer
(Bad Rehburg, Germany) ——— ?

to U.S. in 1850

Mary
(1845-1933)

. 1866 Wisconsin

Emma	George	Hugo L.	Henrietta
(1873-1954)	(1877-1933)	(1880-1960)	(1883-1972)
m. **Wm F. Pflueger**	m. Olive Proell	m. Vivian Madsen	m. **Joseph Topic**
	(1877-1972)	(1890-1974)	
child			children
Francis	children	children	
m. Ralph Puchner			Edith
	George Jr.	William	d. in childhood
	(1906-1933)		
		Robert	Amy
	Katherine		m. Charles Brady
	(no dates)		
	m. **Norman Ott**		

Ira William Place ——— Leila Leslie Place

ikeeter	Ira	Jimmy
	m. Gerta Hempel	m. Toni
		child
		Michael
		(1957-)

Zeman Family

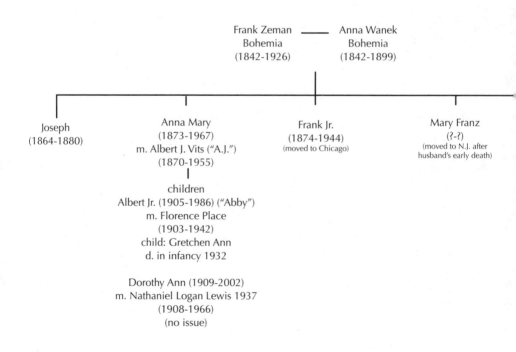

Frank Zeman —— Anna Wanek
Bohemia   Bohemia
(1842-1926)   (1842-1899)

Joseph
(1864-1880)

Anna Mary
(1873-1967)
m. Albert J. Vits ("A.J.")
(1870-1955)

children
Albert Jr. (1905-1986) ("Abby")
m. Florence Place
(1903-1942)
child: Gretchen Ann
d. in infancy 1932

Dorothy Ann (1909-2002)
m. Nathaniel Logan Lewis 1937
(1908-1966)
(no issue)

Frank Jr.
(1874-1944)
(moved to Chicago)

Mary Franz
(?-?)
(moved to N.J. after
husband's early death)

```
├─────────────────────────────┬───────────────────────────────────────────┐
│                             │                                             │
Charles Albert                    Emma                          Edward J.
(1880-1957)                    (1881-1970)                      (1884-1965)
m. Elizabeth Paine            m. Arthur Auton                 m. Minnie Klackner
(1886-1977)                                                     (1888-1964)
│                                                                 │
child                                                          children
Valerie                                                         Jane
m. William C. Muth                                        m. William F. Protz

                                                               Pauline
                                                        m. Robert M. Langenfield

                                                               Marion
                                                         m. Edward Schussler
```

Lewis Family

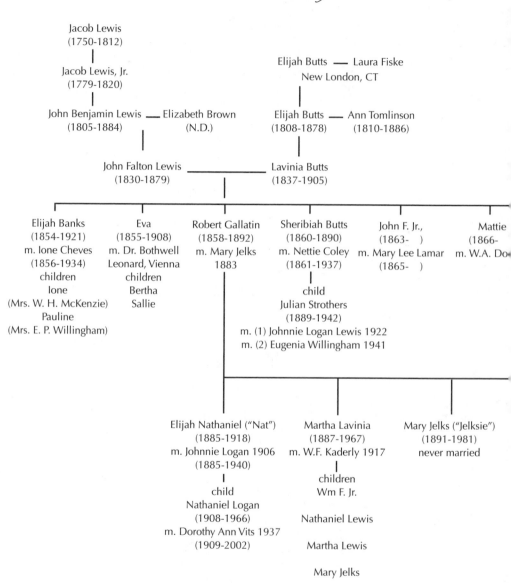

Jacob Lewis
(1750-1812)

Jacob Lewis, Jr.
(1779-1820)

Elijah Butts —— Laura Fiske
New London, CT

John Benjamin Lewis —— Elizabeth Brown
(1805-1884)　　　　　　(N.D.)

Elijah Butts —— Ann Tomlinson
(1808-1878)　　　(1810-1886)

John Falton Lewis ———————— Lavinia Butts
(1830-1879)　　　　　　　　　(1837-1905)

Elijah Banks	Eva	Robert Gallatin	Sheribiah Butts	John F. Jr.,	Mattie
(1854-1921)	(1855-1908)	(1858-1892)	(1860-1890)	(1863-　)	(1866-
m. Ione Cheves	m. Dr. Bothwell	m. Mary Jelks	m. Nettie Coley	m. Mary Lee Lamar	m. W.A. Do◦
(1856-1934)	Leonard, Vienna	1883	(1861-1937)	(1865-　)	
children	children				
Ione	Bertha		child		
(Mrs. W. H. McKenzie)	Sallie		Julian Strothers		
Pauline			(1889-1942)		
(Mrs. E. P. Willingham)			m. (1) Johnnie Logan Lewis 1922		
			m. (2) Eugenia Willingham 1941		

Elijah Nathaniel ("Nat")
(1885-1918)
m. Johnnie Logan 1906
(1885-1940)

child
Nathaniel Logan
(1908-1966)
m. Dorothy Ann Vits 1937
(1909-2002)

Martha Lavinia
(1887-1967)
m. W.F. Kaderly 1917

children
Wm F. Jr.

Nathaniel Lewis

Martha Lewis

Mary Jelks

Mary Jelks ("Jelksie")
(1891-1981)
never married

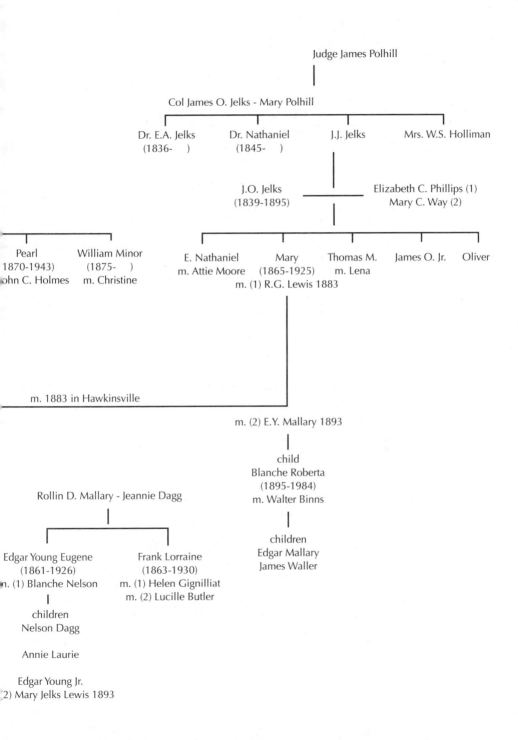

Judge James Polhill

Col James O. Jelks - Mary Polhill

Dr. E.A. Jelks   Dr. Nathaniel   J.J. Jelks   Mrs. W.S. Holliman
(1836-   )   (1845-   )

J.O. Jelks   Elizabeth C. Phillips (1)
(1839-1895)   Mary C. Way (2)

Pearl   William Minor   E. Nathaniel   Mary   Thomas M.   James O. Jr.   Oliver
1870-1943)   (1875-)   m. Attie Moore   (1865-1925)   m. Lena
ohn C. Holmes   m. Christine   m. (1) R.G. Lewis 1883

m. 1883 in Hawkinsville

m. (2) E.Y. Mallary 1893

child
Blanche Roberta
(1895-1984)
m. Walter Binns

Rollin D. Mallary - Jeannie Dagg

children
Edgar Mallary
James Waller

Edgar Young Eugene   Frank Lorraine
(1861-1926)   (1863-1930)
n. (1) Blanche Nelson   m. (1) Helen Gignilliat
                 m. (2) Lucille Butler
children
Nelson Dagg

Annie Laurie

Edgar Young Jr.
2) Mary Jelks Lewis 1893

Logan Family

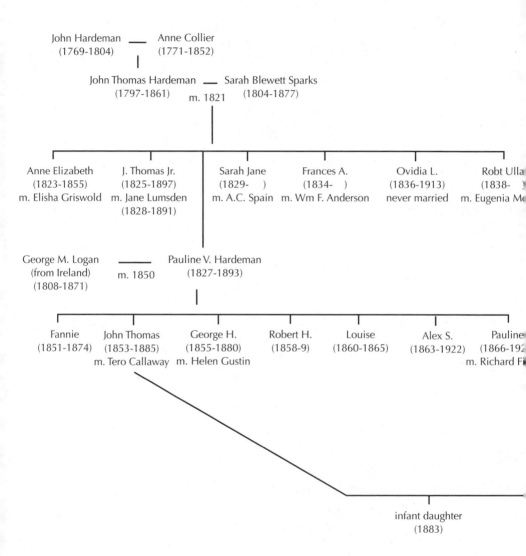

John Hardeman ___ Anne Collier
(1769-1804)   (1771-1852)

John Thomas Hardeman ___ Sarah Blewett Sparks
(1797-1861)   m. 1821   (1804-1877)

Anne Elizabeth   J. Thomas Jr.   Sarah Jane   Frances A.   Ovidia L.   Robt Ulla
(1823-1855)   (1825-1897)   (1829-)   (1834-)   (1836-1913)   (1838-)
m. Elisha Griswold   m. Jane Lumsden   m. A.C. Spain   m. Wm F. Anderson   never married   m. Eugenia M
(1828-1891)

George M. Logan   _____   Pauline V. Hardeman
(from Ireland)   m. 1850   (1827-1893)
(1808-1871)

Fannie   John Thomas   George H.   Robert H.   Louise   Alex S.   Pauline
(1851-1874)   (1853-1885)   (1855-1880)   (1858-9)   (1860-1865)   (1863-1922)   (1866-192
m. Tero Callaway   m. Helen Gustin   m. Richard Fi

infant daughter
(1883)

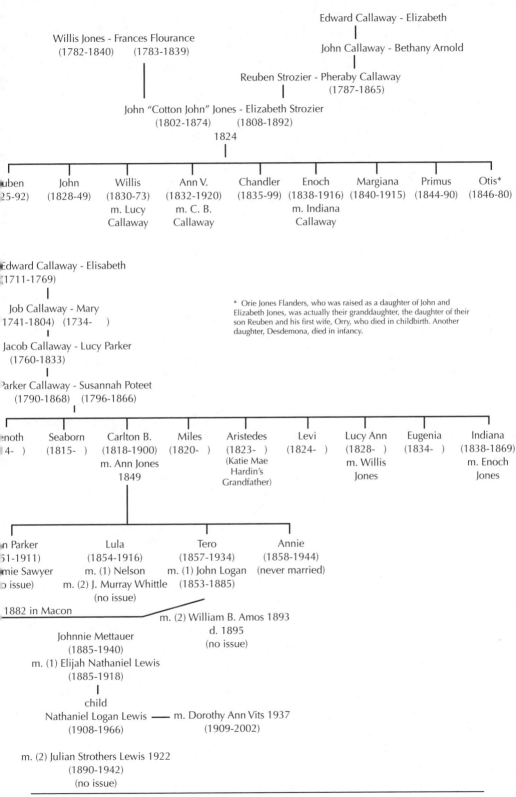

Edward Callaway - Elizabeth

John Callaway - Bethany Arnold

Reuben Strozier - Pheraby Callaway
(1787-1865)

Willis Jones - Frances Flourance
(1782-1840)   (1783-1839)

John "Cotton John" Jones - Elizabeth Strozier
(1802-1874)   (1808-1892)
1824

…uben	John	Willis	Ann V.	Chandler	Enoch	Margiana	Primus	Otis*
…5-92)	(1828-49)	(1830-73) m. Lucy Callaway	(1832-1920) m. C. B. Callaway	(1835-99)	(1838-1916) m. Indiana Callaway	(1840-1915)	(1844-90)	(1846-80)

Edward Callaway - Elisabeth
(1711-1769)

Job Callaway - Mary
1741-1804)   (1734-   )

Jacob Callaway - Lucy Parker
(1760-1833)

Parker Callaway - Susannah Poteet
(1790-1868)   (1796-1866)

* Orie Jones Flanders, who was raised as a daughter of John and Elizabeth Jones, was actually their granddaughter, the daughter of their son Reuben and his first wife, Orry, who died in childbirth. Another daughter, Desdemona, died in infancy.

…noth	Seaborn	Carlton B.	Miles	Aristedes	Levi	Lucy Ann	Eugenia	Indiana
4-)	(1815-)	(1818-1900) m. Ann Jones 1849	(1820-)	(1823-) (Katie Mae Hardin's Grandfather)	(1824-)	(1828-) m. Willis Jones	(1834-)	(1838-1869) m. Enoch Jones

…n Parker	Lula	Tero	Annie
51-1911)	(1854-1916)	(1857-1934)	(1858-1944)
…mie Sawyer	m. (1) Nelson	m. (1) John Logan	(never married)
o issue)	m. (2) J. Murray Whittle	(1853-1885)	
	(no issue)		

1882 in Macon

m. (2) William B. Amos 1893
d. 1895
(no issue)

Johnnie Mettauer
(1885-1940)
m. (1) Elijah Nathaniel Lewis
(1885-1918)

child
Nathaniel Logan Lewis —— m. Dorothy Ann Vits 1937
(1908-1966)   (1909-2002)

m. (2) Julian Strothers Lewis 1922
(1890-1942)
(no issue)

Oral Interviews

* Vivian Hay Anderson, May 18, 2000
  Mrs. Anderson, "Bib," was one of Dorothy Vits's classmates at the Finch School in New York City, and they remained close friends after their respective marriages.
* Sister Fidelis Barragan, April 14, 2004
  A member of the Sisters of Mercy, the order which owns Mt. De Sales School, Sister Fidelis met Dorothy Lewis shortly after becoming principal of the school, a position she held from 1970 to 1988.
* Sister Rosina Bayliss, June 8, 2000
  Following Sister Fidelis as principal of Mt. De Sales School, Sister Rosina visited Mrs. Lewis frequently in the last years of her life.
* Oliver Bateman, Phone Interview, April 26, 2003
  Mr. Bateman was a leader of the emerging Republican Party in the 1960s, a time during which Dorothy and Logan Lewis were active supporters.
* James A. Berg, December 11, 2002
  Mr. Berg, an architect, designed the Lewises Old Club Road home in 1955 as well as the new headquarters for the Georgia Bank at Mulberry and Third in 1963.
* Ralph Talmadge Birdsey, October 16, 2002
  Mr. Birdsey's father, Herbert, grew up down the street from Logan Lewis, and was Logan's classmate at both Vineville School and Lanier High School.
* Amy Topic Brady, October 17, 2000 and October 20, 2000
  Mrs. Brady's mother, Henrietta Vits Topic, was the youngest sister of Dorothy Lewis's father, A. J. Vits. She lives in Manitowoc, Wisconsin.
* Cecil Coke Jr., April 14, 2005
  Mr. Coke is the President of Riverside Cemetery, on the board of which both Logan and Dorothy Lewis served.
* John Drewry Comer, October 2, 2002
  Mr. Comer served on the C & S Macon advisory board with Logan Lewis in the 1950s, and his older sister, Cynthia, had been a friend of Logan's in their youth.
* Monsignor John Cuddy, September 14, 2000; March 15, 2004
  Msg. Cuddy was the pastor of St. Joseph's Church from 1974 until after Dorothy Lewis' death; he also serves on the board of the Lewis Foundation.
* Betty Hay McCook Curtis, June 15, 2000; June 23, 2003; February 17, 2004; and April 26, 2004

The younger sister of Bib Hay Anderson, Mrs. Curtis met Dorothy Lewis when she visited the Hay home in Macon, and she was a student at Finch when Dorothy boarded there while studying theater in the early thirties. Mrs. Curtis's first husband, Jimmy McCook, was a good friend of Logan Lewis's, and the two women remained close throughout Dorothy's life.

* Richard Domingos, February 17, 2004
  Mr. Domingos served on the Georgia Bank Board of Directors while Logan Lewis was President.
* William H. Epps, Jr., May 31, 2005
  Mr. Epps worked closely with Mrs. Lewis' accountant, Sidney McNair, during the later years of Dorothy Lewis's life.
* Arlan Ettinger, July 18, 2003 and July 25, 2003
  Mr. Ettinger, President of the Guernsey Auction House in New York City, befriended Dorothy Lewis in the 1980s as he negotiated the purchase of Logan Lewis's prized Maserati.
* Lucy Gordon, January 24, 2004
  Mrs. Gordon, widow of long time Georgia Bank President Don W. Gordon, first met the Lewises when she moved to Macon in 1960.
* George Hall, May 31, 2000
  Mr. Hall joined Georgia Bank in 1966, and followed Don Gordon to the presidency in 1983.
* Robert C. "Neal" Ham, November 19, 2003 and August 2, 2004
  Logan Lewis recruited Mr. Ham to work for Georgia Bank in 1962; Ham was involved in Logan's acquisition of the Farmers National Bank, and later served on its board at the behest of Dorothy Lewis.
* Edward J. Harrell, May 17, 2000; June 9, 2005, and numerous other times
  Mr. Harrell was Mrs. Lewis's attorney from 1979 until her death, doing the legal work that established her foundation. He had also done the lion's share of the work to establish Georgia Bancshares.
* David C. Jeffords, May 11, 2000; June 16, 2005, and numerous other times
  Mr. Jeffords joined the Georgia Bank Trust Department in 1982 when Dorothy Lewis was a member of the Board Committee which oversaw that department; he later became Mrs. Lewis's Trust Officer.
* Frank Cater Jones, November 11, 2003
  Mr. Jones, like his father, Baxter Jones, represented Logan Lewis in numerous legal matters in the 1950s and '60s (notably in a condemnation case involving property belonging to Dorothy Lewis), and he helped to settle Logan's estate.
* James W. "Jimmy" McCook, III, February 5, 2004
  Logan Lewis recruited McCook, the son of one of his best friends, to serve on

Georgia Bank's board of directors in the early 1960s; he was Chair during much of Dorothy Lewis' tenure.

* Robert L. McCommon Jr., February 21, 2003
  Mr. McCommon and his wife bought the Lewis family home in 1956 and he later served on the Georgia Bank board with Dorothy Lewis.

* William C. McCowen, May 17, 2000
  As a tennis-loving youngster growing up in nearby Cherokee Heights, Mr. McCowen shagged balls for Logan Lewis; as an adult he worked with both Lewises while managing property for Murphey, Taylor, and Ellis. He and his family were already living on Old Club Road when the Lewises moved there in 1956, and he was particularly kind to Dorothy Lewis after her stroke.

* RoseMary McKelvey, February 13, 2004
  Mrs. McKelvey has been a communicant at St. Joseph's Catholic Church since the early 1960s.

* Alan Neal, April 20, 2005
  Mr. Neal came to Macon in the 1970s as a senior executive with what was then First National, later SunTrust Bank of Middle Georgia. He was a knowledgeable source on banking in late twentieth century Macon.

* Laura Nelle Anderson O'Callaghan, September 15, 2000; September 23, 2002; February 20, 2003; April 22, 2003; June 2, 2005
  Mrs. O'Callaghan was a devoted friend of Logan Lewis's from school days through adulthood, and attended his and Dorothy's wedding in Manitowoc.

* Dr. John O'Shaughnessey, March 12, 2004
  Dr. O'Shaughnessey was Mrs. Lewis's doctor, and a member of her church.

* Henry Pinckney "Pink" Persons, Jr., June 14, 2000; June 11, 2003; February 12, 2004; and August 6, 2004
  Mr. Persons was a close friend and longtime business associate of Logan Lewis. One of the principals of Idle Hour Development Company (which developed Country Club Estates), he was also an early member of the Georgia Bank Board of Directors.

* Michael Place, October 20, 2002
  Mr. Place, of Manitowoc, Wisconsin, is the son of Florence Place Vits's youngest brother, Jimmy, and spent a lot of time at the Vits's Michigan Avenue home while growing up. (Flo Vits was the wife of Dorothy Lewis's older brother, Abby.)

* Herbert M. "Buddy" Ponder, Jr., July 10, 2000
  Mr. Ponder joined Georgia Bank in 1978 and became a member of both its board, and that of Bank South Monticello, in the 1980s.

* Albert P. Reichert, April 23, 2003
  Mr. Reichert served in the United States Navy in the South Pacific during

World War II, aboard a vessel similar to that on which Logan Lewis served.

* Bebe Walker Reichert, February 25, 2004
As a convert to Catholicism, Mrs. Reichert was able to give the non-Catholic author better insight into Dorothy Lewis's faith.

* John R. Rogers, Jr., April 14, 2005
Mr. Rogers served on the Georgia Bank Board of Directors with Dorothy Lewis.

* Jane Zeman Protz, September 28, 2000; March 10, 2004
Mrs. Protz is the daughter of Dorothy Lewis's mother's youngest (and favorite) brother. She lived in Manitowoc for many years before she and her husband retired to Savannah in the 1980s.

* Betty Sweet Simmons, June 2, 2000
While younger than Dorothy Lewis, and not particularly close to her, Mrs. Simmons has lived in Macon since the 1930s and is familiar with many facets of the community.

* Cubbedge Snow Jr., June 30, 2000
Mr. Snow grew up down the street from Logan Lewis's family home. Later, his father was the attorney for the Georgia Bank; he himself served on the board of Directors with Dorothy Lewis from 1976 until her retirement.
Additionally, his firm, Martin, Snow, Grant and Napier, represented Mrs. Lewis after 1979.

* John Spindler, October 19, 2000
Mr. Spindler, a retired attorney, was a member of the Manitowoc firm of Clark, Rankin, Nash and Spindler, which represented the Vits family for many years.

* Dixie Stewart, September 9, 2005
Mrs. Stewart's travel agency planned the trips Dorothy Lewis took after her 1990 stroke.

* Joe E. Timberlake III, November 20, 2003
Mr. Timberlake's father was one of the original Georgia Bank board members and he was a knowledgeable source on banks and banking.

* Thurman Willis Jr., June 7, 2000; April 25, 2005
Mr. Willis met Dorothy Lewis, who was then on its board, when he went to work for the Farmers National Bank in 1971; she mentored him and was fond of his wife and children.

Index